Race, Place and Globalization

Race, Place and Globalization

Youth Cultures in a Changing World

Anoop Nayak

Oxford • New York

First published in 2003 by
Berg
Editorial offices:
1st Floor, Angel Court, 81 St Clements Street, Oxford OX4 1AW, UK
175 Fifth Avenue, New York, NY 10010, USA

Paperback edition reprinted in 2004

Berg is an imprint of Oxford International Publishers Ltd.

Library of Congress Cataloging-in-Publication Data
Nayak, Anoop.
    Race, place and globalization : youth cultures in a changing world /
Anoop Nayak.— 1st ed.
        p. cm.
    ISBN 1-85973-604-1 (cloth) — ISBN 1-85973-609-2 (pbk.)
    1. Youth. 2. Globalization. I. Title.

    HQ796.N3677 2003
    305.235—dc22

                                                            2003015449

British Library Cataloguing-in-Publication Data
A catalogue record for this book is available from the British Library.

ISBN 1 85973 604 1 (Cloth)
        1 85973 609 2 (Paper)

Typeset by JS Typesetting Ltd, Wellingborough, Northants.
Printed in the United Kingdom by Biddles Ltd, King's Lynn.

www.bergpublishers.com

In memory of my mother Kanti Nayak, always loved and ever missed.

Contents

Contents

Acknowledgements

This book would not have been possible without the friendship, support and practical aid of a number people.

Les Back, Alastair Bonnett, Robert Hollands and Peter Jackson each influenced the structure and shape of the work through gentle but persuasive criticism. Richard Collier, Kate Corr, Stuart Dawley, Richard Johnson, Hilary Pilkington and Tracey Skelton provided comments or thoughts – however small or large – on parts of the work. Mary Jane Kehily has offered wisdom, care and dialogue throughout. Kathryn Earle has been a willing and patient editor, ably supported by Ian Critchley and the meticulous hand of Justin Dyer. Nicki Carter helped with photocopying. Carmen Booth, Fiona Coleman and Bethan Gulliver each opened doors that would otherwise have stayed firmly shut. The debates in this book are also formed in transnational communication with colleagues in the UK, Scandinavia and Australia – long may this dialogue continue. I would also like to thank David Gillborn and Carfax for allowing me to revise the article '"White English Ethnicities": Racism, anti-racism and student perspectives', *Race, Ethnicity and Education*, 2(2) (1999), pp. 177–202 for Chapter 7, and Pion Ltd for allowing me to revise 'Last of the "Real Geordies"? White masculinities and the subcultural response to deindustrialisation', *Environment and Planning D: Society and Space*, 20(6) (2002), pp. 7–25 for Chapter 4. Finally, I would like to thank the young people who took part in this research for letting me into your lives. This is your work as much mine.

Every effort has been made to trace copyright holders for permission to reproduce their material. Any copyright holders wishing to amend information presented in this book should contact the publisher.

Cover Image

'My parents see me as Indian, but my friends see me as British. I see myself as both British and Indian.'
Baljit Balrow for Self Portrait UK

Self Portrait UK – the national self-portrait campaign, devised and produced by Media 19 in partnership with Channel 4, the National Portrait Gallery and Arts Council England, North East. © Media 19

Part I
Passing Times

–1–

Introduction: Local – Global

Writing a book about young people is perhaps a final admission that one no longer belongs to this group. That we can stand apart from, and coolly record our observations about youth in the certain knowledge that 'we were once young' but no longer are becomes something of a silent shibboleth.

In somewhat teasing fashion, the harder we try to explain the conditions of 'being young', the more estranged we become from these experiences. The rational can only ever approximate the experiential. This makes writing this book something of an impossible project. Unable to express the inexplicable and know the unknowable, even ethnographic research struggles to breach the representational mould and deliver a truly embodied knowledge of young lives. With these caveats in mind my intentions remain more modest. *Race, Place and Globalization: Youth Cultures in a Changing World* brings together 'historical', 'structural' and 'cultural' approaches to the study of youth.[1] It represents an attempt to map the contours of a new *spatial cultural studies*.

Recent years have witnessed profound social, economic, political and cultural change in young people's life experiences and employment aspirations. This book explores the scale of these transformations and their impact upon young people's lives. Indeed, the period of late-modernity has been characterized by widespread economic restructuring and exacerbated labour insecurity. This is exemplified in the decline of a traditional manufacturing core and a rapid expansion in service sector economies. For many young people these changes have seen expectations of life-long labour give way to the prospect of long-term unemployment, part-time work, unskilled jobs, fixed-term contracts and more 'flexible' patterns of employment. At a global scale the wider proliferation of capital within developing countries and former Eastern Bloc nations has further accelerated the 'flows' of capital, people and goods across the world. As social relations become increasingly 'stretched' across time and space and the web of interconnections grows more

---

1. Terms such as 'youth' and 'young people' are used for their economical ease. These terms have been subject to critique and should not be seen as biological stages (e.g. 'the pubescent teens') or psychological phases (e.g. 'adolescence') in an individual's development. Instead, 'youth' is treated here as a social and mutable category that continues to have different meanings in different times and places.

extensive and intricate, it has been suggested that we are now living in a 'shrinking' world where time and space are no longer the barriers they once were (Leyshon, 1995; Waters, 1995). So, in essence, globalization comes to represent the crystallization of the entire world into a single space.

Despite the thoroughly uneven aspects of global processes, which vary across time and place, it has remained theoretically convenient to speculate on the growth of 'risk', uncertainty and insecurity as they come to surround labour market aspirations for future generations (Harvey, 1990 [1989]; Beck, 1998 [1992]; Vail et al., 1999). This work has provided important insights into the problematic nature of economic restructuring in 'new times' by highlighting the power of multi-national corporations and global networks of capital to produce and reproduce inequalities in communities that are far removed from their business headquarters. For a number of writers this has a particularly damaging effect upon youth transitions into local labour markets in post-industrial cities (Hollands, 1997; Mac-Donald, 1999; McDowell, 2002a). And yet at the same time there is a sense that 'something else is going on', where far less is known about how young people are positively adapting to global change at a local scale. As Anthony King has noted, 'differing configurations of the global and the local are producing and transforming different subject positions' (1997 [1991]: 14). Within these relations young people are also active agents who participate, albeit unequally, in the global economy. They are cultural innovators and consumers involved in a complex negotiation with social transformations.

Alongside the 'historical' and 'structural' transformations outlined are also to be found a dazzling array of new 'cultural' processes, practices and ways of being. If de-industrialization has become the primary context upon which structural approaches to youth are situated, then diaspora, multiculture and urban settlement are the brightly embroidered backcloth against which a detailed cultural approach to youth must now also be stitched. This entails developing a richer understanding of race and ethnicity in young lives to see how these relations configure around work, leisure and consumption practices. Supported by new technologies and improvements in communication and transport networks, the current age of migration has spawned a diverse range of diasporic movement and settlement. Moreover, these transformations are changing our daily habitation to the extent that the 'local' and the 'global' are no longer set apart from one another, if indeed they ever were. The focus of this book is then upon the new spaces that emerge in the local–global nexus, and in particular upon the different subject positions young people create in response to global change.

Whilst recognizing the scale and depth of these changes it is important not to oversimplify these processes by purporting that globalization coats each and every place in the thick veneer of its own residue. Instead, many places are given several different coatings over a sustained period of time; others are uniquely textured to resist many of the broad brushstrokes; some locales are patterned in such a way that their imprints unexpectedly emerge despite successive applications; and others still are left untouched as rusting post-industrial surfaces beyond all modern refurbishment. Consequently globalization has not followed a basic 'painting by numbers' schema designed around predictable colour charts and anticipated natural finishes. Closer inspection reveals a gloss that is patchy and spread unevenly by the sweeping roller-brush of change as it comes into direct contact with the unexpected surfaces, ridges and contours of locality and identity. Local cultures have not been entirely superseded by global change either, but rather shape these processes and in doing so influence the opportunities, lifestyles and cultural identities of young people.

In this sense, young people in different places negotiate change in different ways. Rather than witnessing the 'death of geography', through the annihilation of space and time, we find instead that place and geography matter more than ever (Massey and Allen, 1994 [1984]). Global cultures, then, do not operate independently but connect and interact differently at national, regional or local scales (McEwan, 2001). As Anthony Giddens explains, 'Globalization concerns the intersection of presence and absence, the interlacing of social events and social relations "at distance" with local contextualities' (1991:22). The importance of place and locality is nowhere more apparent than in the dialectical relationship 'local–global', or in Roland Robertson's melting of the couplet as 'glocalisation' (1997 [1995]:28). For Robertson, this involves the inter-penetration of 'local' and 'global' forces: ' . . . globalization – in the broadest sense, the compression of the world - has involved and increasingly involves the creation and incorporation of locality, processes which in themselves largely shape, in turn, the compression of the world as a whole' (p. 40). It follows, then, that globalization is as uneven as it is contradictory; moreover, 'homogenising and heterogenising tendencies are mutually implicative' (p. 27). Increasingly there is recognition that people and place also shape the contours of global change. The global encounter, thus, constitutes a new logic of economic and cultural development. However, the extent to which we truly are living in a 'global village' or 'borderless world' where the power of nation states is dissolving and the particularity of local cultures disintegrating is subject to debate. Indeed, for global sceptics such as Hirst and Thompson (1999 [1996]), many of the transformations ascribed to the term 'globalization' - the world as 'one place', the resort to genuinely transnational corporations, the 'death' of nation states, and so forth - are 'mythic' (see also Bradley *et al.*, 2000). What is not in dispute is that the period of late-modernity is characterized by widespread change. It is the contention of this book that in a changing world place and identity continue to matter. Empirically grounded place-based analyses of young lives may now offer a challenge to wider perceptions of globalization as an omnipotent, homogenizing force that goes unheeded, in favour of a more textured and contingent portrayal of youth cultures. *Race, Place and Globalization* is, an attempt to thread together theoretical understandings of large-scale 'macro' transformations with a detailed ethnography into the micro-politics of youth life worlds.

The Fieldwork

The fieldwork takes place in the Northeast region of England. Features of this de-industrial context are discussed at length preceding the ethnography and include detailed descriptions of migration, economy and culture in the locality. The three-year study involves speaking to, observing and interacting with young people over time and within particular spatial contexts. The ethnography incorporates participant observation of young people in multiple settings, 'thick' description of people and place, and taped semi-structured interviews with groups and individuals. A fieldwork journal was also used to recount events happening 'on the move', maintain a sense of chronology and provide biographical information on particular individuals. This meant that an in-depth insight into individual social life-paths could be garnered over time and participants could be observed in different places and situations. Observations and semi-structured interviews with groups and individuals were conducted in neighbourhood, city centre and school settings. These sites were chosen for pragmatic and ethical reasons as they offered key zones where young people could be observed and interviewed in spaces and conditions that were familiar and accessible. Confidentiality was assured and the names of all respondents have been altered to preserve anonymity.

The school-based research was undertaken in two institutions, renamed here Emblevale School and Snowhill Comprehensive. An outline of key respondents accompanies a skeleton description of the institutions and is attached in the Appendices. The research process was also enriched through a series of daily interactions. As I rented a flat on the same estate as a large proportion of the respondents I gained a deeper insight into their daily life-paths. As a number of fieldwork encounters occurred in neighbourhood, city centre spaces and other informal settings they cannot be easily classified. They remain part and parcel of a 'lived' ethnography. Local knowledge and interactions with young people in neighbourhood or city centre zones was ultimately invaluable: it enabled me to develop trust and gain an insight into young people's place within the family and local community. Unexpectedly, it also offered a means of observing truants and gaining insight into the 'curricula of the street', designed around a syllabus of 'hardness', 'scams' and an informal but highly organized economy (Chapter 5).

Moving beyond the institutional level is essential since traditional 'Research on schooling is usually confined to schooling, and thus has difficulty seeing where the school is located in a larger process' (Connell, 1989:292). If the majority of educational studies tend to focus in upon what Ball (1990) terms the 'micro-politics' of schooling, Willis (1977) offers an important exception by connecting processes of schooling to community relations and the local labour market. Looking beyond the institutional level can then broaden the research scale to encompass homes, neighbourhoods, regions and nations as sites for the formation of identities. Moreover, places shape the character of institutions and the identities that lie therein. As the inter-penetration of local–global processes continues, it is now high time to scale the school walls.

Structure

The present volume is interleaved with vignettes from my past and present research histories. As a Masters student, and later researcher at the Department of Cultural Studies in Birmingham, I found debates and writings on race politics, youth cultures and critical ethnography to be highly inspirational. These ideas were given a razor-sharp edge when conducting an ethnography of a Skinhead 'gang' with a colleague, Les Back, as part of an ESRC (Economic and Social Science Research Council) project investigating young perpetrators of racist violence. This research made evident the need to connect 'good theory' with a reflexive and critically informed 'good practice'. Indeed, it later led me to consider the possibilities for white youth to construct a positive ethnicity unencumbered by the baggage of whiteness, racism and nationalism (Nayak, 1999a). Theoretically convenient it may have been to consider race through a standard black/white binary and the old formula that racism = power + prejudice. But what happens when the perpetrators of racism also include young men with African-Caribbean fathers who are also involved in racist violence against local Asian shopkeepers (see Back and Nayak, 1999; Nayak, 1999b)? And what if their peers are themselves downtrodden whites whose emotion is overwhelmingly one of powerlessness? Or, to quicken the mix, what does it now mean to be young, English and white in the present post-imperial moment?

The enigmatic question of whiteness was something I addressed during my doctorate research funded by the Department of Geography, University of Newcastle upon Tyne. At the time I was particularly drawn to the cutting-edge debates on space, place and global change that were happening in the discipline. It the light of these arguments it is no longer sufficient to write about young lives in a spatially disconnected way (Massey, 1998). As social geographers have exemplified, 'particular notions of "race" and nation are articulated by different groups of people at different times and at different scales, from the global to the local (Jackson, 1993: 12-13). In an early piece, the geographer Vaughan Robinson highlights the import-ance of bringing spatial perspectives to bear on the subject of race.

The spatial distribution of ethnic groups *produces* inequalities in access to services, employment, desirable housing and ultimately life chances; it *shapes* patterns of social interactions whether these be positive (e.g. whom you marry) or negative (e.g. whom you attack); and it *contributes* to the development of attitudes and stereotypes. Further-more, our emphasis upon place has generated typologies of regions, of towns and cities which have allowed us to show how the different histories, economies and socio-demographics of these types of place refract overarching processes in contrasting ways and, as a result, produce varying local outcomes. (1987:194)

Linking cultural studies methods, theories and perspectives with geographical insights is, then, an important part of the inter-disciplinary bridge-building exercise that has culminated in this study.

The book is divided into three sections: 'Passing Times', 'Changing Times' and 'Coming Times'. With an emphasis on transition, Part I addresses *'Passing Times'*, and in particular the transformations that have seen materialist studies of youth become displaced by more complex cultural accounts of youth lifestyles. Chapter 2 critically evaluates the shift from structural–materialist perspectives to cultural–postmodernist tendencies. It also addresses the movement from subcultures to new youth 'tribes'. Chapter 3 explores the embedded historical and material context in which the research takes place, with an emphasis upon the erosion of an older industrial culture and the major impact this is having upon people and place. Part II, *'Changing Times'*, attempts to capture the process of transition in young lives before exploring the divergent impacts this is having upon youth formations that occupy different 'youthscapes' distinguished by unique geographical, historical and cultural variations. It addresses the multiple and creative ways in which young people respond to change through elaborating 'localist' (Chapter 4), 'survivalist' (Chapter 5) and 'globalist' (Chapter 6) subcultural tendencies. In Part III, *'Coming Times'*, I explore the changing youth debates surrounding race, place and ethnicity. The section argues for a need to traverse black/white racial binaries in favour of a more complex multiculturalism in tune with new global rhythms. It concludes by reconsidering youth cultures in the contemporary moment and offering clear pointers for challenging social and racial inequalities.

Passing Times

The following chapter *'Placing Subcultures'*, maps the study of youth cultures historically, theoretically and geographically. It begins by outlining the emergence of subcultural studies in the US before exploring its growth and development, most notably in the UK. The chapter then considers the varied critiques that have been made of subcultural methods. In particular, it contains a critical engagement with postmodernism, a paradigm which has asked some of the most challenging questions of subcultural research in recent times, especially in the light of previous analyses of political economy. The chapter concludes by arguing for a deeper engagement with issues of place and location in young lives. To achieve this goal it suggests that productive synergies can occur by intertwining social geography with cultural studies perspectives to provide new 'maps of meaning' (Jackson, 1995 [1989]). These are used to provide an enriched ethnographic focus on people and place.

Chapter 3 reveals how the globalization of migration is altering even the most ostensibly white regions. The chapter explores the ways in which diasporic movement and settlement have impacted upon the Northeast region of England and the possibilities for new local identities. Drawing upon local historiography, the work seeks to move beyond the conventional 'white highlands' assumption that has come to mark the region to date. By illustrating the complex, sometimes hidden histories of settlement, the account aims to provide more inclusive ways of thinking about place and locality. In particular, the chapter illuminates the competing and contradictory role that racism and anti-racism have played in the region (Gilroy, 1994 [1992]). The aim is not simply to reiterate that peripheral white regions are areas in which parochialism has flourished (Gaine, 1987, 1995) but also to reveal authentic struggles for social justice. It is argued that a turn to recent labour and anti-fascist points of resistance provides an important means for conceptualizing the region in a way that is entirely in keeping with 'tradition', place and local identity. If recent history is anything to go by, sewing together the 'local' and the 'global' does not have to be an act of surgical trauma.

Changing Times

The following three chapters each provide case studies of different subcultural responses to global change and economic restructuring in the North East of England. *'Real Geordies'* begins by outlining the profound labour market transformations that have occurred in the region. These changes have most directly impinged upon the lives of this once skilled stratum of the English working class whose attitudes and aspirations are equated with a former labour aristocracy. It then turns to the meaning of 'Geordie' and its relevance in contemporary times. Here, the subculture of young men known as the *Real Geordies* is seen to produce a resilient and localized response to the period of change and fluctuation. The celebration of the 'local' through felt identifications with people, place and what Raymond Williams has called 'structures of feeling' become a way of revitalizing the fading fabric of local pride in the context of de-industrialization. It is argued that the recuperation of local identity occurs not in the traditional sphere of labour and production, but in the creatively re-worked zone of consumption. Here, the 'traditional' values and attachments associated with manual culture are displaced and symbolically retrieved in the corporeal tasks of football and drinking. For these 'local lads' living in insecure times, being a *Real Geordie* is not a mark of shame but a badge of honour used to signal white male pride and working-class 'respectability'.

Chapter 5 considers a second local subculture, *Charver Kids*. It reveals how the *Charver* subculture have been 'stained' by long-term familial unemployment, blocked opportunities and a distinct lack of social mobility. As a stigmatized 'underclass', these families are subject to a longstanding urban discourse that consistently portrays them as the 'undeserving' poor, 'parasitic' and 'beyond the pale'. At the same time, this group and the places they inhabit are frequently deemed 'dangerous', 'undisciplined' and 'untouchable'. In other words, if the *Real Geordies* are aspiring, upwardly mobile carriers of a 'respectable' white working-class lineage, then the *Charver Kids* are the 'rough', irredeemable Other whose lives spiral down and regress in Tyneside's urban 'sink' estates. In view of these conditions, *Charvers* have established new ways of living, through the development of an alternative market economy. Unable to achieve white respectability through legitimate economic means, the subculture resort to survivalist strategies of existence - street-crime, 'scams' and the participation in an informal or 'black' economy. These actions further augment the not-quite-white status of this group and are seen as biting responses to the uneven processes of globalization and the increasing polarization of different socio-economic groups.

After the 'localist' and 'suvivalist' responses to global change pursued respectively by the *Real Geordies* and *Charver Kids*, Chapter 6 considers the take-up of a 'global' perspective by a colourful patchwork of experimental and outwardly looking youth. '"*Wiggers*", "*Wannabes*" and "*White Negroes*"' explores the new forms of cultural identity being enacted by young people even in mainly white areas. The chapter focuses upon four zones of bodily consumption - sport, fashion, hairstyles and music - to see how young people are experimenting with a new corporeal canvas that is in keeping with the cultural excess of global times. The chapter explains how these embodied performances offer new ways of thinking about identity that traverse and rework the bounded restrictions of place, locality and nationhood. Cross-cultural fusion is found to be a refreshing tonic that can at once loosen local vernacular and enable a new multiculture to speak. This act of creolization is 'spoken' through the body and articulated across the multiple surfaces of youth culture. However, Chapter 6 also engages with the limits of cultural syncretism and the contradictory global forms of consumption that re-inscribe racial difference through a reification of blackness.

Coming Times

Chapter 7, on 'Contemporary Racisms and Ethnicities', seeks to go beyond the established black/white racial dualism. It provides an empirically grounded and theoretically informed debate about the political limits of black/white racial dichotomies. Through an ethnographic excavation of the lives of young people, the chapter reveals the complex and contingent ways in which racism and anti-racism feature in their lives. The work identifies how anti-racist practice may be deemed by young people to be 'favouring' minorities and thereby seen as an unfair, 'anti-white' mode of regulation. This unspoken resentment is illustrated in a 'white backlash' that has seen orthodox anti-racism disappear underground, after it fleetingly placed its head above the parapet in the 1980s. At a local level anti-racism is seen to be subject to a widespread 'discourse of derision' which, though seldom deserved, has become deeply ingrained in local myth and folklore. Rescuing some of the relevant components of the project, where anti-racism may appear a Southern English, 'anti-white' form of politicking, is shown to be highly problematic in Northern white bastions with once strong labouring traditions.

The concluding chapter pulls out three thematic strands from the research. The reconsideration of youth cultures includes a discussion of change and continuity; the meaning of whiteness; and the role of place and identity. To this extent, post-industrialism is treated throughout not as an incisive breach with manufacturing and industry, but as an ongoing process fraught with contradiction and uncertainties that young people must negotiate. The section is cautious not to over-exaggerate the depth and extent of change whilst recognizing the significance of recent transformations. However, economic and cultural changes are embedded and inscribed within one another, meaning that gender, ethnicity and class identities cannot be held apart from de-industrialization but are central to this process. In addressing the rarely spoken question of white ethnicities, the chapter seeks to go beyond a black/white racial dualism. Instead it argues for a critical engagement with the meaning of whiteness in young lives and an evaluation of the new subject positions available for emerging white-Anglo identities. The chapter provides clear insight into how the binds of whiteness can be untied by drawing upon young people's cultural and material histories and situating these in a manner more favourable to the complexity of coming times. Finally, despite the social, economic, political and cultural transformations we are witnessing in late-modernity, the study suggests that place and locality continue to be of marked significance in the landscape of youth. Here, the material and cultural significance of place is juxtaposed with postmodern theories of 'placelessness', fragmentation and dis-integration. It is argued that richer engagement with theory and practice is required if we are to do genuine justice to the multiple complexities of everyday life.

To conclude, this is a book about young people, ethnicity and social change. It is a theoretically informed historical ethnography. As part of a spatial cultural studies it seeks to situate young people in time and place. It also encourages readers to reconsider the value of social class in debates on race and ethnicity at a time when more fashionable post-colonial theories have come to the fore. In doing so, it deploys a form of discursive materialism that is in critical dialogue with recent postmodern perspectives. The work is split into three sections that relate to recent transformations: 'Passing Times', 'Changing Times' and 'Coming Times'. The monograph uses historical, structural and cultural perspectives to provide a multi-layered analysis of young lives. It also draws upon inter-disciplinary research including cultural studies writings on youth; human geography perspectives on globalization, space and place; and the wider sociology of race and ethnic relations. While the book may inevitably disappoint certain disciplinary purists, it is envisaged that working across these boundaries may enable creative tensions and new harmonies to speak. *Race, Place and Globalization* is a port-hole into this trans-disciplinary debate, not a point of closure.

–2–

Placing Subcultures:
Ethnographic Methods and Youth Studies

The History of Subcultural Studies

In anthropology, sociology, criminology, cultural studies and education the concept of 'subculture' has been an important theoretical mode of analysis and methodological technique with which to interpret young people's social lives. Originally imposed on 'underground' groups that were felt to differ from the social 'mainstream', the term had connotations that suggested these groups were subterranean, subordinate and, at least potentially, subversive social formations (Gelder and Thornton, 1997). Over time these subcultures would acquire labels and identities such as Teddy Boys, Mods, Skinheads, Rastas, Punks and Goths. Classically subcultures were thought to operate with a different ethos that could challenge or transgress the values held by wider society, for example through the Rastafarian ideology of Jah, the anarchism of Punk or the nomadic lifestyles of Travellers, Squatters and Eco-warriors. To this extent, subcultures were frequently theorized as 'counter-cultures' defined 'as against' the values, beliefs and social practices of the prevailing society. In less spectacular fashion, youth writers began to suggest that subcultures may coalesce around a loose configuration of values that may materialize through a given activity: skateboarding, break-dancing, or an interest in the Nu-Metal music scene, for example.

More recently, the epistemological and methodological status of subculture has been subject to an unflinching critique, as we shall go on to discover. In this chapter I seek to highlight some of the main issues that have emerged in debates on youth, subculture and ethnography. To shed light upon these themes I will briefly refer to key 'moments' in the recent history of youth studies. The review will draw upon important urban studies undertaken at the University of Chicago, USA; the subcultural work that took place at the University of Birmingham, UK; the Marxist critical theory pursued by scholars at the University of Frankfurt in Germany; and the new studies of 'deviancy' proposed at the National Deviancy Conference by UK criminologists. This international dialogue, compressed here so as not to test the patience of the reader, reveals how different theoretical, empirical and methodological techniques were being developed in the study of youth subcultures. These approaches were often complementary and drew inspiration from the work already undertaken in respective fields. This body of work represents the rich diversity of research within youth studies and the developing interest in urban ethnographies.

Producing a surfeit of material from the 1920s onwards, scholars based at the Department of Sociology and Anthropology at the University of Chicago, USA, were early pioneers of subcultural investigation. The 'Chicago School', as the group became known, were associated with a specific brand of urban micro-sociology that explored what were then thought to be the shadier recesses of polite society, including subcultural studies of youth gangs, table-dancing, cock-fighting and drug-taking. In contrast to criminological studies propagating that 'deviant' behaviour was the product of individual traits and personality defects, the Chicago School persuasively argued that crime and juvenile delinquency must be under-stood within the context of the working-class neighbourhoods, ghettos and slums from whence they arose. For example, William Foote Whyte's (1981 [1943]) analysis of Boston gang-life reveals not the chaos and breakdown of social rules in an Italian-American slum, but the emergence of an organized, hierarchical and highly ordered *Street Corner Society*, the title of this enduring study.

Later Chicago studies pursued this theme, with deviance regarded as a *normative* outcome when the perspective of subcultural actors was given primacy. For these writers, subcultural analysis offers a window on the world that enables us to see and understand people's social actions in their immediate cultural context. Thus, Albert Cohen (1997 [1955]) speculated that subcultures emerge when individuals with similar experiences and concerns come together to provide meaningful solutions to their problems. Although these collective responses may facilitate the development of a subculture with its own norms and values, for Cohen this invariably entails a sharper distancing from and by the dominant culture, as witnessed in Howard Becker's (1973 [1963]) detailed account *Outsiders*. The emphasis on subcultures as 'outsiders' operating on the dark margins of society began to recede as working-class youth cultures grew more visible with the advent of Rock 'n' Roll and the increased spending power obtained during the early post-war consumerist years (Osgerby, 1998). The creation of elaborate working-class youth styles, coupled with the attendant public fears that surrounded them, encouraged writers to reconsider the meaning of subculture beyond the trope of being social deviants or outsiders. Gradually subcultures were seen as micro-communities, groups within groups, who came to share similar felt and understood interests in music, taste, fashion, politics, art, sport, dance and a whole spectrum of embodied social practices.

The move away from the dominating discourse of 'deviancy' and 'delinquency' proposed by Becker and other Chicago academics was powerfully augmented in Britain with a series of dynamic presentations delivered to the National Deviancy Conference from the late sixties to the early seventies. Thus, in *Images of Deviance*, Stanley Cohen's (1971) edited collection deriving from the conference papers, we find a proliferation of essays on such topics as drug use, policing, thieving, football hooliganism and industrial sabotage. Jock Young's (1972 [1971]) study on the social meaning of drug use and Stanley Cohen's (1973 [1972]) later, expert analysis *Folk Devils and Moral Panics* were evidence of a new, highly influential approach to youth subculture and the question of 'deviancy'. Through a detailed account of Mods and Rockers in South East England between 1963 and 1966, Cohen demonstrated how youth subcultures were portrayed as national 'folk devils' in press and media reports, thereby becoming a repository for 'deviance' and a broader set of social 'moral panics'. For Cohen, the alternative vocabulary through which youth subcultures were now being discussed by critical commentators and contributors to the National Deviancy Conference was part of a new 'transactional' response to 'deviancy'. Cohen explained:

> The older tradition was *canonical* in the sense that it saw the concepts it worked with as authoritative, standard, accepted, given and unquestionable. The new tradition is sceptical in the sense that when it sees terms like 'deviant', it asks 'deviant to whom?' or 'deviant from what?'; when told that something is a social problem, it asks 'problematic to whom?'; when certain conditions or behaviour are described as dysfunctional, embarrassing, threatening or dangerous, it asks 'says who?' and 'why?'. In other words, these concepts and descriptions are not assumed to have a taken-for-granted status. (1973 [1972]:12)

The new 'transactional' ideas, then, offer a feisty challenge to pathological studies of youth and accounts that view young people as morally responsible for their low social status as 'outsiders' or 'delinquents'.

The Centre for Contemporary Cultural Studies

Throughout the 1970s and 1980s, British writers from the University of Birmingham's Centre for Contemporary Cultural Studies (CCCS) were to emerge as some of the most eloquent and influential exponents of youth subculture. Their writings reflect a deep commitment to Marxist and neo-Marxist traditions, the roots of which can be found in the work of Karl Marx, Frederich Engels, Louis Althusser and most evidently in Antonio Gramsci's theories of power and hegemony. The CCCS was also furnished with a wealth of pioneering labour historians and cultural writers, including Raymond Williams, Richard Hoggart, Richard Johnson and Stuart Hall, whose early intellectual writings on social class and education were to provide the historical apparatus for an incisive, material cultural studies. A key contribution made by these writers was their acute sensitivity to popular histories and everyday life, a recognition that stretched to encompass the 'making' of histories as complex ideological activity that is subjectively given meaning through selective acts of remembrance and forgetting (Johnson *et al.*, 1982).

The vigorous engagement with the popular was to develop and extend the early 'critical theory' approach adopted by associates from the Institute for Social Research at the University of Frankfurt. More popularly termed the 'Frankfurt School', Theodor Adorno, Walter Benjamin, Herbert Marcuse and Max Horkheimer were established leading lights of German Marxist critiques on 'mass culture'. Utilizing Marxist notions of 'false consciousness', the Frankfurt School viewed popular culture as a type of saccharin bubble-gum, ideologically imposed from above for ordinary people to ruminate upon in an uncritical, de-politicized manner. In contrast, by adapting Gramsci's theories of hegemony, the CCCS were able to conceptualize popular culture in a more complex form as a shifting terrain in a 'war of manoeuvre' that was marked not only by coercion but also by consent. Moreover, hegemonic consensus was not an ideological given – the culmination of dominant ruling ideas holding sway over subordinated classes – but achieved by an ongoing process of resistance, negotiation and incorporation. In this dynamic reworking, popular culture was no longer the pink candy-floss imposed from above to mask ideology but was *itself an arena for class conflict and struggle* between dominant and opposing groups. For the early CCCS writers, youth subcultures, then, are 'smaller, more localised and differentiated structures' which must be placed in 'relation to the wider class-cultural networks of which they form a distinctive part' (Clarke *et al.*, 1977 [1975]:16). In this reading, subcultural practices are 'rituals of resistance' enacted by working-class youth in response to the break-up of traditional communities and an unbridled post-war consumerism that was creating a sharply visible, unequal distribution of wealth.

Phil Cohen's (1972) seminal work on subcultural conflict and working-class community, which was to evolve into a detailed cultural geography of social relations in London's East End (see Robins and Cohen, 1978), was in many respects a template for future CCCS work on youth subcultures. Cohen argued that post-war British youth subcultures engage in an 'imaginary' relationship with older working-class traditions and past times. Here, the exhibition of a subcultural identity is a means of expressing and 'magically resolving' the crisis of class relations – at least at the level of the symbolic – through territorial practices and stylistic gestures. The symbolic aspects of class resistance are then obliquely signified and circuitously carried in youth subcultures. Consequently, John Clarke, in his analysis of Skinhead subcultures claims members had a 'subordinated view' of their situation where 'acceptance of racial scapegoating . . . displaced antagonisms from their real structural sources' (1974:279). Embellishing on Cohen's thesis, he remarks in a later study:

Our basic thesis about the Skinheads centres around the notion of community. We would argue that the Skinhead style represents an attempt to re-create through the 'mob' the traditional working class community, as a substitution for the real decline of the latter. The underlying social dynamic for style, in this light, is the relative worsening of the situation of the working class . . . . (Clarke, 1977 [1975]:99)

The focus on subculture, social class and resistance is emblematic of a number of essays found in the CCCS youth studies collection *Resistance through Rituals* (Hall and Jefferson, 1977). The majority of these Marxist-inspired essays apply a complex form of textual semiotics (described below) to interpret the cultural meanings of youth styles and activities. Here the focus on youth subcultures is derived from visual representation, press reports, historical and secondary sources.

Lest we forget, members from the CCCS also undertook some detailed ethnographic research that was closer (if not politically then at least methodologically) to the traditions pursued by Chicago sociologists. Key ethnographic studies were to include Paul Willis's (1978) vibrant analysis of Hippy and Biker subcultures, Chris Griffin's (1985) research concerning young women's transitions from school to work, Simon Jones's (1988) exemplary neighbourhood ethnography of multiethnic youth relations and Angela McRobbie's (1991) youth club observations of teenage girls. Most famous, amidst this rich and diverse collection, is Willis's landmark text, *Learning to Labour* (1977), which is certainly worthy of further discussion here for its attempt to bring together structural processes with cultural formations.

In this latter study, Willis divulges 'how working-class kids get working-class jobs'. The author argues that schools are sites for the reproduction of class relations; however, it is only by observing, speaking to and interacting with a 'counterculture' of working-class boys known as the 'Lads' that Willis is able to deliver a fascinating account of their daily existence. He describes how the 'Lads' adopt a 'counter-cultural' response to education that demarcates them from 'Ear'oles', that is, conformist academically orientated youth and the bourgeois institution of schooling. On the surface this stance appears anti-authoritarian in outlook, but in actuality it is transposed into perfect preparation for the world of manual work. Through rituals of non-conformity, the 'Lads' hasten their departure into factory work, a world in which their codes and values are endorsed and mutually understood. Consequently Willis remarks upon a 'parallelism' between the counterculture of the 'Lads' and the culture of the shop-floor, where a masculine ethos, trickery and subversion are the essence of factory life. Thus, 'When the lad reaches the factory there is no shock, only recognition', asserts Willis, since 'he is immediately familiar with many of the shop-floor practices: defeating boredom, timewasting, heavy and physical humour'(1977:193), and so forth. However, the conventional CCCS focus on young men and class reproduction became increasingly difficult to sustain as feminism and race-conscious critiques of subculture came to the fore.

The Critique of Subculture

Since the prominent writings of the Birmingham CCCS in the seventies and eighties there have been two other significant approaches to subculture which derive from a 'structuralist anti-oppressive' sensibility and a later 'postmodernist' tradition. Where the former has attempted to foreground the subordinated identities of girls, women and ethnic minorities (see Fuller, 1982; Griffin, 1985; Mac an Ghaill, 1988; McRobbie, 1991; Mirza, 1992), the latter has sought to fragment, disperse and question notions of subcultural identity altogether. A defining component of the structuralist subcultural approach was to maintain a focus on relations of power but extend these insights to a more thought-out consideration of institutional racism and sexism (example, see Hollands, 1990). As we shall discover, these standpoints offered ontological and epistemological critiques of the masculinist subcultural tradition. However, it is the cluster of ideas associated with postmodernist tendencies that have become the new flora and fauna upon which contemporary critiques of subculture now thrive. Although this volume will engage with key ideas and recent writings from each of these traditions, it works across these tensions in an attempt to wed together structural and cultural approaches to youth. The aim, then, is not to do away with subcultural studies, as some postmodern writers propose, but to encourage a more critical and reflexive use of the term 'subculture' that can enable us to situate young lives culturally and materially in changing times. The recent criticisms of subculture discussed below can, then, allow us to develop a richer understanding of youth cultures befitting of global times.

Typologies

For postmodernist thinkers a fallacy of the subcultural approach is the overwhelming sense that young people are somehow the living embodiments of the subcultures they come to represent. Their subjectivities are only 'revealed', then, by the researcher through a discursive register of well-worn sociological 'types', such as the hell-bent football Hooligan, the anarchic Punk or the ecstasy-fuelled Raver. Here, there is a danger that young lives are reduced to the atomized essences of an imagined authenticity. Furthermore, these portraits may actually serve to reinforce social stereotypes by viewing young people only through the restrictive lens of subculture. The tendency to create typologies is, according to Andrew Tolson, a feature of subcultural portraits that dates back to the early character studies of Henry Mayhew. Tolson declares, 'Social identities are not really *constructed* in this type of interview, they are presupposed. They are defined in terms of an individual already possessing a certain role or status . . . which provides a prior qualification from which to speak' (1990:19).

More subtle approaches that illustrate complexity and inconsistency within youth formations may enable stereotypes to be more readily imploded. Crucially we must not lose sight of the fact that subcultural studies are, after all, 'exercises in representation' (Thornton, 1997:1). This is evident in the work of Widdicombe and Wooffitt, who use language as the medium to interpret 'how it was that specific subcultural identities became salient in specific moments in the accounts' (1995:2) of young people. By investigating 'the constitutive nature of language' (p. 1), the authors are able to place a sharper focus on subculture as a performative act of being and becoming.

In an attempt to avoid portraying youth subcultures as monolithic, hermetically sealed entities, contemporary writers have drawn upon the postmodernist language of 'hybridity',[2] 'tribes', 'neo-tribes', 'lifestyles', 'clubcultures', 'taste cultures' and 'pseudo-communities' (see for example, Brake, 1993 [1985]; Redhead, 1995; Thornton, 1995; McRobbie, 1996 [1994]; Featherstone, 1998 [1991]; Bennett, 1999a). For postmodern writers this 'slippery' terminology is more appropriate for explaining the changing morphology of club cultures, or the 'virtual communities' evoked when 'surfing' the net, using home entertainment systems or interacting on-line through new media technologies of communication. These approaches have enabled us to appreciate that youth cultures are not static formations but comprise 'a series of temporal gatherings characterized by fluid boundaries and floating memberships' (Bennett, 1999a: 600). Rather than being caught in suspended animation, subcultures orbit around a moving constellation of signs, symbols, practices and motifs. To this extent, it may be more accurate to consider subcultures as 'discursive clusters' that momentarily coalesce around a configuration of values only to transform and mutate again, in a perpetual state of flux and cultural repositioning. Indeed, '*youthscapes*' is a phrase I have used throughout the book to indicate the potential diversity and mobility of youth subcultural formations and their unique relationships to place. Interpreting subcultures in this way is my attempt to recognize not only that young people insert themselves within particular subject positions, but also that their youthscapes are discursively positioned through the magnetic pull of others – peer groups, media reports or the accounts of sociologists. The different youthscapes envisioned here – *Real Geordies*, *Charver Kids* and *Wannabes* – are labels internally generated by the groups themselves, or remain the popular terms used by other youth groups to identify these stylistic formations.

In light of postmodernist critiques, subculture cannot be read as a fixed, stable and determining point of existence around which youth identities are organized but rather forms a transitional and nebulous *moment of being* in young people's

---

2. There remains a concern that the postmodernist lexicon of 'hybridity', 'tribes' and 'neo-tribes' could unwittingly reproduce older anthropological distinctions and serve to racialize bodies of working-class youth as 'Other'. For a racial critique of hybridity, see R. Young, 1995.

coming-of-age. The new emphasis on the hybrid experiences of youth have enabled researchers to move away from any sense of these cultures as bounded typologies whose values are consistent and without contradiction. In recent writings on youth we are perhaps witnessing the 'death of subculture', as exemplified in the title of Muggleton and Weinzierl's collection *The Post-Subcultures Reader* (in press). Thus, in a renunciation of older class-based models of youth, Steve Redhead has gone as far as to argue that it is opportune to move from 'subculture' to 'clubcultures' (1997). The passing of subculture is also evident in Bennett's clarion call to speak of 'neo-tribes' and Featherstone's claim that youth subcultures 'operated as fixed symbolic structures which are now rejected or ironically parodied and collaged' (1998:100). Despite these invaluable insights, *Race, Place and Globalization* suggests that places and material cultures do shape contemporary youthscapes, albeit in complex and variable ways.

Class Reductionism

Studies on the relationship between subculture and economy provide some of the most thoughtful, detailed and inspiring analyses of young lives. This body of work supplies a compelling rationale for the need to place youth studies in relation to the structural components of education, training, employment, housing and welfare. With a keen radical edge, Marxist and neo-Marxist accounts of subculture have sliced through superficial representations of youth as 'mindless hooligans' to produce a rigorous, informed analysis of political economy. British post-war subcultural theorists in particular began to see these social groups not as youthful formations to be cajoled and nursed back into line but rather as critical segments of society that contained the seeds of resistance and working-class empowerment.

A concern that dogged early cultural studies of youth was the underlying premise that subcultures are necessarily formed in opposition to an authoritarian bourgeois state. For example, early social studies such as T.R. Fyvel's (1963 [1961]) analysis of Teddy Boys portrayed them as 'Rebellious youth in the welfare state'. The neo-Marxist approach adopted by the CCCS studies was to see young people as the agents of social change where their actions are, in the final analysis, 'rituals of resistance'. In contrast, postmodernist approaches to subculture have asserted that such youth formations are organized as much through commercial enterprise as in 'resistance' to the capitalist economy. Here, a subcultural identity can be purchased over the counter as it is made available through clever niche marketing and an increased availability of select music, clothes, accessories and memorabilia. In the contemporary global marketplace this has meant many young lives are marked as much by conformity with capitalism as opposed to blunt socio-economic resistance (Klein, 2000), with a greater awareness of parody, mixing

and creative innovation. In contrast to the authentic class struggles depicted in
Resistance through Rituals and a range of CCCS stencilled papers, postmodernist
writers have been less convinced by the 'genuine' qualities they feel were ascribed
to subcultures and social class formations. Thus, Redhead insists that 'authentic
subcultures' were 'produced by the sub-cultural theorists, not the other way round'
(1990:25). Elsewhere, he notes how 'The fragmentation of the audience(s) for
popular music and its culture in the 1990s makes *Subculture* theory outdated.'
However, he continues, 'It does not mean there are no subcultures any longer:
these abound in youth culture today, but are frequently grounded in market niches
of the contemporary global music industry' (1995:103).

The theory-led and occasionally deterministic approach of Marxist scholars
has also been accused of instigating a *reductionist* analysis whereby the economic
base is given primacy over other social relations and systems of oppression.
Consider how Pearson's early observations of 'paki-basing' in the Northern
English town of Lancashire become wedded to an all-encompassing analysis of
economy.

> Only if we enter into the heart of working class life can we understand these beliefs and
> actions. 'Paki-bashing' is a primitive form of political and economic struggle. It is an
> inarticulate and finally impotent attempt to act directly on the conditions of the market
> – whether the exchange value which is contested concerns housing, labour power or
> girls. (1976: 69)

This 'ruling ideas'[3] framework operates as a grand narrative through which
complex and diverse social phenomena – violence, sexual politics and racism –
come to be subsumed in what appears an over-arching philosophical line of
inquiry. In this analysis, the 'impotent' Skins occupy a castrated/subordinate
masculinity vis-à-vis their socio-economic location, the anger for which is displaced into violent outbursts. Here, the Skins are shadow-boxers *extraordinaire*,
flexing their muscles in pumped-up exhibitions that never truly alter their 'real'
social class situation. However, the overly rational economic account may not
capture the deep investments and 'structures of feeling' entailed when adopting
subcultural style and practice. There is also more to some of these antagonistic
practices than mere shadow-boxing, as the perspectives of 'paki-bashing' victims
and the female recipients cited above could no doubt inform. As such, the focus on
class at the expense of other 'subordinated' identities can lead to an unabashed
celebration of white masculinity, seen in Pearson's romantic notion of the 'mis-
directed heroism of the "pakibasher"' (1976: 86). Here, there remains an absence
of individual agency, with white patriots viewed as passive victims of the state,

3. I am grateful to Richard Johnson for the use of this term. It is drawn from the Marxist notion
that the ideas of the ruling class are, in every epoch, the ruling ideas.

acting under a 'mis-directed' false consciousness. The question of why *some* working-class youth may assume a subcultural identity whilst others do not is never fully reckoned with. Rather than treating white, racist activities as the pointless stretching of symbolic sinew, recent ethnographies have revealed how such activities are in part a response to material deprivation but also a core way of asserting an unequivocal white masculinity in uncertain times (Healy, 1996; Nayak, 1999b).

Masculinism

The issue of masculinism has haunted subcultural theory since its inception and continued to dominate American, British and Canadian research up until the late 1970s and early 1980s (Brake, 1993 [1985]; Griffin, 1993). Feminist critiques of subcultural theory have focused upon the implicit and even explicit identifications male researchers made with their all-male research groups. This homosocial act, itself a form of male bonding, was to see the experience of white working-class boys come to be 'representative' of youth. Consequently, the lives of girls and ethnic minorities were frequently peripheral or 'invisible' within these accounts. As early as 1975, McRobbie and Garber noted how 'the very term "sub-culture" has acquired such strong masculine overtones' (1977 [1975]: 211). Thus, in a retrospective gaze back at the classic collaborative study *Knuckle Sandwich* (Robins and Cohen, 1978), a tale of urban, working-class life, Phil Cohen admits that 'the book was lambasted by feminists for its masculinist standpoint. Even though we had definitely not celebrated the laddish culture of violence which we described, we had certainly failed to frame it with an equally strongly weighted account of working-class cultures of femininity' (1997:87).

This raises a further question about gender: are girls even active in the public spectacle of subculture? Closer inspection reveals that many girls have participated in subcultures but to a large extent have evaded the male gaze. Girls may even be involved in different subcultural activities to their male counterparts, indicating further subdivisions within youth. Even in an aggressively masculine subculture such as that of the Skinheads there is evidence of female participation (McRobbie and Garber, 1977 [1975]). This is seen in the striking Skinhead girls of the 1970s who adopted feather-cut hairstyles as they began to re-position that once iconic symbol of working-class masculinity, the Doc Marten's boot. In Daniel and McGuire's (1972) early portrait of an East End Skinhead gang known as the Collinwood, the emphasis is solely on male respondents, yet group members themselves refer to the presence of female Skins. As one Collinwood member reported, 'Even the birds used to go round and beat the blokes up, we see two birds one day with a shorter crop than ours' (p. 34). Also, in Richard Allen's eponymous

Skinhead fiction novels of the 1970s, which were renowned for their macho bravado, volumes entitled *Skinhead Girls*, *Sorts* and *Knuckle Girls* were readily available (Allen, 1992); this at least suggests a circuit of female subcultural readership, if not participation (see Walter, 1998). The multiple relationships girls and young women may have with subcultures was to imply a methodological re-conceptualization of youth.

> It may, then, be a matter, not of the absence or presence of girls in sub-cultures, but of a whole alternative network of responses and activities through which girls negotiate their relation to the sub-cultures or even make positive moves away from the subcultural option. (McRobbie and Garber, 1977 [1975]:216).

In response, the early eighties witnessed feminist studies of girls and women as a challenge to the accepted orthodoxy of subculture as an inherently masculine pursuit. However, as Stanley and Wise (1983) have commented in their study of epistemology, a more radical perspective is required than simply including women within research – this perspective would entail challenging the masculinist values of the research process itself. Research into what Angela McRobbie (1997) has called 'different, youthful subjectivities' gradually came to the fore in this period, where gender and ethnicity began to compete with social class for primacy in British youth-based studies. Examples of feminist work in the field include Anna Pollert's (1981) workplace excavation, *Girls, Wives, Factory Lives*; Christine Griffin's (1985) educational study, *Typical Girls?*; Angela McRobbie's research on teenage femininities (1991, 1996 [1994]); Sue Lees's (1986) work with adolescent girls, *Losing Out*; Mary Fuller's (1982) study of black girls in the comprehensive system; and Anne Campbell's (1991 [1984] recognized volume, *Girls in the Gang*. The aim in this work was to make girls 'visible' in studies of youth and thereby challenge the conventional 'view from the boys', the unapologetic title of Parker's (1974) famous study of youth in inner-city Liverpool.

This body of work (and much more besides) has rescued girls from the margins of youth studies and offered a searing critique of the masculinism inherent in much early work. But the problem of girls' invisibility within subculture may not rest entirely with masculinist ascription. The gendering of space has also impacted upon the issue of who researchers whom and in what contexts. As David Morgan asserts, 'Qualitative methodology and ethnography after all has its own brand of *machismo* with its image of the male sociologist bringing back news from the fringes of society, the lower depths, the mean streets, areas traditionally "off limits" to women investigators' (1981:86–7). While most subcultural studies explore the public terrain of leisure spaces, streets and youth institutions, girls may in fact be negotiating a private subculture at home that is cemented through make-up routines, a fascination for teen-magazines, dancing/listening to particular records and 'girl-talk' (see McRobbie, 1991).[4] Due to the structural relationships that women have with domesticity, these writers have pointed to the centrality of a 'culture of the bedroom' (McRobbie and Garber, 1977 [1975]:213) when it comes to the production of teenage femininities and the importance of popular culture (Kehily, 2002).

In a self-proclaimed 'ethnographic and feminist account' of New Wave Girls, Blackman (1997) chose to enter the domestic setting to gather data on female friendship groups by observing girls 'skiving' (truanting) or by learning about sleep-overs. In another ethnographic exploration of these friendships Val Hey (1997) displays admirable initiative in accessing 'girls' worlds' by examining the scribbled notes and messages passed between girls in classroom contexts and later discarded in the bin. Exploring these 'hidden' spaces (homes, bedrooms and intimate cultural worlds) is always difficult and raises a number of methodological and ethical issues. Moreover, when girls do engage in subcultural activity which involves experimentation with drugs, alcohol, sex or violence, say, they may be less likely to brag about these accounts publicly for fear of usurping the stringently sexist codes of teenage femininity (Canaan, 1986; Lees, 1986, 1993). In other words, the very actions that may be read as a *positive* assertion of masculinity and 'growing-up' for young men may have *negative* consequences for the social and sexual lives and reputations of young women.

Furthermore, a heterosexual presumption has come to mark most studies of youth subculture. As Michael Brake points out, 'Youth culture has been male dominated and predominantly heterosexual, thus celebrating masculinity and excluding girls to the periphery' (1993 [1985]:29). With only a small number of studies on *young* gay and lesbian lives (see Trenchard and Warren, 1984; Mac an Ghaill, 1991; Unks, 1995), Murray Healy's (1996) book *Gay Skins* forms an important exception to this trend. Within, Healy skilfully demonstrates how the gay Skinhead 'short-circuits accepted beliefs about real masculinity' (p. 5), since 'the queer skin's value is that he opens the closed signifier of masculine authority' (p. 200). Moreover, Healy's respondents give way to the end of 'innocent' notions of a gay subject in their life-histories, with a number implicated in the full repertoire of racist practices associated with the second wave of Skinhead youth in the late seventies and early eighties.

As feminist studies of youth began to question the inherent masculinism of subcultural representations, writers grew increasingly aware of the overbearing whiteness of many of these studies (Amos and Parmar, 1984). Thus, in a critique of working-class subculture, Mary Fuller elaborated on the silent issues of gender and race rarely discussed by sociological investigators: 'Their efforts have been almost exclusively concentrated on white sub-cultures . . . the balance being

4. However, Griffin (1993) has pointed out that the 'public' and 'private' spheres are themselves interrelated and drawn attention to the dangers of pathologizing young women as simply domestic inhabitants.

heavily towards male (and white) adolescent experiences and cultural expressions. In other words not only does this tradition in sociology treat the world of adolescence as essentially male, but it also considers adolescents to be racially undifferentiated' (1982: 270).

Since Fuller's remarks, there have been a series of studies on black youth subcultures (Hebdige, 1977; Mac an Ghaill, 1988; Alexander,1996, 2000; Sewell, 1997). However, the fact that a cursory glance through the existing sociological literature on youth reveals a distinct lack of engagement with the ethnicities of young, *white* people does not render the process of racialization any less significant. Here, my aim is not to 'get white boys off the hook' by reclaiming their status as the vanguard of a new 'victimhood', nor is it to depict them as the forerunners of popular radicalism. Instead, the approach seeks to lay open for inspection the ascendant, yet hitherto less visible social categories of whiteness and masculinities. Thus, in reflecting on right-wing diatribes concerning youth 'hooliganism', Robert Hollands perceptively remarks, 'What is odd about the hooligan ideology is that two of its main elements – the affirmation of working-class masculine identities and its peculiarly white ethnic character – are rarely mentioned or addressed' (1990:140). Elsewhere, the relationship between heterosexuality and masculinities has been the focus of a school-based ethnography, informed by new queer theory thinking on the body, identity and performativity (Nayak and Kehily, 1996). Disrupting the normalcy of these categories marks a shift in previous subcultural studies that have rarely addressed the gendered and ethnic configurations of able-bodied, heterosexual, young, white, working-class males.

An unintended consequence of feminist and anti-oppressive subcultural studies has been the emergence of an academic, reactionary response to working-class, masculine styles of culture. In his recent work, Phil Cohen discusses the irony of this predicament: 'By the end of the 1970s the romantic idealisation of "the lads" (alias white male working-class youth) had begun to give way to its opposite – an all too ready denunciation of their inherent and irredeemable racism and sexism' (1997:11). Cohen goes on to declare how anti-racist and feminist critiques of white working-class culture throughout the eighties began to resonate with New Right expressions of class condemnation in what became a mutual coalition heralding a 'new Yob culture' (p. 11). In contrast, this study seeks to engage with the subordinated existence of many white, working-class males, while avoiding the rose-tinted tendency to equate their hostilities with a heroic, economic resistance.

Methods

Deriving from structural linguistics, *semiotics* is the study of signs, symbols, texts, images, myth and meaning. It is premised on a belief that the modern world is made up of a series of signs that are 'encoded' with hidden meanings to the extent that 'there is an ideological dimension to every signification' (Hebdige, 1987 [1979]:13) waiting to be 'decoded'. A trenchant critique laid at the door of the CCCS concerns the overwhelming degree to which their analyses of youth have relied upon a Marxist-influenced semiotics. The complex knowledge readers required of Marxist socio-linguistics has led to complaints of 'overtheorization' (Widdecombe and Wooffitt, 1995:20). There is also a concern that by devoting endless prose to such items as the Punk's safety-pin, the Acid House 'smiley' or the Rapper's gold tooth, rather than decoding the 'sign' we are in fact fetishizing it, so endowing it with further 'coded', mystical meaning.

Although *Resistance through Rituals* is based in large part upon semiotics and textual analysis, perhaps the most adroit application of these methods can be found in the work of Dick Hebdige, himself a former member of the Centre. In Hebdige's highly polished text *Subculture: The Meaning of Style* (1987 [1979]), a comprehensive account of black–white subcultural relations, the textual reconstruction draws influence from Marxist, structuralist and semiotic insights. Despite the author's great articulacy and its numerous achievements, however, *Subculture* is in keeping with most other cultural studies of youth of the period in its failure to engage with the *lived experience* of young people. Thus, Les Back points to the way Hebdige 'tends to read off meanings from style formations without paying any attention to the interactional components of racial dialogue at the level of everyday experience' (1996:12). In essence, Hebdige provides an account of post-war British subculture that is stripped from the lived social context of experience. The absence of structural context is all the more surprising given that the author himself acknowledges that 'the experiences encoded in subcultures is shaped in a variety of locales (work, home, school etc.)'. In admitting to the geographical specificity of subcultures he goes on to reflect how 'Each of these locales impose its own unique structure, its own rules and meanings, its own hierarchy of values' (1987 [1979]:84). The question we must ask semiologists, then, concerns the extent to which we can impose meaning and interpret the sign, signifier or signified if these motifs are systematically torn from their daily, mutable contexts.

A further concern with such forms of textual analysis is the over-reliance upon second-hand data and the superficiality of signs. This is especially problematic given that much of what is written about youth cultures is penned by outsiders and couched in the discourse of 'moral panics', the 'romantic' or the 'spectacular'. David Moore (1994) provides a vivid ethnography of a Skinhead collective in Perth, Australia. The book is entitled *The Lads in Action* and, as the name suggests, there is an emphasis on the *performative*, rather than the textual aspects of subculture. Basil Samson's foreword to the research alerts the reader to the knowledge that 'There is a difference between reading culture as observed text and deriving culture from the texts of others' (1994 [1993]:x). Moore himself is scathing of the academic distance derived from textual tendencies: 'These studies comprise a sociology of appearances, for they fail to make the crucial distinction between what people say they do (representation) and what they actually do (presentation). The findings and arguments of these studies contain little information about or discussion of the performative aspects of the respective study populations' (1994:15).

In textual analyses there is a frequent tendency to treat discussants as dry artefacts from which a number of signs can be 'read off' and 'decoded' by a theoretically adept, academic 'expert'. Ethnography challenges this 'sociology of appearances'. In essence, this marks a shift from textual approaches, towards an interpretation of young people's subcultures as 'what they actually *do*' (Gelder, 1997:145). Embodied examples of what subcultures 'do' may include the social activities of drug use, fighting on the terraces, sexual practices, body-piercing, dancing, drinking or tattooing. Semiotic methods are also reliant upon secondary data, for, according to Moore, 'If we construct a distinction between youth studies which base their findings and argument on media reports, interviews, question-naires, and such like, and studies firmly anchored in ethnographic research, the majority fall into the former category' (1994:15). To develop a more refined analysis of process, and garner a deeper understanding of what young people actually do in particular places, ethnography can be a unique instrument with which to probe young people's life worlds. For Herbert, a main advantage of the method is that it 'explores the tissue of everyday life to reveal the processes and meanings which undergird social action' (2000:551). Not least for these reasons, ethnography is my chosen method with which to trace the rich textures of young lives (see Appendix 1).

Ethnography, People and Place

This work brings together historical, structural and cultural approaches to the study of youth, the aim being to provide a place-specific analysis of youth identities in changing times. The focus, then, is upon the multiple connections between people and place and the many tangled synergies that emerge in 'new times'. This involves rethinking 'local' places in 'global' times to ask how local–global processes impinge upon young lives. This study has a strong *spatial* component to it, which is increasingly a feature of contemporary social science research into the spatial construction of youth cultures (Massey, 1998). To facilitate something akin to a 'spatial turn' within the social sciences, John Urry (2000) has recently argued for a 'mobile sociology' that is more attuned to the flows and diverse mobilities of people, objects, finance, images and information. Where sociology has tradit-ionally focused upon 'occupational, income, educational and social mobility', for

Urry, it has 'failed to register the geographical intersections of region, city and place, with the social categories of class, gender and ethnicity' (p. 186).

Presently, human geographers are questioning the tendency of some subcultural writers (especially textual and postmodernist adherents) to produce *aspatial* accounts of youth cultures. For example Valentine *et al.* (1998) call for a deeper interrogation of the 'geographies of youth', as most youth studies ignore or underplay the significance of place and spatial variation at different scales and in multiple sites. For social geographers, places and identities are mutually con-stitutive in that not only does 'place' shape youth identities, but also youth iden-tities shape and influence the character of places. Indeed, 'it is by means of the body that space is perceived, lived – and produced (Lefebvre, 2001 [1974]:162). As Lefebvre has shown, the multiple ways in which spaces are imagined represents a means of living in those spaces. The elaboration of space and place is increas-ingly evident in recent work on youth culture and nightlife such as Malbon's (1999) research on clubbing (see also Ingham *et al.* 1999), Bennett's discussion of 'local' music scenes (1999b:63–7) and Chatterton and Hollands' (2002:95) con-ceptualization of the night-time economy as comprising a series of 'urban play-scapes'. At an institutional scale, Gordon *et al.* (2000) have also explored the micro-spatial dimensions of the official, informal and physical school in Finland and England.

In contrast to arguments concerning the materiality of place, a main thrust of postmodernism has been to indicate that we now live in 'placeless' times where attachments to nation, neighbourhood or work institutions may be dwindling. As Featherstone intimates, 'the focus turns away from lifestyle as class- or neigh-bourhood-based to lifestyle as the active stylization of life in which coherence and unity give way to the playful exploration of transitory experiences and surface aesthetic effects' (1998 [1991]:95). Of course, globalization is also assumed to be a major driving force behind these processes, disregarding state borders in the endless pursuit of capital, obliterating local cultures and bringing about more general social and economic upheaval. The sense in this moment is, as Miles has recently claimed, that 'youth lifestyles have become de-territorialized' (2000:159). In this way, 'Young people no longer depend on subcultural affirmation for the construction of their identities (if indeed they ever did) but construct lifestyles that are as adaptable and flexible as the world around them' (pp. 159–60). Despite the merits of these contentions, the close analysis of different youthscapes undertaken here suggests otherwise. Overall the ethnography comes much closer to Watt's empirical observation 'that the everyday lives of many young people living in cities are far more place-bound and prosaic than postmodern theory might suggest' (1998:692).

Whilst human geography has been important in developing spatial analyses of social formations, there remains a paucity of detailed ethnographic research that meticulously engages with the socially embedded qualities of lived experience.[5] This is in stark contrast to the fields of sociology, anthropology and cultural studies. By marrying geographical theories of space and place with ethnographic traditions it is suggested that a more detailed treatment of people and place can be achieved. Indeed, it is argued that ethnography is an excellent meeting point for geographers and other social scientists wishing to pursue spatially embedded analyses of cultural identity. For the place-based subcultural research undertaken, the method is especially appropriate since 'intensive analysis and fine-grained detail provide the optimal way to illustrate and explicate the oft-stated connection between the life world of a social group and the geographic world they construct' (Herbert, 2000:551). The purpose here is to provide rich description of how groups and individuals respond to change within their immediate everyday contexts. The emphasis in this book is, then, upon locally embedded experience and the manner in which social interactions are situated in time and place. To this extent, ethnographies are vital to geographic study as they may 'capture varying tempos and rhythms of movement and connection, illuminating implications for both people and places' (McHugh, 2000:72).

This study seeks to map a *cultural geography* of people and place through a multi-site analysis of young lives. It deploys ethnography for its incisive ability to 'elucidate the linkages between the macrological and the micrological, between the enduring and structured aspects of social life and the particulars of the everyday' (Herbert, 2000:554). In other words, the research politicises the complex minutiae of everyday life by placing identities within broader social, economic and cultural processes. It is the contention of this text that the changing economic geographies of places and regions are still primary landscapes upon which the cultural lives of young people are situated. Ethnographic observation and 'thick' description are deployed to provide an *embodied* account of young people coming-of-age in de-industrial times. These methods have allowed me to 'flesh out' interviews with participant observation, field-note accounts, visual evidence, historical data and biographical material (Atkinson, 1990). The method of interpretation is clarified in Appendix 3.

As such, I have attempted to produce an 'embodied' account of subculture that recognizes performance, action and experience, and situates this firmly within the context of young people's immediate local circumstances. Finally, although criticisms pertaining to specific elements of ethnographic research (e.g. ethical issues, concerns over 'objectivity' or establishing a 'representative' sample) are well rehearsed (see Hammersley and Atkinson, 1989 [1983]; Silverman, 1994

5. For example, the social geography journal *Environment and Planning D: Society and Space* retains an exclusive focus upon human geography and frequently utilizes qualitative analyses. However, it has been pointed out that only 8 of 161 (5 per cent) papers have used ethnographic field data (Herbert, 2000:550).

[1993]), the method can also break down a number of research conventions. For example, ethnography may implode established dichotomies between structure/ agency, public/private, theory/practice, talk/action, fact/fiction and even researcher/ researched What is presented in this account, then, is a series of positioned responses that are contingent upon the fluidity of context, situation and group dynamics (see Frosh *et al.*, 2002). The story related is as much about my own immersion and place within youth communities as it is about the respondents themselves. Furthermore, ethnographies are not only about the relationship between the researcher and the researched but are also the products of an 'intertextuality' between other ethnographic accounts of other social worlds (Atkinson, 1992). The multi-layered dimensions of ethnography means it remains an invaluable technique through which to refine geographical or sociological concepts and to provide empirical specificity from which new positions and critical theoretical perspectives may arise (Katz, 1994; Kobayashi, 1994; Nast, 1994).

The Challenge and Limits of Postmodernism

Since its emergence in the late 1980s, postmodernism has been, and continues to remain, one of the most influential, if frustrating, paradigms in the social sciences. It has been eagerly taken up in youth cultural studies, leading at least one prominent writer to herald it as a 'breath of fresh air' (McRobbie, 1996 [1994]:4). Postmodernism is also one of the least understood and most maligned theoretical frameworks. One of the reasons for a theoretical and conceptual fuzziness is that postmodernism is not a fixed or logocentric theory but instead comprises an eclectic cluster of philosophic and artistic ideas and approaches. Emerging from artistic movements, its influence can be felt *stylistically* in architecture, literature, fashion, music, art and popular culture. Here, postmodernism is associated with a stylistic borrowing from different epochs and cultures. This pick-'n'-mix is evident in contemporary youth cultures and popular music, for example the development of a British Asian Bhangra scene in places such as London, Birmingham, Manchester and Leicester. Once associated with traditional Punjabi folk music, Bhangra music has been transmuted and translated through Western beats, Ragga and Hip-Hop influences to emerge as a distinct badge of cultural pride for young Punjabis and many other Asian youth. The new sounds evident in Hip-Hop and Bhangra also draw upon music from different historical time frames and diverse geographical locations (e.g. Africa, Asia, the USA or Jamaica). There is no authentic, original, set of notes here, but rather a melody that segues between past and present and resonates with the timbre that this is forever a copy, of a copy, of a copy, that in turn will be 'cut-'n'-mixed' anew. At the level of style, then, postmodernism can be likened to a 'dissonant symphony', a phrase that perhaps captures the impossible ambiguities that derive therein, making it at once decipherable yet incoherent.

As such, it is a complex *bricolage* upon which fragmentation, simulation, parody and pastiche play upon the surface.

A second way of interpreting postmodernism is to understand it *periodically* as the time after modernity in which many of the certainties associated with the modern era have disintegrated This approach is particularly relevant to the study undertaken. Here, postmodern societies are characterized by social and economic change, underpinned by the post-Fordist move away from a conveyor-belt culture of mass production that once produced standardized products for a standardized market. While the extent to which we are living in new postmodern times continues to be hotly debated (a preferred term is to speak of late- or high-modernity), it is generally agreed that the age of manufacturing, Fordism and industrialization is in decline. Contemporary societies no longer cohere around the symbols of heavy industry such as the pit, the shipyard or the factory plant but are increasingly seen as dispersed, fragmented and intricately diverse in their structure, composition and cultural ties. Thus, while the period of postmodernity is often characterized by greater choice, flexibility and individuality, paradoxically it is also associated with 'risk', uncertainty and insecurity.

A final way (there are many others) of understanding postmodernism is by seeing it as a *critical practice* that has permeated the arts, social sciences and humanities in particular. Here, the postmodern 'turn' is associated epistemo-logically and ontologically with the collapse of 'meta-narratives' – big stories that seek to understand our place in the world through recourse to the grand theories of Neo-Liberalism, Marxism, Christianity, Islam, Western Science or even Radical Feminism. The rejection of the universal truths propagated by modernism has led to a movement away from what Jean-François Lyotard (1991 [1984]) identifies as the 'tyranny' of rationalism. Increasingly, researchers are moving to more reflexive interpretations of the socially constructed nature of truth and value systems by giving greater recognition to contextual contingency and partiality. In a series of postmodern displacements, truth is replaced by representation, fact-finding by deconstruction, centring by dispersal, biological roots by 'routes' or rhizomes, master *logos* by inter-textuality, order by fragmentation, familiarity by parody, reality by simulation, self by identities, singularity by plurality, originality by hybridity. In particular, postmodernism as critical practice has brought the margins to the centre. In doing so it has given way to a greater recognition of difference and the ways in which gender, ethnicity and sexualities intersect with, and so com-plicate, modern beliefs in truth, knowledge and experience. For example, we can consider the increased recognition given by Western medicine to Chinese herbal remedies and 'alternative' healing practices, or, by way of another example, the increasing awareness that older Aboriginal land rights in Australia have been displaced by modern colonial geographies. If the margins are returning to the centre, clearly this will not happen overnight, but is part of a more prolonged struggle for international recognition within and beyond the territory of race (Bonnett and Nayak, 2003).

In the field of youth cultural studies I have highlighted how postmodernism has provided sophisticated critiques of classic subcultural studies. This critical appraisal encompasses the tendency to rely upon rigid typologies; focus on production rather than consumption; emphasize resistance over conformity; impose masculine norms and values; claim authenticity rather than representation. There is much food for thought in the criticisms outlined. However, in my attempt to unite 'structural' with 'cultural' approaches I have been keen to explore some of the limits of postmodernism for youth studies. The geographer David Harvey, in his opus *The Condition of Postmodernity*, is a scholar at the forefront of a blistering criticism of postmodern tendencies. He critiques postmodernism on account of its nihilism, arguing that it lends itself to nothingness and 'swims, even wallows, in the fragmentary and chaotic currents of change as if that is all there is' (Harvey, 1990 [1989]:44). For Marxist intellectuals such as Harvey, postmodernism is little more than the 'cultural clothing of flexible accumulation', the dressing up of material inequalities in fake designer fabrics that soon fade as the spin of the political wash quickens. Postmodernity is, if Frederic Jameson (1991) is to be believed, not the breach with modernity we may have conceived but the 'cultural logic of late capitalism'. For many Marxist scholars, postmodernism is vacuous, 'apolitical', theoretically pretentious and ultimately, I would posit, located in the superstructure. Central to this is the idea that postmodernism is a *relativist* project, tip-toeing across the thin white picket fence in times of great uncertainty and inequality when a confident stride and firm foothold in one camp or another is patently required

This split is evident in studies of youth when McRobbie (1997:30) contrasts the 'wild style' of (contemporary) cultural studies with what she sees as the 'materialist steadfastness' of sociology. The more experimental postmodernist approach has given way to the 'fragile, "shaggy", hybrid identities' (p. 42) she identifies as being more in keeping with 'new times'. However, the difficulty of inter-linking 'cultural' and 'structural' approaches has led to a bifurcation in youth studies between small-scale studies of 'cool youth' and more mechanistic attempts to identify the 'pathways' and defining markers associated with 'youth transitions'. Thus, on the one hand, Gary Clarke, writing in the Thatcherite era of British mass youth unemployment, questioned 'the value of decoding the stylistic appearances of particular tribes during a period in which young adults are the prime victims of unemployment' (1981:1), whilst, on the other, Miles has argued that 'a structural perspective on transitions has been counter-productive, primarily because of its failure to prioritise the actual views, experiences, interests and perspectives of young people as they see them, in favour of bland discussions, most commonly of trends in employment and education patterns' (2000:10). In summary, for Miles,

'The most damaging problem with the "transitions debate" is that it has tended to take young people out of the youth equation' (p. 10). More than ever, a reflexive and flexible understanding of 'youth transitions' is required if the concept is to retain future credibility (see MacDonald *et al.*, 2000 for discussion). Surprisingly then, there has been little dialogue across the structural–cultural divide, a debate the ethnography brings to the foreground, and holds in tension.

One of the most lasting aspects of the recent cultural studies and postmodernist agenda is that it has achieved a shift away from monochrome studies on education, labour and political economy (e.g. Willis, 1977; Corrigan, 1981 [1979]; Griffin, 1985; Hollands, 1990) in favour of colourful studies on dance, popular music and consumption (see Thornton, 1995; McRobbie, 1996 [1994]; Redhead, 1993, 1997; Bennett, 1999b, 2000; Malbon, 1999). The movement from workplaces to 'cool places' (Skelton and Valentine, 1998), and the question of why this change has happened and what are its implications is, to my mind, currently under-theorized. What does it mean to design a new youth studies agenda around a geographical focus of the night-club, shopping mall or Rave event? What does this tell us, if anything, about the perceptions held by adult researchers of young people's life worlds? And what happens to theory and politics when we explore youth identities outside of the school, labour market, family or crime-ridden neighbourhood? Indeed, as Chatterton and Hollands (2002) demonstrate, the night-time economy is itself a zone that can only be understood in the 'interrelationships between production, consumption and regulation' (2002:95).[6] For as Beck recounts, institutions *are directly intermeshed with phases in the biographies of people. Insitu*tional determinations and interventions are (implicitly) also determinations of and interventions in human biographies' (1998 [1992]: 132). This suggests that more integrative approaches to youth studies are required if we are to achieve a greater sense of how 'cultural' and 'structural' processes impact upon young lives. In the light of postmodernist critiques of the unitary subject, it is now no longer sufficient to provide unreflective sociological accounts of youth transitions. Similarly, 'spectacular' youth studies on the cultural aesthetics of Rave scenes, fashion and music can still learn much from the less celebratory but lucid depictions of young lives portrayed in materialist analyses. *Race, Place and Globalization* is an attempt to open up this dialogue, a discussion that needs to occur at international levels and across disciplines if it is to be taken further.

6. In a review of political economy the geographer Jane Wills has noted that

> While the encounter with poststructuralism and cultural studies has been a productive one for economic geography, it would seem less productive as far as political economy is concerned . . . in much recent research there is a tendency for the bigger political questions and matters of policy prognosis to be sidelined in the important empirical detail concerning issues such as identity, everyday life and consumption. (1999:444)

–3–

Diasporic Movement and Settlement in the North East of England

Introduction

It would appear that the contours of race and ethnicity are shifting under the auspices of major structural and cultural changes associated with late modernity. The twentieth century witnessed a steady process of de-colonization, an age of mass migration and the spread of dense social networks as a consequence of major improvements in transport and communication technologies (see Waters, 1995). It has been suggested that these changes have helped bring people and places closer together, in what has been referred to as a 'shrinking world' where the barriers of time and space have been, at least in part, 'annihilated' (Leyshon, 1995). In particular, the globalization of migration has meant that diasporic groups – displaced peoples who share cultural, ethnic or religious ties – are increasingly able to maintain linkages as social relations become 'stretched' over time and space.

Diasporic communities have also had an impact upon their new places of habitation, altering the social, economic and cultural milieu of these environments (Massey, 1995; McEwan, 2001). This is exemplified in the rise of 'Chinatowns', 'Little Indias' or 'Little Irelands' across the globe (Chang, 1999), and of course the more mundane, taken-for-granted aspects of multiculturalism that permeate many of our daily lives. This has led writers to rethink the meaning of 'place' in global times by appreciating how the contemporary landscape is now made up of a myriad of different peoples with a diverse array of attachments to their locales. For Appadurai (1990), the new urban environment may better be conceived of as an 'ethnoscape', a liminal zone comprising a landscape of shifting subjects: tourists, immigrants, refugees, exiles, guestworkers, and other moving groups and persons. Amidst this space of 'flows' and the various 'cartographies of diaspora' (Brah, 1996) we may distinguish the 'disarticulation of place-based societies' (Robins, 1991:13). Here, communities are no longer formed over successive generations and built around traditional industries such as the pit, shipyard or factory, but are increasingly more mobile and, as a consequence, now more diverse than ever.

But that is not all. At the same time are also to be found more stable communities attracted to the social 'stickiness' of kinship, work, leisure and neighbourhood networks. As we shall find, local attachments to place have not entirely disappeared, indeed, they may have become reworked (Taylor *et al.*, 1996). At the national scale too, it remains premature to write uncritically of the death of the nation state. For Manuel Castells, 'The fading away of the nation-state is a fallacy', since states remain 'strategic actors, playing their interests, and the interests of those they are supposed to represent, on a global system of interaction, in a condition of systematically shared sovereignty' (1997:307). Moreover, in terms of collective identity there has been a resurgence of nationalism, tribalism and xenophobia across nation states throughout parts of Eastern Europe, Africa, Asia and the Middle East. The question we must ask, then, is whether global change and diasporic movement have eradicated or exacerbated popular racism. There is no straightforward answer to this, but in the contemporary global economy migration can also be seen as an expression or reinforcement of uneven spatial development.

To explore these issues in more detail, the present chapter will illustrate the changing histories of race and migration in the North East. The aim is to provide a geographic and historical context for examining emerging youth ethnicities in the region. The chapter begins by deconstructing the popular conception of the region as the homogeneous 'white highlands'. It will then examine how racism has featured in particular areas and the impact that this has had upon ethnic minorities. Finally, I will turn to the legacy of race and class histories to show how the region can be 'culturally re-imagined' as a potentially inclusive place, befitting of global population movements.

'Beyond the Pale': Deconstructing the White Highlands

Located in the Northeast periphery of England, the Tyneside conurbation epitomizes a region that has strong local roots but an uncertain relationship to nationhood. The distinctive regional identity of Tyneside, combined with its proximity to the Scottish border, has seen a greater emphasis given to Northern peculiarities by locals at the expense of an homogeneous 'Englishness'. Some writers have noted how the Northeast concept of Englishness 'has long been ambivalent', and that this version of the nation 'was high up and far away' (Carr, 1992:143). David Bean identifies the shipping links the region maintains with Northern Europe, and notes that 'Tyneside isn't really part of England at all . . . being out of Britain altogether and somewhere in Pan-Scandinavia' (1971:4–5). Others have gone as far as regarding Northeast peoples as the 'Unenglish' (Taylor, 1993), claiming that they do not fit into Southern definitions of nationhood, premised on the rural 'home counties', and, as such, regionalism remains a reaction to this.[7] Thus, Taylor (1993) has gone on to depict this area as England's 'foreign country' within (see also Lanigan, 1996). Evidence of this insular local culture is also given support in Corrigan's Sunderland-based research when the London ethnographer reflects, 'In getting to know the north-east, I found a fiercely regionally partisan place' (1981 [1979]:9).

Given the tenuous relationship the North East has with the nation at large, it may seem strange that the region is widely recognized as a bastion of English whiteness, far removed from the urban, multi-ethnic metropolis. Writing about perceptions of the North East in the late nineteenth century, Robert Colls points out, '"Northernness" was not the same as "Englishness"' (1992:3). Paul Gilroy remarks on this dissonance, claiming 'regional or local subjectivities simply do not articulate with "race" in quite the same way as their national equivalent' (1995 [1987]:54). Despite these overt tensions, the local and the national are not entirely exclusive categories, but co-exist in a complex inter-dependent relationship with one another. It is suggested that some of the most nationalistic sentiments of the nation at large are *translated* onto the local culture as a type of 'parochial patriotism'. The majority of ethnographic accounts I collected displayed a marked identification with the region to such an extent that 'Geordie' was regarded as an overriding ethnicity within the context of Britain. Young people were keen to assert commonalities of language, behaviour, beliefs and values as evidence of 'Geordie' ethnicity, and often remarked on the disparities with other localities, especially London and 'the South' generally. These young people were keen to stress the distinctive nature of being 'Geordie'.

Anoop:	*What's distinctive about being a Geordie?*
Alan:	The language.
Danielle:	Language!
Alan:	Well the accent.
Anoop:	*But there are some different words?*
Danielle:	'Gannin".
Alan:	'Aye', we say, 'aye'.
Lucy:	We'd say, 'Eeeh, ya wanna pack't in!' or summit. Say things like that.

In a study of Newcastle's flamboyant nightlife Hollands equates the term 'Geordie' directly with a 'strong patriarchal and masculine occupational identity' (1995:12). Indeed, the term 'Geordie' was associated with being a *pit-worker* at a

---

7. In a previous study of two Northern towns, Taylor *et al.* comment, 'the North has always been a region that is defined by its residual and subordinate relation to London and the South-East'. They recall how 'Being "of the North", in this sense has always involved a recognition that one is "peripheral"' (1996:18).

time when the phrase 'carrying coals to Newcastle' radiated with regional prosperity as the colloquialism entered common parlance. The way that notions of
locality have dovetailed with manual labour in this way is nowhere more apparent
than during the miners' strike of 1984–5, when neighbourhoods mobilized around
the slogan 'Save our Pits! Save our Communities!'

The North East has a population of around 2.6 million and its principal city is
Newcastle upon Tyne, containing around 260,000 residents. It is a mainly white
region, reputed to contain the 'whitest place in England' by way of the old colliery
town, Easington. Perhaps Newcastle's chalk- white Civic Centre is an apt monolith
to the area. Built at a cost of £4.5 million, the Civic Centre was nevertheless
constructed from multinational materials: 'there's a lot of Italian marble, Cornish
granite, Lebanese cedar, Aubusson tapestry, French walnut, rosewood from Rio, all
sorts of exotic African hardwoods . . . (Bean, 1980:62). This erasure of a multicultural past is, perhaps, the stigma of a region that has problematically assumed
the mantle of the homogeneous 'white highlands'. However, a scratch beneath the
veneer of 'Geordie' may reveal several inconsistencies and points of resistance to
the apparent, overbearing whiteness of Tyneside culture.

The ethnic composition of the city of Newcastle reveals a white majority of
almost 96 per cent based on 1991 census readings, while early indicators from the
2001 census estimate that around 7 per cent of Newcastle's population are of origin
other than white British. However, these figures may also reflect the extended
repertoires for ethnic classification in the recent census. Although ostensibly white,
(241,684 residents identify as white in 2002), the overall social geography of
Tyneside contains black migrant communities concentrated within the West End
district of the city, whose numbers rise to 11.3 per cent in the Wingrove ward.
Notably these communities are drawn from the South Asian sub-continent, including Indian, Pakistani and Bangladeshi peoples. The convergence of minority
groups within the West End section of the city is therefore somewhat at odds with
the depiction of the region as a cluster of 'white highlands' (Bonnett, 1993a:136).
In a fascinating study of Asian youth in West End Newcastle, J.H. Taylor con-
tradicts conceptions of the city as monolithically white.

> There were plenty of Pakistanis to be found drinking Exhibition Ale or Newcastle Brown
> in the pubs of the area, particularly the Bay Horse, on Westgate Hill, and the High
> Elswick Tavern (known to Asians as the 'small publi') tucked away between Gloucester
> Road and Cromwell Street. In the Tavern they played dominoes. In the Bay Horse they
> monopolized the upstairs dartboard. Many Asians also patronized the Queen's, in
> Campbell Street. (1976:75)

This stark ethnic differentiation between the West End quarter and the rest of
Tyneside has led Beatrix Campbell to depict the sector as 'the only place in the city
that resembled a cosmopolitan, modern metropolis' (1993:74). A closer look at the

Northeast region reveals Hindu temples, Muslim mosques and places of Sikh worship located throughout. There is a Jewish synagogue in the plush Newcastle district of Jesmond and the small town of Gateshead, as well as a Hare Krishna temple along the Westgate Road in the city of Newcastle upon Tyne. We may also reflect upon the Bangledeshi communities that can now be found residing in Newcastle, Sunderland and South Shields. Middlesborough also has small but longstanding Pakistani, German and Irish immigrant communities.

The North East Chinese Association is also to be found on Stowell Street in Newcastle, which in turn has developed its own particular hybrid culture. The small strip of restaurants, shops and take-aways has been developed by successive generations of migrants. The zone is populated by people of Chinese and Viet-namese heritage, some of whom live nearby and run the number of restaurants and small businesses in the area. This city-centre quarter represents Newcastle upon Tyne's 'Chinatown', a space Patrick Ely depicts as 'the stage upon which two separate cultures meet and interact, drawn together through their common desire for Chinese food' (1997:14). Nevertheless, I found that these hybrid exchanges do not necessarily curb more casual racism, as Tyneside youth explained:

[10 years]
James: Chinese people get a lot of hassle as well because people think they can act hard, cos they've learnt all this karate stuff and that. Everyone jus' calls 'em [names].
Anoop: So what gets said?
James: 'Karate man', 'slanty eyes' and stuff like that.

Such hostilities sharply contradict the fallacy of a 'no problem here' attitude that presumes that racism is absent from mainly white areas (Gaine, 1987, 1995). The image of Chinese, Hong Kong or British-Born Chinese (BBCs) as 'Oriental experts' in martial arts is a recurring myth in Western imagination, a theme addressed by David Parker (1995) in his book *Through Different Eyes*. Along with Chinese and South Asian communities in the region one can also trace a history of Arab migration to the area. Peter Fryer recounts how 'Arab and Somali seamen are said to have settled in South Shields in the 1860s, and there were some West African and West Indian seamen in North Shields before the First World War' (1984:299). During the First World War the number of men from the Yemen working in the seafaring trade dramatically increased in South Shields to around 3,000, to the extent that the district of Holborn became synonymous with these migrants. As suggested by the title of Lawless's book *From Ta'izz to Tyneside* (1995), diasporic movement and settlement are an important part of the weaving together of different geographic narratives in the region.

Whereas information pertaining to the numbers of visible minorities in Tyneside can be found, there remains as yet no statistical breakdown relating to the number of 'white' foreign migrants from Irish, Polish, Italian, German and Scandinavian backgrounds who have all settled in the region over the years.[8] In the main these groups have appeared as 'invisible' minorities, though white minority ethnic expression has been etched into the landscape in other ways. For example, St Mary's Catholic Cathedral was built on Clayton Road West in Newcastle city centre in 1844 and there are a burgeoning number of Gaelic pubs and authentic Italian restaurants throughout Tyneside. Indeed, the area contains one of the largest Irish populations in mainland Britain behind Liverpool and Glasgow, with around a quarter of local schools being Catholic. Nestling along the stretch of the River Tyne somewhere between Gateshead and South Shields is found Hebburn, a town that was formerly an Irish-speaking colony. Today, visitors are more likely to frequent the Irish Centre, which can be found on St Andrews Street in the central part of Newcastle upon Tyne, near the so-called 'Chinatown' quarter. The area of Gateshead on the south bank of the Tyne also boasts one of the largest orthodox Jewish communities outside London and is often known as the 'Jerusalem of England' (Donbrow, 1988 [1972]:6). There is also a Polish Club towards the West inner-city. However, aside from shared pockets of migrant settlement, the civic face of Tyneside remains hauntingly white.

A Most Parochial Patriotism: Racism and Regionalism

Despite the symbolic disassociation with 'Englishness' that is a feature of much 'Geordie' life, a legacy of racist struggles pepper the locality to the present day. There is documentation of anti-Irish race riots in 1851, arising from the migratory movements of rural folk from Ireland to the North East during the potato famine. In Stockton near Middlesborough there were violent disturbances between Irishmen and the English in 1872. In South Shields Lawless (1995) recounts a series of hostilities towards Arab seamen that preceded the 1919 'riot'. Evidence of anti-Semitic violence can also be traced as Jewish communities came to settle in Newcastle upon Tyne and then later Gateshead. For example, in 1925, the paramilitary-style British Fascisti was to open up branches in Newcastle and then subsequently Sunderland. More recently, Indian, Bangledeshi, Pakistani, Chinese and Vietnamese communities have, along with a number of Eastern European asylum seekers, become victims of harassment.

The roots of racism in the region are, then, longstanding. They are also interwoven into social class and local cultures. Thus, in the inter-war years economic depression meant that Arab seamen in South Shields were increasingly subject to what Lawless calls a 'rising tide of racial hysteria' (1995:78). This swell grew as white seamen discharged from the Royal Navy demanded their old jobs in the Merchant Marine. Arabs, whose claims to be British subjects had been upheld

8. The 2001 Census for England and Wales has for the first time accounted for Irish ethnicity.

during the war, were now finding legislative attempts were being made to reclass-ify them as 'coloured aliens'. In South Shields, they soon discovered, 'If the Arabs were working, they were accused of depriving white men of jobs; if they were not, then they were lazy spongers who were a financial drain on the town's ratepayers' (Carr, 1992:137). These tensions would later culminate in the so-called 'race riots' of 1919, where Arab seamen retaliated against the racism and violence of white seamen and union officials concerned with preserving white labour privilege in the face of increased competition. In view of the ferocity of anti-Arab racism in the 1920s, it was to be deemed pragmatic to develop a small council estate in Laygate by Holborn that was to be let exclusively by Arabs, colloquially termed 'sand dancers'. Despite the prominent roles played by Arabs, West African and West Indian seamen in both the war and Northeast shipping trade, there is little evidence today of this multicultural past on the waterfront and Quayside districts. This supports Campbell's statement that most dockland developments in the 1980s occupied 'sanitised histories . . . cleansed of ethnicity . . . purged of their cos-mopolitan culture' (1993:26).

Moreover, when the residue of migrant history materializes, it is not necessarily a point of celebration. Thus, Bigg Market watering-holes such as The Black Boy or 'Blackie Boy', which was established in 1923, have names which hint at a nostalgic period of racial inequality. We can also turn to local legend and urban myth. In popular folklore it is commonly said that during the Napoleonic wars a monkey was washed up on the shores of the coastal town of Hartlepool, mistaken as a French spy, and then summarily hung by local Northeast crofters! Remarkably 'H'angus the Monkey', played by Stuart Drummond as the costumed mascot for Hartlepool United Football Club, has turned politician, having been voted in to power on a crest of local support. Of course, myths that represent foreigners through the uncivilized symbol of the ape have a longstanding presence in the English imaginary. Other Northeast myths have also popularly referred to miners leaving the colliery coated in coal dust only to be chased and set upon by locals who believed they were 'blackies'. But beyond these mythic configurations can sometimes lie the deeper markings of racial hatred and imperialism.

In 1929 the region famously hosted the North East Coast Exhibition, which took place upon Newcastle Town Moor and in which some 500 firms exhibited. Mary Wade's memoir *To the Miner Born* provides special insight into how local pride could be translated into a nationalistic sense of white superiority. The author remi-nisces upon her school visit to the Exhibition and recalls how the finest thrill for the class was reserved for a visit to the 'African village'. 'Despite all the poverty around us, perhaps this was our first injection of a superiority complex. With furniture in our home and desks in our classrooms, surely we were fortunate. Home cooking did not vary much, but leek puddings and tettie was certainly more appetising than anything the Africans were eating' (cited in Bourke, 1994:175–6).

Although the Exhibition took place in the wake of a depressed local economy, it did not stop parochial pride from blossoming out of the roots of white imperial fantasy. It was this sense of 'white pride' that was to become a target for Fascist organizations in the period. Notably, the Bigg Market district of Newcastle was, along with Benwell, a popular site for Fascist activity in the 1930s. Further examples of racist violence can also be found in the reports of small-scale anti-Italian riots taking place during 1940 involving the towns of Middlesborough, Sunderland and Newcastle upon Tyne. Fryer also documents the 1961 mob riot in Middlesborough, 'when thousands of whites, chanting "Let's get a wog", smashed the windows of black people's houses and set a café on fire while the terrified Pakistani family that owned it took refuge in cupboards' (1984: 380). At the time, the 1961 census records that there were only 418 Pakistanis living in Middles-borough, many of whom owned small businesses or 'worked on the railway, in the docks and for the iron and steel industry' (Panayi, 1991:141). Prior to the events of 1961, attacks on Pakistani and Indian workers have been recorded in the area. This has led Panikos Panayi to conclude that the uprisings do indeed constitute a race riot as they occurred 'against the background of more general animosity towards minorities' (p. 153).

The more recent history of the region also indicates that diasporic movement and settlement were met with local resistance. J.H. Taylor goes on to remark how 'anyone with ears can have heard anti-Asian sentiments expressed every day in Newcastle' (1976: 226). In the contemporary setting young 'Geordies' I interviewed also expressed a familiarity with street-based racist interactions:

[11–12 years]

Alan: If some people walk into a shop and say there was a Pakistani bloke there and
           he's bein' cheeky they'd think all of them are like that, all of them are nasty.

Anoop: Would there be any trouble?

Alan: Probably.

Anoop: Like what?

Alan: Probably spray-paint the shop.

Danielle: And get called racist names.

Brett: Smash the windows.

Furthermore, Mould's (1987) study of 'racial' attitudes amongst children of various ages in Tyne and Wear revealed that around three-quarters of the pupils held negative attitudes about black people, and from this fraction a third held strongly hostile attitudes. A later study involving 62 children in Tyneside conducted by Lara Bath and Peter Farrel presents a slightly more optimistic picture but still concludes with the damning indictment that 'one-third of the students expressed prejudiced feelings' (1996: 11). This would indicate that racism in mainly white areas is very much alive and that the North East in particular is certainly not immune.

At a local level an ostensibly white image of the region may even be promoted. Sir John Hall, the local multi-millionaire who has financed the resurgence of Newcastle United Football Club (NUFC), has made few apologies concerning the ethnic exclusivity of the 'Toon Army'.[9] In describing his dream of watching eleven 'Geordie' players playing in NUFC colours, this example of fierce regionalism can be read as an exacting form of belonging. It is especially curious given that NUFC have a multinational team drawn from number of different countries. Hall's references to what he calls 'The Geordie Nation' are at once a dis-identification with the nation at large (England/Britain), and a re-inscription of these patriotic values at the level of the local. This jingoistic discourse, what can be likened to a type of 'parochial patriotism', draws on a familiar schema of loyalty, origins and racial authenticity, so defining 'Geordie' as an exclusive ethnicity. The fervent celebration of the Great Geordie Nation along these chauvinistic lines remains problematic in a space Campbell depicts as a 'region where racism is displayed with a certain pride' (1993:162). Furthermore, in the 1980s NUFC's ground, St James' Park in the city centre, was pin-pointed as a recruiting ground for far-Right extremists selling local National Front magazines such as the *Newcastle Patriot* and *Geordie Bulldog*, as well as the British National Party's *Lionheart* (Bonnett, 1993a). These activities have now ceased and the politics of race in football is altering with the widespread influx of black players, public awareness about racism in football and the global branding and commercialization of the game.

Despite these changes to the social landscape, many of Tyneside's minority communities continue to remain constrained by a 'geography of exclusion' (Sibley, 1995). Asian communities are seldom found gathered in city-centre public spaces such as the Bigg Market, football ground or central pubs. The public presence of ethnic minorities may appear at first glance barely visible but in actuality this presence is carefully negotiated across temporal and spatial dimensions in the region. Thus, the segregation of ethnic minority communities within discrete urban quarters encourages the region to appear superficially more white than it actually is. Of particular concern remains the way white ownership of public space has allowed racism to flourish in the area. Campbell refers to the former Dodds Arms in the multi-ethnic West End part of Elswick as associated with 'trouble, pros-titution and skinheads' (1993:80). She notes how this 'piracy of space' can liken young men to 'local imperialists', where 'what was once a shared space becomes a colony' (p. 177). She goes on to describe how visible minorities invariably have to develop a geography or self-preservation by adapting their movements in the city according to learnt notions of safety and danger. 'Asian, Chinese and

9. These disclosures are also gendered, as Hall famously described Geordie women as 'dogs' and compared club captain Alan Shearer to Mary Poppins in a *News of the World* exclusive in which he also derided fans for foolishly purchasing NUFC shirts made for a fiver.

Vietnamese teenagers brought up in Scotswood and Elswick plan their routes as they make their way around their neighbourhoods. There are certain places and bus routes some of them boycott. They are tactical about their movement and their networks – what they do not enjoy in the place they live is freedom of movement' (1993:164).

The socio-spatial markers operating in parts of the region are tightly drawn across lines of racialized demarcation. In his local study of music and culture, Bennett describes areas such as Fenham and Elswick in the West End as 'a self-contained if not ghettoized world for the Asian population of Newcastle' (2000: 106). The racialization of public space in this way could certainly make it 'risky' for minority groups to transgress their allotted spaces and participate in the broader dimensions of Northeast nightlife. These boundaries are an emphatic point of racial closure and may be supported by verbal and physical abuse when the 'colour line' is crossed. For those living in white suburban areas such racialized demarcation kept cross-cultural interaction to a bare minimum. As a consequence I found the existence of residual forms of racism, which may have all but died out in modern multi-ethnic centres, were prevalent. At times the word 'paki' (and especially 'paki-shop') could be used in an unflinching manner with little awareness that it remained a widely recognized term of abuse. A primitive grammar of racism was also apparent in the dialects of some older people that include such archaic terms as 'blackie', 'darkie' and 'nig-nog'. Local cultures are, then, also important in shaping the styles and social formation of racist epithets. The spatial restrictions that racism has upon diasporic movement, settlement and ethnic behaviour mean that the hybrid exchanges associated with globalization do not always come to fruition.

Further research undertaken in the North East has also reflected upon the insular and at times antagonistic culture to racialized 'outsiders'. In his colourful study of Newcastle drinking cultures Robert Hollands found that respondents still viewed the city as hostile to ethnic minorities, in part because 'the region is largely white and that Geordie culture, by its very nature, is somewhat exclusionary' (1995:35). A local respondent in Coffield *et al.*'s study informed them he didn't like London and had 'returned to the North because "There were too many Pakis down there"' (1986 [1985]: 123). These statements can be backed up by the figures of the 1990 Civic Centre survey stating that 57 per cent of black people had endured personal abuse in Tyneside. In recent times the North East has also been host to a variety of refugees and political asylum seekers, many whom herald from Eastern Europe and parts of Africa. The uneven dispersal of asylum seekers has seen a number of refugees located in some of the most impoverished areas of Sunderland, New-castle, South Shields and Middlesborough. The British National Party (BNP) has sought to capitalize on this issue by leafleting in Stockton, Teeside in 2000 and campaigning for political support in Sunderland in 2002. The National Front (NF) has also been politically active and undertaken paper sales in Sunderland and Durham, according to a recent edition of the anti-fascist magazine *International Searchlight* (2002). A recent government Home Office report indicates that Northumbria has the highest levels of racially motivated attacks outside of London with, 1,159 assaults (2.15 per 1,000 of the population) for 1999–2000. Police statistics for the city of Newcastle alone indicate that 690 racist incidents were reported between April 2000 and March 2001, a clear rise from the 460 recorded the previous year. However, this may also reflect an overall improvement in the reporting facilities of Northumbria Police indicating that incidents of racism are now being taken seriously.

Anti-racism, Labour Histories and 'Grassroots' Resistance

Where there has been racism in the region, it must be noted that it has also been met with local resistance. In 1823 the Newcastle upon Tyne Anti-Slavery society was established to combat the injustices that continued after the traffic in slaves had ceased in 1811. Nigel Todd's (1995) elegant monograph on behalf of the Tyne and Wear Anti-Fascist Association (TWAFA) graphically portrays the emergence of – and resistance to – Oswald Mosley's British Union of Fascists (BUF), the infamous 'Blackshirts'. Sir Oswald Mosley's BUF used the Bigg Market place as a space to set up rostrums and deliver propaganda about alleged Jew or Red conspiracies. The uniformed Blackshirts, wearing menacing belts and buckles, surrounded Fascist speaker platforms in case violence ensued. In actuality it frequently did, and it is to the credit of local communities, Tyneside Socialists and a patchwork of anti-Fascist organizations that the success of the BUF was greatly restricted. Here, local culture with its emphasis on resistance and its distrust of Southerners was a vital antidote to Fascist ideologies. Thus, in 1933 a large public meeting was staged at Newcastle's City Hall condemning Nazi anti-Semitism in Germany, a protest that was replicated in Sunderland. Other displays of anti-racist/ Fascist resistance in the region are later evident in a march from Elswick Road to the Town Moor, orchestrated by Tyneside CARD (Campaign Against Racial Discrimination) in protest against Enoch Powell's inflammatory 'Rivers of Blood' speech in 1968.

The North East has a rich legacy of resistance that has stemmed from labour clubs, unions and working men's clubs. This social class history is deeply embedded in the place. Thus, the Bigg Market area has also been a popular site of labour resistance, as witnessed in the Great Strike of 1926, when miners continued to remain in the area some seven months after the dispute. A little over a decade after the 1919 attacks upon Arabs, seamen from the Yemen would stand shoulder to shoulder in South Shields with their white counterparts in protest against a rota system of employment for its 'coloured' members that would effectively divide the workforce. The National Union of Seamen, a corrupt organization tightly linked to the shipping owners, had vainly 'hoped that if a strike materialized, the black seamen, impoverished by the restricted work opportunities of the rota system, could be used as strike-breakers' (Carr, 1992:138). Supported by the Seamen's Minority Movement, the majority of Arabs solidly refused to sign the PC5, which would effectively put them on the rota and undermine their fellow white seamen. Urged on by white seamen to stop other 'scabs' from signing up, a battle ensued at Mill Dam in 1930 in which the police weighed in against the Arabs. After the 1930 riot, resistance to the rota system would collapse, but the event demonstrates the complex, shifting relations between Arab seamen, white seamen, blacklegs and white capitalist proprietors (see Lawless, 1995).

Staunch local resistance is nowhere more apparent than in the Jarrow March of 1936, which was a response to the 75–80 per cent unemployment rate the area suffered as a consequence of brutal economics. Sir Charles Palmer's shipyard and steel works were at the forefront of shipbuilding techniques and had been the economic core of the community until their closure as a result of the emergence of National Shipbuilders' Security, Ltd. The area had also seen the rise and fall of a great coal industry in the form of Jarrow Pit and was now in danger of witnessing the collapse of the shipyard. Moreover, the Jarrow March suggested that economic disenfranchisement was as much a national issue as a local one. Thus, fellow workers from other cities kindly supplied the marchers with food and accommodation as they cheered them on their passage from Jarrow to London. The Jarrow labourers came to symbolize the precarious relations that existed between capitalists and workers nation-wide. Consequently, Tom Pickard reminds us that the marchers 'carried not only Jarrow but bits of all England with them' (1982:16). Unlike other 'hunger marches', the Jarrow crusade could not be dismissed as a Communist-inspired demonstration (from a population of 35,000, some 23,000 were claiming relief). The March was led by MP Ellen Wilkinson, who has recorded her historic memoirs of the struggle in a moving account, *The Town that was Murdered* (1939). This noble protest was all the more emphatic given the suggestion that British Fascists in the 1930s had been far more entrenched within the ranks of industrial proprietorship than was hitherto recognized (Pickard, 1982).

The traditional hospitality associated with the North East was later to be extended to Basque refugees in the late 1930s. The Spanish War saw the fiercest assaults on the civilian population carried out in the Basque region. The conflict was soon to be overtaken by the Second World War, with German and Italian aircraft bombing the area as Fascism increased its stranglehold on world politics. Under these conditions the Basque regional government appealed to other countries to shelter refugee children. Unlike France, Belgium and the Soviet Union, who willingly provided state support, Britain begrudgingly admitted 4,000 Basque children on the strict understanding that no public expenditure would be incurred

The children were dispersed throughout the country and along the Northeast coastline. *The Shields News* on Friday, 30th July 1937 ran with the headline, 'Basque Refugees on Way to Tynemouth – Residents' Protest'. However, in the absence of public sector support and on viewing the dishevelled children, families in Tynemouth, Gateshead and North Shields played invaluable roles in housing and educating the children. The miners' lodge, church groups and other community organizations provided essential financial relief and even set up a hostel for the refugees. Spanish sailors would drop into the Tyne port and visit the hostel providing news of the war and information on particular families. According to Watson and Corcoran, the case represents an 'inspiring example', since 'The Basque children were the biggest single influx of refugees into Britain in modern times and the only one to be completely composed of children' (1996:82).

Such moments of organized social class and anti-Fascist protest sit uneasily with recent disturbances in the region, exemplified in the 1991 riots, which began on the outlying Meadow Well Estate and then spread towards parts of West End Newcastle (see Campbell, 1993; Collier, 1998). These parochial 'white riots' had little in common with the multi-ethnic uprisings in Britain throughout the early and mid-1980s in protest against social deprivation, racism and the brutal policing strategies deployed in black and inner-city neighbourhoods. Consequently, Campbell depicts the riots as having a strange 'political emptiness' (1993:x), being, 'as much *against* the community as they are *about* it' (p. xi). Carr (1992) takes a more positive view and is at pains to disassociate the violence from race politics. 'It was gratifying to see that the riots of September 1991 did not contain a racial element,' he notes, 'but, as the traditions and values of the area are eroded, racism may become a more dominant force that will come to exclude the new immigrants and their children' (p. 146). As the violence meted out against asylum seekers in Tyneside reveals, these tensions have already given way to an unapologetic racism.

The aftermath of the 1991 riots was characterized by high fear of crime, plummeting house prices in nearby areas and the suspicion of further violence. The echo of these uprisings was later to resound during my first year in Tyneside, notably in the Bigg Market district, an area renowned for the excessive consumption of alcohol. The space, named after 'biggs', an old word for barley, has also been known as the 'Bere Market' and the 'Oate Market' (Bean, 1971:70). As barley is the basis for beer, the interconnections between drinking, industry and locality can be easily identified. During festivals such as George IV's coronation, nearby Middle Street was also said to contain fountains that flowed with free alcohol on days of public celebration (Bean, 1980). Today the Bigg Market is a unique composition of pubs, clubs, restaurants, (male) public toilets, take-aways and taxi ranks, all clustered together as the basis for a frenzied 'going out' community. Designed for the 'Bigg Night Out', the area is populated by a thronging mass of young people moving between pubs and commercial eateries to the pumping bass of the latest dance tunes. It was in this zone – a space where strike workers had picketed and the BUF were repelled – that a rather different brand of violence was to occur.

In the 1995–6 football season, NUFC held what appeared to be an unassailable lead in the English football Premiership. Unexpectedly they capitulated, losing many of their final games before eventually conceding the League title in their final home game of the season. On a hot afternoon hordes of men, women and children had gathered in NUFC shirts as a buzz of distant expectation rang through the streets. In the aftermath of the game, exuberant emotion had become translated into harsh disappointment, anger and hostility. Walking past the normally bois- terous watering-holes that evening, I was struck by the latent volatile atmosphere. The resentment was compounded by the news that arch rivals Sunderland FC were being promoted as Division One Champions to the Premiership. Somewhere along the line an idea emerged to descend on Newcastle Central Station to await Sunder- land fans changing trains on returning from their final away fixture of the season. Police had anticipated this move and stood armed with batons and shields in ranks outside the station. The NUFC fans (here, all men) were funnelled through Pink Lane by around fifty baton-wielding policemen. Windows were smashed and stones were thrown as the police randomly charged into sections of the crowds in a concerted effort to disperse as many supporters as possible. The fans were ushered back into the Bigg Market and the district was cordoned off as rioting ensued till the early hours of the morning. Walking through the Market the next day, shattered glass and debris lay scattered throughout and the old-fashioned public toilets in the area were no longer topped with a roof. The scenes were to be repeated when NUFC lost in the 1998 and then 1999 FA Cup Finals, when 30 arrests were made for drunk and violent behaviour after the latter defeat. In a narrow sense these battles mimicked the two earlier moments of protest violence in the Bigg Market: by 'the people' against the Blackshirts and by the mining strike-leaders who valiantly resisted the authority of proprietors and the strong arm of the law. In contrast to these events, the recent football violence that occurred appeared as a kind of self-mutilated anguish, a hollow riposte to wounded local pride. This time anger was not targeted at local political economy but concerned a dissatisfaction with consumption and the failed investments of NUFC.

Even so, there is evidence of alternative spaces and practices in the Northeast night-time economy. The Trent House pub in Newcastle is owned and run by descendants of one of the first black families in Tyneside. This heritage continues to be signalled through the pub's traditional decor and kitsch memorabilia. The walls are studded with black, vinyl 45 rpm records produced by a number of soul, motown and reggae artists. The jukebox continues to favour black styles of music from artists such as James Brown, Aretha Franklin, Prince Buster, UB40, Public Enemy and Desmond Dekker. There is an emphasis on multicultural representation in the fliers and postcards positioned strategically on the tables and by the door. This Leazes Lane pub is famed for its relaxed and hassle-free atmosphere and regarded as a space for open-minded locals. The Trent is also linked to the excellent after-hours club World Head Quarters (WHQ). The globally named institution continues to promote black music and remains one of the city's least aggressive night-spots, tucked away in Malborough Cresent near Newcastle Central Station. The Newcastle University Student Union Handbook describes it as 'Specialising in black music' with a 'formidable reputation for quality sounds' (1996: 65). Other pubs which play black music include The Head of Steam on Neville Street, playing a fusion of jazz, funk and soul; and The Telegraph behind Central Station, where resident DJs bang out Drum 'n' Bass.

In spring 1997 WHQ, which is now undertaking relocation, opened a new café bar which it named the 'Muhammad Ali Club/Café as a sign of respect to black pride. Posters of Ali (a one-time visitor to the North East) and Stephen Lawrence in the bar display a clear political sensitivity to racism. The WHQ symbol of a multi-ethnic handshake between a black and white hand is embossed with the caption, 'UNITING ALL COMMUNITIES'. This symbolic intertwining of black and white local histories on Tyneside inverts John Hall's exclusive 'Geordie Nation' portrayal of the district. The WHQ drinking club is a doubly conscious alternative to old style Working Men's Clubs and new style Bigg Market drinking. WHQ also declares that 'Geordies are black and white', in a dual reference to multicultural legacies and to NUFC, who play in the monochrome striped kit. This redefinition of local culture does not denigrate the unique labour history of Tyneside but offers other points for identification in global times beyond the narrow confines of white parochialism. Another example of the reconfiguration of the 'local' can be found in the Newcastle Mela festival. The event has taken place in Exhibition Park, a space we previously saw to have been a site for the celebration of industry and empire. The two-day festival is supported by NAAM (Newcastle Asian Arts and Music) and is used to promote Asian arts, music and culture within Newcastle and the North East. In the August bank holiday weekend of 1999 the event was reputed to have drawn 30,000 people who partook in the music, cuisine and bazaars available on site.

It would, then, be somewhat misleading to suggest that the North East is necessarily 'more racist' than other English districts. Dynamics of race and ethnicity are contextually contingent, they are embedded in the culture of their geographical location, and come to operate differently within specific sites and institutions such as the school, the street, the pub or the domestic home. I found that those young people who had grown up living alongside minority ethnic communities were less likely to view them as 'outsiders' and more prone to see these neighbours as 'Geordies'. Such expression of multi-ethnic belonging may exist in pockets where close, longstanding relationships have been forged within working-class communities. The feeling that 'some coloured people are English' and thereby are an integrated part of the local landscape was endorsed by other young people, especially those with multi-ethnic schooling and/or neighbourhood experiences (Chapter 6). At these moments Tyneside school students proved capable of making a qualitative distinction between skin colour and nationality.

Concluding Remarks

This chapter began by examining the legacy of diasporic movement and settlement in the North East of England. In doing so, it questioned the pervasive view of the region as the quintessential 'white highlands'. Though ostensibly white, closer inspection also uncovered diverse patterns of migration and settlement within the locality. It is argued that recognizing the longstanding histories of population movement may enable more inclusive notions of 'Geordie' identity to be achieved. Furthermore, the historical analysis reveals a significant paradox. There is evidence to indicate that nationalism has taken something of a backseat in Tyneside, an outpost that has been geographically, economically and socially cut off from the English mainland. Nevertheless, the disassociation from the nation large did not go hand in hand with the relinquishing of whiteness and popular racism. Instead, these identifications were often sublimated through an affirmation of local identity that hardens into a form of parochial patriotism.

It was such marked investments in white regional identity that exacerbated hostilities to outsiders. In particular, the position of ethnic minority groups was especially precarious as the past and present histories of Northeast racist violence came to testify. In most cases ethnic minorities were socially excluded from representations of 'Geordie' identity and lifestyle. Indeed, the overbearing white-ness of the region had all but marginalized these groups and placed them as the hidden Other within the already dislocated periphery of the North East. At the same time there remained powerful histories of anti-oppressive action in the locality. Most notably, this could be seen in the defiant actions of miners and steelworkers as well as in 'grassroots' anti-racism. This included the 1926 Miners' Strike, the Jarrow March, the rebuttal of Fascism in the 1930s and beyond, and the integration of Arab communities in South Shields. At these points the local culture and the region's radical working-class tradition most poignantly came to the fore. The accounts of young people also revealed hope for the future. Alongside the hostilities expressed towards asylum seekers and recent newcomers were to be found a creative reworking of localism that included minority ethnic groups. Not least for these reasons, in a concluding chapter I have provided routes for challenging racism in ways that do not alienate working-class children, but are embedded in a new 'pedagogy of place'.

Part II
Changing Times

–4–

Real Geordies:
White Masculinities and the Localized
Response to De-industrialization

Introduction

In the British post-war period, manufacturing employment continued to offer viable, if restricted, options for working-class males. However arduous these jobs were, they were seen to provide stability, life-long labour, masculine camaraderie and a pride in either 'craft' or 'graft'. Correspondingly a number of authors were keen to investigate social class disparities with a view to understanding 'how working-class kids get working-class jobs' (Willis, 1977) as opposed to professional and office-based careers (see also Lacey, 1970; Hargreaves *et al.*, 1975; Corrigan, 1981 [1979]). As a consequence of widespread de-industrialization, which has impacted most heavily upon old manufacturing towns in the North of England, today these jobs barely exist. At the same time the erosion of robust apprenticeship and youth training schemes mean that young people are rarely offered a reliable bridge with which to make a smooth transition into adulthood and manual employment as was once expected (Griffin, 1985; Hollands, 1990; Mc-Dowell, 2002a). The story, then, no longer concerns blocked opportunities and 'dead-end' factory jobs. Rather, we must ask how young people with familial labouring histories are adapting their identities to fit the demands of the new post-industrial economy.[10]

In an attempt to integrate 'structural' and 'cultural' approaches to the study of youth, this chapter embarks upon a detailed analysis of economic transitions. It explores the depth and scale of transformations in a working-class region to investigate how a group of young white men are negotiating the transition to a post-industrial society. The insular, subcultural practices of the group are seen as

10. With the decline of apprenticeship training schemes there has been an increase in the numbers of students continuing in education. While post-16 education rates are higher in the North East than they were in the 1960s, they compare less favourably with many other UK regions. Such findings have led others to map educational inequalities through the prism of a North–South divide (Bradford & Burdett, 1989). For a global discussion of masculinities and boys' underachievement debates, see Martino & Meyenn (2001).

complex, materially orchestrated responses to the 'new times' of the changing local–global economy. In the context of de-industrialization the chapter considers how a white, industrial masculinity could be recuperated in the field of consumption, notably through embodied rituals of football support, drinking and going out. These practices offer compelling insight into how young men 'learn to be local' in a service sector culture that has restructured their identities. Here, it has been noted that young men are more likely to be 'learning to serve' (McDowell, 2000) than 'learning to labour' (Willis, 1977).

While a few important studies have been completed on the meaning of race and ethnicity in the lives of white youth, this work has focused upon large multi-ethnic conurbations and most notably the London metropolis (Hewitt, 1986; Back, 1996; Cohen, 1993, 1997). The urban focus has perpetuated what Watt has called 'the hegemonic status of the inner-city discourse in relation to race and space' (1998:688), offering little challenge to the ascendancy of whiteness as a dominant and normative power in mainly white preserves (Nayak, 1999a, 1999b). By focusing upon a peripheral white region, this study of white identities aims to interconnect local political economy with cultural analysis. In doing so, it will contribute to new studies on the 'geographies of youth' at a time of marked global change and uneven development (Skelton and Valentine, 1998). This place-based analysis considers how a group of young white men negotiate the transition to a post-industrial economy (McDowell, 2002a, 2002b). It investigates how global change impacts upon the local economy and influences the practices and aspirations of this once upwardly mobile social class group. Drawing upon historically informed ethnographic material the longitudinal analysis aims to distil the contradictions that lie behind their blunted ambitions and the need to elicit a 'spectacular' performance of white masculinity in institutional, neighbourhood and city-centre settings.

The chapter begins by outlining the socio-economic context of the region to examine how local–global relations have impacted upon 'Geordie' youthscapes in the North East. It then focuses upon the labour histories and future aspirations of a local white masculine, school subculture known as the *Real Geordies*. Ethnography is used to consider the meaning of 'Geordie' identity in the post-industrial moment and is undertaken at an urban scale in two key masculine zones, football and drinking. Finally, the geographical analysis intertwines theories of globalization, political economy and cultural studies to explore why a cluster of young white men should enact a narrow and vituperative subcultural response to de-industrialization. The chapter concludes by arguing that scholars need to be more attentive to local nuances and regional identities in their theoretical analysis of economic restructuring and globalization.

Economic Restructuring and Labour Market Transitions in the North East

Perhaps that is all there is left of white working-class culture when you take the work away: football and beer. [...] It seemed to me a celebration of nothingness.

Darcus Howe, *White Tribe*, Channel 4, 13 January 2000

The history of the North East is built upon an industrial spine of shipbuilding, coal mining and heavy engineering. This heritage has been wrought into the very architecture of the landscape by nineteenth-century industrialists. Such captains of industry include Richard Grainger, John Dobson, Charles Palmer, William Armstrong and the Stephensons, who combine to establish a strong masculine tradition. Indeed, Massey has indicated that there were possibilities in the region for a 'genuine local ruling class' (1995 [1984]: 194) designed around this firm engineering base and a relative lack of reliance upon colonial trading legacies. Rich in local resources, the city of Newcastle has been compared to Peru on account of its coal mines, but it has always been something of a 'plantation economy', with most of the money flowing out of the region.

Nevertheless it was coal mining, or what Hudson calls 'carboniferous capital' (2000:31), that was the initial catalyst behind the region's industrial development. The scale of the region's international standing can be measured through its mineral economy. Before the First World War around 15–20 million tons of coal were being exported world-wide from the River Tyne. Indeed, the North East once contained the oldest coal mining district, powering international economic and commercial success in Britain before the last remaining pit closed in Ellington in 1994. The closure was all the more dramatic when we consider that a quarter of the nation's coal had once come from Gibside alone. The closure of the Swan Hunter shipyard in 1993 and the subsequent struggle to resuscitate the shipbuilding industry are another part of the story of a region's changing economic infrastructure (Tomaney *et al.*, 1998). Despite periods of biting economic recession in the interim war years and prior to the take-up of arms, during the 1950s unemployment rates rarely exceeded 3 per cent in what was mainly a burgeoning local economy.

However, the more recent history of the North East has concerned the painful transformation of a region relinquishing its strong industrial base and adapting to a new 'condition of postmodernity' (Harvey, 1990 [1989]). By the 1970s, employment patterns were split between the declining manufacturing core and the expanding service sector economy. The trend continued apace in the eighties, when less than a third of jobs were to be found in the traditional manufacturing economy (see Robinson, 1988:12–19). Under the Thatcherite administration the North–South divide was exacerbated as the government invested in infrastructures in London, the South East and especially along the M4 corridor (Lewis and Townsend, 1989). With a mainly manufacturing base, the North East was especially affected by de-industrialization, losing 38 per cent of jobs between 1978 and 1984. These spatial divisions have continued, albeit with their own internal, complex configurations of poverty and unemployment (Massey and Meegan, 1984). Between 1978 and 1991 the region saw a population exodus of 22 per cent, while it has been demo-graphically estimated that the South East will witness a population rise of 13 per cent over the next twenty years. With youth unemployment standing at 50 per cent in 1995, the limited opportunities for work may encourage further out-migration. In this respect the *Real Geordies* inhabit a de-industrial landscape, not dissimilar to that of the 'Valley Girls' identified in T. Skelton's (2000) study of the Rhondda, South Wales.

Economic restructuring in the region has also led to changes in the conceptions of gender identity and the relationship between masculinity, work and leisure. Indeed, some authors have suggested that the once familiar sexual division of labour – organized around a male 'breadwinner' and an expectation of women's domestic work – is increasingly an outdated practice, even in the North East (Wheelock, 1994). Instead, unemployment, part-time work, fixed-term contracts, shared parental duties and female labour are growing features of the rapidly changing household economy (Jarvis *et al.*, 2001). Women's employment has increased significantly, with the growth of the service sector making up nearly half of the labour force in a region where male employment continues to fall. The placeless, 'de-masculinizing' aspects of labour are exemplified in that famous 'non-place space' of consumption located just off the A1: the Gateshead Metrocentre. More lately, this displacement is apparent with the development of telephone call centres, which are particularly salient to the North East economy and prize 'feminized' attributes such as keyboard skills and communication proficiency over the robust 'masculine' qualities associated with the culture of manual labour. Within the sphere of local political economy the decline of male-dominated manual labour, accompanied by a growth in office work and service sector employ-ment, has generated more gender-mixed workplaces and different cultural codes of practice.

The spatial division of labour in the North East – once concentrated around heavy industry, the shipyard and the pit – has now been further fragmented and splintered in the nexus of a new, intensified global economy. This in turn has encouraged what we may tentatively call a new 'spatial division of leisure' which has seen the replacement of old workingmen's clubs and pubs with new corporate leisure industries, owned by large national and multinational companies (Chatter-ton and Hollands, 2001). On the one hand, this has encouraged urban regeneration in city-centre and dockland areas and led to greater participation from women in the Northeast night-time economy. On the other hand, the new spatial divisions of leisure have eroded older past-time drinking traditions and led to the new local–global articulations we shall investigate.

In place of the declining industrial economy, a number of international investors have attempted to capitalize on the often non-unionized skilled and semi-skilled labour supply so abundantly available. The new global economy has further witnessed the arrival of inward Foreign Direct Investment (FDI) by way of East Asian multinational corporations (MNCs), including micro-electronics companies Siemens in North Tyneside, Fujitsu near Darlington, Samsung at Billingham in Cleveland and the establishment of the Japanese Nissan car plant in Washington near Sunderland. The North East now has a new history of being a 'branch-plant' economy: many companies relocated to the region but their head-quarters have remained elsewhere. One attraction for the new micro-electronics plants had been the availability of mechanical labour and a belief that the region's local engineering skills were transferable and compliant with the technical dexterity now required. Multinationals such as Siemens and Fujitsu were also cognizant that the imposition of shift work in the North East, involving 'unsociable' working hours, would be met with little resistance by a local labour force deeply familiar with these practices from colliery work and heavy engineering. The region's knowledge-based economy, the availability of cheap skilled and semi-skilled labour, the lack of unionization and the culture of industrial labour were all key facets in enticing FDI (see also Thrift, 1989).[11]

However, the 'footloose' nature of MNCs has brought with it a need for new skills, greater social mobility and more flexible patterns of work that may sit less easily with the aspirations of traditional youth masculinities designed around an investment in older occupations. Where the factory, shipyard or colliery offered a masculine point of contact in the public world of work, these sites were, like workingmen's clubs, also a breeding ground for community solidarity and trade union activity (as witnessed in the famous Jarrow March of 1936). In these 'new times' such strong local networks of support may find it more difficult to organize around foreign multinationals whose fleet-of-foot movements frequently demand cheap flexible labour, fixed-term contracts and non-unionized activity in the global market. Thus, the mayfly life-span of Siemen's semiconductor industry in North Tyneside saw the creation and loss of 1,200 jobs between 1997 and 1998; similarly,

11. For the Nissan car plant the region was also viewed as a 'green area' without a history of motorcar production and therefore lacking the labour rights established in comparative regions such as the Longbridge car plant in the British Midlands and the Ford manufacturer at Haylewood in the North West. The untapped female labour in the region also enabled MNCs to forgo many traditional rights associated with industry and introduce 'flexible' and part-time patterns of work. At the same time, the cost of Northeast labour compared very favourably with an equivalent workforce in Germany.

the opening of the Fujitsu plant in 1991 led to 555 redundancies when it closed only seven years later (see Dawley, 2000).

It is within these 'new' and increasingly uncertain times that the *Real Geordies* – a white, masculine, working-class youth subculture – are negotiating the transition to adulthood and the uncertain promise of a white masculine labouring identity. The challenge for the young men in this study lies in coming to terms with the end of an industrial empire and the region's declining economic status in the competitive global economy. At present a considerable amount of quantitative (and some qualitative) research has been undertaken concerning the economic geography of Northeast England (Robinson, 1988; Garrahan and Stewart, 1994; Hudson, 2000; Tomaney and Ward, 2001). However, there remains a paucity of detailed ethnographic research that explores how young people's subjectivities are culturally and materially embedded within their places of habitation and how such relations shape regions and identities. As Bauder has recently argued, labour market geographers need to engage more carefully with 'local uniqueness, situatedness and contingency' (2001:47) to understand how place influences life-choices in the area of employment. This analysis explores how the *Real Geordies* negotiate the transition from an industrial to a post-industrial (or, more accurately, neo-industrial economy), where the effects of globalization are manifest at economic, social, political and cultural levels within the locality. Though it is rarely referred to directly we shall see how class operates as a 'structuring absence' (Skeggs, 1997:74) in the lives of these young men, permeating their aspirations, social activities and broader value systems.

The Real Geordies

> I decree today that life is simply taking and not giving
> England is mine and it owes me a living
>
> 'Still Ill', The Smiths, 1984

The *Real Geordies* were white, working-class young men aged 16 years who were born and raised in the North East of England. The core members comprised Jason, Shaun, Steve, Filo, Carl, Fat Mal, Dave, Cambo, Duane and Spencer, although others, including Jono and Bill, occassionally joined the group. Aside from Carl, whose parents lived in council dwellings, each of the *Real Geordies* came from families who were now classified as owner-occupiers, having purchased properties in the Northeast housing chain. Some were participants of 'white flight' from the inner city and now lived in districts that ranged from leafy suburban quarters to humble residential estates on the city outskirts. A prominent masculine legacy of manual labour ran through their familial biographies. With few exceptions, all spoke of fathers, uncles and grandfathers who had developed specialist skills refined as sheet-metal workers, construction workers, offshore operators, glaziers, fitters and mechanics.[12] However, some members came from backgrounds where the tradition of manual labour had been sustained through the heavy industries of engineering, coal mining and dock work. A smaller fraction also came from families connected to small businesses, including Jason's dad, who ran a fish stall in North Shields, Jono's dad, who was a cab driver for a local taxi firm, and Shaun's father, who was a publican. Even so, these individuals shared the same subcultural status as their peers and also had male relatives with an established tradition of hard manual labour in the North East. For these 'local lads' the relationship between political economy and their masculine youthscape is implicitly one in which 'occupation serves as a mutual identification pattern' (Beck, 1998 [1992]:140).

By and large, then, the *Real Geordies* came from a stratum of the skilled English working class, once the 'aristocracy of labour'. This habitation enabled them to invest in what Gray has described as the cult of the 'respectable artisan' (1981:31). This masculine heritage involved an element of craftmanship in which labouring skills and techniques were acquired through apprenticeships and tutoring schemes. Skilled and semi-skilled occupations related to the construction industry and the higher echelons of the manufacturing economy commonly featured in their familial biographies. Cambo, Dave, Carl and Spencer had fathers and elder brothers who were employed in recognized trades, including that of plumbers, plasterers, tilers, joiners, 'brickies' and glaziers. Duane hoped to become a car-mechanic like his father; Filo's dad had worked as a docker before gaining an engineering qualification that enabled him to fit and repair central heating boilers; Steve said his dad was a 'sparkey' (a skilled electrician); Fat Mal's was a foreman in a factory; and Bill's father was reputed to have a relatively lucrative job in a sheet-metal plant.

Moreover, the traces of this specific labour history had left their mark upon the practices of the *Real Geordies*. Elements of an industrial heritage were embodied in an appreciation of skilled physical labour over mental agility, a collective sharing of heavy, often sexual adult humour and an established drinking capability (see Taylor and Jamieson, 1997). As Cohen writes, 'Growing up working-class has for many meant an apprenticeship to such an inheritance – a patrimony of skill entailed in the body and its techniques, forging a quasi-congenital link between origins and destinies' (1997:205). Most recognizably, members took it upon themselves to enact the image of the 'Geordie hard man' in classroom interactions,

---

12. The employment situation of female members (grandmothers, mothers and sisters) was more diverse. For example, this included a number of housewives as well as shop workers, childminders, packers, secretaries, cleaners and a teacher.

in football matches on the playground and upon the wider social landscape of the city (Hollands, 1995). The *Real Geordies* promoted the values of a muscular puritan work ethic (honesty, loyalty, self-sufficiency, 'a fair day's work for a fair day's pay') in a situation where manual *unemployment* was increasingly the norm. The economic situation of the *Real Geordies* was especially uncertain in view of what now appears to be the permanent collapse of the local 'hard' economic infrastructure. The *Real Geordies* believed in 'hard graft' when it came to physical labour but felt the school did nothing to prepare them for what they invariably described as 'the reel world' (Fat Mal). Consequently, they repeatedly informed me that lessons were 'borin' mon' and claimed they could not see the point in learning about Shakespearean literature or complex mathematical formulae when this would be of little use beyond the classroom.[13] When I pointed out that these skills might be transferable and could enable them to become more employable in the long term, a familiar reply remained, 'There's nee' propa jobs anyway' (Cambo). Instead, the *Real Geordies* knew that access to the jobs they required involved contacts, 'It's who yer kna, like' (Shaun), and as such saw through the contradiction in the national curriculum – 'Laarnin'? Far us! Nee point waat so ever' (Bill) – in an institution where 'Teachers only favour the posh'uns – the only thing I larnt aboot is to hay'ut school' (Filo).

The industrial credentials of the subculture were also embodied in their name. 'Geordie' once encompassed people from Newcastle upon Tyne, the Tyne Valley, Northumberland, Wearside, South Tyneside and Durham, though it is a label whose geographical boundaries are rapidly shrinking and growing ever more parochial. Formerly, as noted above, 'Geordie' was synonymous with industrial labour and was literally, amongst other competing definitions, a term for *pit-workers* that grew in prominence as local labourers would later secure a bond to work in other Northern coal-fields (see Colls and Lancaster, 1992:ix–xvi). The question then arises, if the *Real Geordies* could no longer be 'Real' in the true occupational sense, then what does it mean to be Geordie in the late-industrial economy, and, more pertinently, have we witnessed the last of the *Real Geordies*? Instead, the ethnography reveals that in the out-of-work situation the meaning of 'Geordie' is being constituted elsewhere, in the realm of leisure and consumption. For E.P. Thompson, class-consciousness can better be understood in terms of historical materialist relations that have cultural meaning, 'embodied in traditions, value-systems, ideas, and institutional forms' (1982 [1968]:8). As we shall find, a *Real*

13. This was deeply contradictory as the young men had chosen to stay on in the Sixth Form, though many reflected that a number of peers had previously left. Many were ambivalent about staying on but provided various responses. Sixth Form could forestall the dole queue; give them time to consider their options; give them 'headspace'; 'get them out of bed in the morning'; provide qualifications that may allow for higher wages in the future; keep parents off their back.

Geordie identity was being consolidated in other social arenas beyond that of the traditional workplace.

In the main the *Real Geordies* had already rejected the upwardly mobile passage into further or higher education, careers and deskwork. But this did not mean they had rejected the work ethic itself. Indeed, many were critical of 'scroungers' and 'spongers', that is, those who relied on unemployment benefits for long periods (see Willott and Griffin, 1996), or were thought to be entangled in criminal networks. The young men sought to establish a symbolic boundary of white 'respectability' (see Skeggs, 1997) between themselves and *Charver Kids* from unemployed families, whose lives shall be the focus of the following chapter. In keeping with E.P. Thompson's (1982 [1968]) portrait of nineteenth-century rural artisans and skilled members of the working class, the *Real Geordies* also construed themselves to be a 'cut above' other local youth cultures on account of a proclaimed labouring heritage. They were found to construct a sense of white entitlement not only in relation to the local economy but also through and against other youth cultures. This revealed the relational connectivity that existed between the different local youth formations. Here, the emphasis is upon the discursive enactment of whiteness through labour and the variety of ways young people respond to global change. For the *Real Geordies*, relegating other youth subcultures to the margins of whiteness was a means of performing an imagined 'authentic' white masculinity. In the absence of a significant ethnic minority population the *Real Geordies* affirmed their whiteness not simply in relation to blackness, as other writers have shown (Hewitt, 1986; Cohen, 1993; Back, 1996), but also through and against other forms of white subjectivity. Through these subtle distinctions the *Real Geordies* could exert a flickering sense of authority over other working-class young people on account of their 'superior' white labouring credentials.

Although publicly the *Real Geordies* appeared to hold similar attitudes, opinions and desires, privately there were some notable differences. While a few respondents expressed upwardly mobile tendencies, many did not, revealing the biographically contingent aspects of labour transitions, despite shared experiences mediated by gender, class and ethnicity (see also Hollands, 1990; MacDonald *et al.*, 2000). Such accounts fracture any simple notions of the subculture as a monolithic, hermetically sealed unit. For example, Steve may have been somewhat exceptional in viewing A-levels as a direct means to improve his chances of working in a bank. Moreover, he spoke discretely to me about considering options for higher education.[14] Also, Duane wanted to do an HND in mechanical engineering at a local college, while a number of others showed preferences for

14. Such accounts made problematic the notion that the *Real Geordies* were as homogeneous in their desires as they may have appeared Indeed, individuals would frequently present themselves in a different manner when with the peer-group as opposed to one-to-one conversations. This validated the longitudinal methodology as it enabled me to situate respondents within multiple, sometimes conflicting, accounts.

vocational training courses. Filo, meanwhile, had learnt much about fitting boilers from his father but at present lacked approved qualifications. Similarly, Cambo frequently speculated that there was 'stacks' to be made in building conservatories but was unsure quite how to put this plan into action. Carl and Jason, meanwhile, wanted to extend their current part-time employment in the service sector. They felt assured in the knowledge that while such work meant it remained financially difficult to leave the parental home, employment offered them the opportunities to work a regular 'nine-to-five' shift and the possibilities of future managerial training in the quest for a 'reel job' (Carl). This temporary lifestyle would also enable them to maintain subcultural affiliations based on a commitment to 'birds, booze and a fuckin' nite oot once in a while!' (Jason). Consequently, they saw little point in saving money and were determined to spend what they earned on clothes, drink, music, football and what Carl termed 'living for the weekend'. The emphasis here was less on future aspirations and more on 'making do'. In this context attachments to locality and an extending dependency on the parental household become increasingly widespread features of working-class young lives (Hollands, 1997).

When it came to the world of labour, the *Real Geordies* were neither 'work shy' or 'lazy' as some teachers and had claimed, nor were they devoid of employment strategies. Instead, they were concerned with practical knowledge and negotiating various life-paths that would *preserve* rather than eradicate their subcultural allegiance to football, drinking and going out. They regarded themselves as would-be-workers, in contradistinction to the masculine criminal underclass identified in Campbell's (1993) analysis of the region. For the *Real Geordies* the notion of the 'breadwinner' identity encompassed a virtuous sense of masculine pride, labour and white credentials, forming a potent symbol that the American historian David Roediger (1992, 1994) has discussed at length (see also Allen, 1994). Roediger explains how, 'In popular usage, the very term *worker* often presumes whiteness (and maleness) . . . its actual usage also suggests a *racial* identity, an identification with whiteness and work so strong that it need not even be spoken' (1992:19; see also Allen, 1994). It was this 'unspoken' concept of workmanship that the *Real Geordies* evoked in their day-to-day activities. In many ways gender and ethnicity were displaced into locally specific practices and forms of identification sym-bolized in being a *Real Geordie*. Thus, the *Real Geordies* were similar to the 'Geordie' youth referred to by Coffield *et al.* whose 'localism operated sometimes as a fortification behind which new ideas (like a multi-cultural society) could be ignored and parochialism flourish' (1986 [1985]:143–4). In this respect, the sub-culture deployed regional identity in a more stringent manner than other youth and carefully 'policed' who could rightly lay claim to being an authentic 'Geordie'. Most certainly, the *Real Geordies* believed they resided within the 'respectable' rather than the 'rough' wedge of working-class culture.

With its once famous shipbuilding industry, the North East has became a symbol of the 'Iron North', and its workers are regularly depicted as having an iron, masculine constitution to match. In the late-industrial period the muscular prowess of white Geordie masculinity is being called into question. This has resulted in the surrender of the concept of life-long employment with a firm, in which the cultivated attributes of the *Real Geordies* – loyalty, hard graft and routine – would now go unappreciated. The closure and general uncertainty surrounding Northeast micro-electronics plants has already incurred large-scale job losses that have severely impinged upon the work-based horizons of the *Real Geordies*. At present, the plants at Siemens and Fujitsu have been reoccupied by Atmel and Filtronic Plc, respectively, though it remains to be seen whether the new employment on offer will carry the cache of long-term job security. Indeed, the closure of these former sites most directly affected the group, who had witnessed the devastating impact of redundancy on neighbours, immediate family and other relatives. For the subculture concerned, 'Geordie' identity was now most noticeably being re-fashioned in two zones – football and the practice of going out drinking. Each of these arenas held parallels with the workplace in offering a space for masculine bonding, routine and regulation in 'risky' and uncertain times. Accordingly, if a shared labour heritage was a subtle point of commonality used by the *Real Geordies* to invoke an imaginary sense of community, then football and public house drinking were equally important as others. Each of these practices will be described in detail before an analysis of work, leisure and labour history is undertaken in order to illuminate the cultural specificity of these youthscapes. With the local employment situation so unstable, the transition into the masculine world of work would remain, in many cases, as if in a perpetual state of deferral. As such, the *Real Geordies* were like flies in amber, having become petrified in the hardened solution of an older period from which their values descended

Refashioning 'Geordie': Football-Fandom

At the end of the day, we're the *Real Geordies* and no-one can take that away from us.

Dave

Sporting traditions, including horse racing, running, athletics, dog racing, football, rugby and pigeon racing, have all played a prominent role in the North East. Tailor's (1992) historical study of sport in the region implies strong connections between the industrial economy, leisure pursuits and local identity. For example, the early fascination with rowing competitions was seen as a symbolic means by which the region could assert a muscular prosperity over London rowers on the

Thames. Here, the River Tyne was seen as the economic life-blood of the region, offering a counterpoint to the nation's capital. The decline of rowing is thereby linked to the reduced significance of working watermen on the Tyne and the popularization of football. The fusion of sport and local identity is nowhere more apparent when one considers how the 1862 spectacle of the Blaydon Races has become immortalized as a regional anthem. However, by the 1890s local sporting pride had began to shift towards football, where 'it took only a short time to become integrated into the regional male identity' (p. 120). Over a century on, football is still at the forefront of sporting consumption in the North East, though rugby, ice-hockey, basketball and other sports are gaining in popularity with the development of professional teams. Moreover, in a period when many football stadia are located outside of city centres, St James' Park in Newcastle occupies a central location and is of core significance to an area where regional identity has been concentrated around local infrastructures such as the factory, shipyard and colliery. For the young men I researched, football continued to retain its signif-icance as 'Tyneside's greatest modern passion' (Bean, 1971:208).

Most *Real Geordies* held season tickets at St James's Park and were critical of 'armchair' supporters, viewers who only watched the team in domestic settings on television. Supporting the 'Mags'[15] was an embodied, full-time occupation and involved considerable expense for a hard-core minority who followed the team home and away. Escapades relating to fighting, drinking, being chased, etc., were recounted with as much gusto as were goals. For the group, being 'Geordie' meant *physically* supporting the team on the terraces and beyond. They insisted that it was important to 'stand up for yersel' both against official authority (teachers, the police, public figures) and in other situations (during disputes with family mem-bers or girlfriends, in response to opposing football supporters, in street-fights). Moreover, they pointed out how their fathers had done the same thing when they were young and even encouraged this masculine posture as a sign of developing manhood: perfect preparation for the industrial world of work.[16] Crucially it was at the symbolic level (a father's dream, a running commentary on the back-streets, the wearing of a football-shirt with the name of Alan Shearer) that football and football-support became a substitute for work.

The young men in this study epitomized John Hall's 'Geordie Nation', that is, they saw NUFC as the cornerstone on which *Real Geordies* can be brought into being. Recent work has already suggested a peculiarly intense relationship exists between 'the great leviathan of football' (Tailor, 1992:120) and local masculinities

15. NUFC are known as 'the Magpies' on account of their black and white team colours.

16. The impact that 'spectacular' masculine practices can have upon girls and young women has been the focus of feminist accounts of subculture (McRobbie & Garber, 1977 [1975]), while more recent research has examined how these rituals impact upon subordinated masculinities (Connell, 1995; Nayak & Kehily, 2001).

in the region (C. Skelton, 2000, 2001). The attachment to place was such that a number of respondents expressed how friends, family and ownership of a NUFC season ticket were too much to relinquish. On match-days the *Real Geordies* took pride in being part of a social collective, NUFC's 'Toon Army'. Even so, the practices of the group served to highlight the difficulty in affirming this identity when creative economic negotiations had to take place in order *to be seen* to support the club. Overall, many of the *Real Geordies* displayed a startling creativity when it came to financing their support of NUFC. For example, some shared season tickets in an attempt to spread the expense; a few had taken up part-time jobs, including paper-rounds, work in petrol stations, supermarkets and fast-food chains; some relied on parental sacrifices which were paid back in other ways; a couple of members claimed to simply 'know people'; others got fast cash as reputed dealers in 'dodgy goods'. As MacDonald's portraits of young people in the Northeast community of Teesside show, 'fiddly jobs' (1999:177) form a core part of the local youth economy and can also be seen as a creative response towards future labour insecurity. Another means of balancing support for the team against economic hardship was to watch games screened in pubs and a local cinema as a compensatory manoeuvre. This secondary viewing activity, though no substitute for 'gannin' the gemme', was recognized as a reaction to a tight financial situation, and symbolically given prestige over the practices of the 'armchair supporter'. Significantly, drinking and collective viewing allowed for the match-time experience to be recreated in the male environment of the public house. Furthermore, just as certain parts of the ground are mythologized as 'home ends', particular 'standing room only' pubs were seen as more appropriate viewing points for these 'celluloid supporters'. As the phrase suggests, these latter supporters could *simulate* being at the match, but would have to authenticate their allegiances further if they wanted to be taken seriously as 'Real'.

Being a *Real Geordie* became an embodied activity that stretched from donning the shirt to having NUFC emblems tattooed on the skin, as undertaken by Cambo and Fat Mal. Fighting, drinking and vociferously cheering the team on were all part of the corporeal labour involved. It was with some precision that the *Real Geordies* could recall match results, names of goal-scorers and times at which goals had been taken, yet at the same time they looked down on some other NUFC supporters who had achieved this knowledge second-hand and derided them as 'anoraks'. The *Real Geordies* depicted 'anoraks' as supporters who studiously supported the team, had a penchant for statistics, but were ultimately (like the 'ear'oles' Willis [1977] encountered) passive observers. The split between having a 'mental' knowledge of the team and a 'physical' know-how gleaned from first-hand experience (pre-match drinking, cheering the lads on, fighting and chasing other supporters) was used to distinguish them as 'Real' in comparison with other school student supporters. Local youth who supported the club, then, broadly consisted of

Real Geordies, who regularly went to 'the gemme', 'celluloid supporters', who gathered in a pub, and 'armchair supporters' and 'anoraks', who watched quietly or listened to NUFC on Sky TV or local radio in the privacy of a domestic setting. Notably, this 'armchair' viewing was regarded as a feminized activity, a move away from the male bonding achieved in the public house or stadium, towards women, the family and the global media enterprise. The *Real Geordies* distinguished between such gendered public and private viewing, discriminating positively in favour of the former and negatively against the latter. These viewing practices were neither separate nor distinct, however, as members would often combine each of these activities depending on finances, if NUFC were playing away, or if they had other social commitments. Thus, the claim to be 'authentic' or 'Real' was in actuality more complex than it first appeared since it involved negotiation and a continual performance of renewal.

Refashioning 'Geordie': Drinking and Going Out

A pint with the boys
In a buffle of noise
That's livin' alright.

'Livin' alright' – original theme from *Auf Wiedersehen, Pet*

Newcastle is rightly famed for its pubs. After all, where else in the country is the Friday/Saturday night session such an institution?

Newcastle University Student Union Handbook, 1996.

The current fascination with a 'Night on the Toon' has seen the North East represented less as an area with a declining manufacturing infrastructure, and more as a 'Party City' for the hedonistic activities of drinking and clubbing (Hollands, 1995). Accordingly, some writers have commented that the region has 'rarely been far from the top of the nation's drunkenness table' (Bean, 1971:223). Coffield *et al.* also found that 'The strongest tradition followed by the young adults we knew was drinking alcohol' (1986 [1985]:132–3). They go on to point towards how, 'The importance of drinking to the local community was reflected in the large number of words used for being drunk, including "stottin", "mortal", "pissed" and "smashed".' When an oft-cited survey by US travel consultants Weismann Travel was reported in the UK national press, rating the region's principal city Newcastle as the eighth party city in the world, the new image of the 'Geordie' was globally cultivated well beyond the former boundaries of an occupational legacy. Such good-time images may tell us less about the actual night-time economy of a region and more about the regard with which working-class cities such as Dublin, Liverpool or Newcastle are deemed to be places for excessive partying and wild stag/hen nights (Chatterton and Hollands, 2001). These current representations are a sharp contrast to the drab, industrial image of the city as replete with old miners in flat-caps, grey factories, dog racing and fog on the Tyne.

Drinking culture remains firmly tied to the Northeast industrial heritage. Today pubs with names such as The Baltic Tavern, The Free Trade, The Ship Inn and Offshore 44 testify to the working-class ancestry of shipping, trade and labour upon the River Tyne. Bean has alluded to other pubs called 'the Hydraulic Crane, the Rifle, the Gun, the Ordnance Arms, the Forge Hammer, the Crooked Billet, the Moulders Arms, the Mechanics Arms, the Shipwrights Hotel, the Vulcan, the Blast Furnace – and many, many more' (1971:97). Elsewhere, he compares the former row of drinking establishments nearby a cluster of local engineering traders to 'a chain of industrial oases' (1980:5). However, as most residual pubs have now either vanished or come under new ownership in the late-industrial context, the ties between drinking and work have been spatially and culturally displaced. This cultural history provides an interpretative backcloth against which contemporary drinking cultures are being produced.

The *Real Geordies* enjoyed dressing in smart shirts and meeting up with one another in city-centre spaces. They would pass through a series of pubs, usually having just one drink in each as they linked up with other members to form a chain for 'circuit drinking'. This hedonistic display allowed them to be seen in a number of public places and so belied the appearance that money could be a meagre resource.[17] Furthermore, the circuit ritual enabled those who missed the pre-liminary meeting place to join the chain at another venue. Circuit drinking remained, then, a highly regulated activity forged through familiar rituals and routine practices. The *Real Geordies* all dressed in subtle variations of a recognized style, they knew which pubs would be frequented and in exactly which spots the others could be found; at all times, they never lost sight of whose turn it was to get the drinking round in. Moreover, they had a detailed knowledge of the price of drinks in corresponding venues, and on special weekdays (e.g. to mark the end of exams or a birthday celebration) were able to map out their drinking circuit to take advantage of 'happy hours', 'two-for-one' offers, and the like. Bottled lagers were favoured at the time of the research as they allowed the 'lads' to encompass a larger drinking territory than would otherwise have been possible if pints were drank at each establishment. Bottled larger enabled drinks to be sipped slowly if money was tight with less obvious attention and had the added benefit of being harder to 'spike' in dimly lit clubs. New places were always given a try, assessed accordingly and subsequently incorporated or rejected from future drinking routes. Favourite 'watering-holes' included those with a club-style atmosphere where DJs would be

17. To facilitate under-age drinking, certain bars that were renowned for younger age drinkers were frequented. Another trick to by-pass wary doormen was to enter with a group of young women, 'cos the bouncers neva turn lasses away - not in a group anyway' (Shaun).

playing loud house and chart music. Visiting a number of venues provided a structure for the evening, it offered variety and allowed the subculture to have a heightened public display in the city centre.

Moreover, circuit drinking appeared to increase the potential of 'funny happenings' in what can be understood as a modern-day form of promenading. In this way, the subculture recuperated older forms of an industrial white masculine culture through collective rituals related to male drinking, fighting, football and sexual conquest. Thus, 'funny stories' referring to passing out, throwing up or acting completely out of character when under the influence of alcohol were reported – such as the time Filo insisted on urinating from the Tyne Bridge and ended up with 'pissed-streaked troowsers!', or the occasion when Fat Mal ruined his best silk shirt when he fell asleep on top of his kebab and chilli sauce after a heavy night out with the 'lads', and so on and so forth. The *Real Geordies* appeared to derive great satisfaction from relating humorous events, sexual narratives and tales of casual, 'funny' violence (see Nayak and Kehily, 2001 for discussion). Narration was a means of pruning and cultivating a harmonious youthscape that at least on the surface appeared homogeneous, if in practice it was anything but. Indeed, these shared stories served to bind the group together and provided them with a sense of collective history and mutual experience.

On an unplanned night out with the *Real Geordies* I saw how one such event could provide ammunition for further narration. Outside a chip-shop we encountered a raucous crowd of Bigg Market 'lasses' who taunted us with a colloquial rhyme, 'Buy us some chips, and you can feel me greasy tits!' High spirits instigated a scene where Steve and Spencer were attempting to nibble chips from the cleavage of two giggling 'lasses' while a boisterous food fight erupted between the others, as a set of sheepish customers looked on. As a consequence we were barred from the chip-shop, but for the *Real Geordies*, 'It wor worth it' (Duane) as 'It were a *reet* laff mon' (Cambo) and 'We even got a bit of breast with wor chips!' (Steve).[18] In the absence of a regular wage, such masculine exhibitionism appeared to be of pronounced symbolic importance. It enabled the subculture to displace, and so retain, the occupational meaning of 'Geordie' in the dead-zone of industrial inactivity. These actions also provided the group with a repertoire of narratives to further augment their investments in the culture of 'hard' labour. Evidently the *Real Geordies* were nostalgic about a time they had never experienced. In this respect it is not past events themselves that were of significance but the emotional investments that were felt to be embodied in these real or imagined social practices.

18. Such 'hyper-masculine' displays could at times present tensions in the research process (see Gough & Edwards, 1998). While I did not wish to be seen to endorse the 'laddish' behaviour of the group, I was equally conscious not to appear over-patronizing as this could result in respondents monitoring their behaviour in ways that would not have been in keeping with the method of participant observation.

Despite changes to the manufacturing base, the *Real Geordies* maintained 'felt' investments in the traditional basis of working-class culture. These emotions were present in their nostalgic affection for the region; the emphasis on male drinking pursuits; a heavy, physical humour; the smattering of stories about fighting and sexual exploits; the abundant parochial conservatism which coloured much of their opinions on gender, sexuality and ethnicity. Indeed, such leisure activities related to terrace chanting or Bigg Market drinking may not be so far removed from emotional investments present within masculine work-based cultures. Local writers such as Lancaster have emphasized the role of the 'carnivalesque':

> "Pit-hardened" young males, with no pit or shipyard within which to vent their mach-
> ismo, sublimate their traditional industrial toughness into the carnivalesque. . . . Indeed,
> it could be argued that the carnivalization of popular culture provides a vital emotional
> prop for coping with rapid change' (1992:61).

By interpreting the diverse social practices of the *Real Geordies* ('gannin' the match', Bigg Market drinking, having a 'laff') as a 'vital emotional prop' in uncertain times, we gain further insight into the deep investments made in these activities. As Massey has noted, '"traditions" are often themselves hard to grasp in an increas-ingly globalised world, and may be reduced to the "commodified", "pastiche", "often romanticised" and "partially illusory" presentations' (1995:49). Indeed, the postmodern language of carnivalesque, masquerade, parody and pastiche may offer a more playful means of interpreting the plight of the *Real Geordies* in the post-industrial city than the version presented here. Instead, this analysis has concentrated on the 'risk' and uncertainty of the global economy, the fragmentation of labour markets and the upheaval experienced by locally embedded commun-ities. Critically, the meaning of 'Geordie' was no longer about *production* (the colliery, shipyard or factory) but had been displaced into the arena of *consumption* (football, drinking and going out). Lacking advanced qualifications, social mobil-ity and solid training experience, the task of securing stable employment would not be easy for the *Real Geordies*. The extent to which subcultural practices can retain their 'magical' properties of recuperation in the adult world now remains especially problematic.

The Anatomy of Labour: The Price of an Industrial Inheritance

> When people speak of . . . having "coal in their bones", they are talking about an
> apprenticeship to this kind of inheritance . . . the assertion of this kind of pro-
> prietal pride involves strategies of social closure which define all those who are
> held to lack such credentials as 'outsiders' and a potential threat.
>
> (Phil Cohen, 'The perversions of inheritance' 1993[1988])

While the concept of 'Geordie' has changed over time, the identity prevails despite the complete closure of collieries in the North East. We would be mistaken in believing that, because the *Real Geordies* could never be 'Real' in the true occupational sense as pit-workers, a number of symbolic associations did not take place. As Cohen remarks above, the idea of 'coal in your bones' is itself a type of apprenticeship literally embodied in the sublimated white, male, working-class practices presented.[19] Thus, the *Real Geordies* continued to retain a locally specific investment in the declining regional work-based activities of mining, shipping and steel-related industries in a period of increased fragmentation and globalization. As a birthright, symbols of industry have a privileged place in the psychic economy of this particular subculture though the 'anatomy of labour' was now displaced into other cultural activities. To this extent, in the North East, 'The legacy of a culture of waged labour has thus proved highly resistant to change' (Hudson, 2000:82).

In a study of post-industrial masculinities in Sheffield, Taylor and Jamieson (1997) draw attention to the economic and cultural value still retained through the nostalgic remembrance of former apprenticeship schemes in the steel industry. Drawing on the work of Connell (1995), they found that the cult of being 'Little Mesters' – that is, the 'master cutler' – was symbolically carried by contemporary generations of young men and experienced as a 'protest' form of masculinity. The authors point out that although masculinity is recognized as closely tied to the concept of labour, unemployment does not entail 'the sudden and total evacuation of men from the *symbolic terrain* of work, or the loss of work references in the discursive construction of hegemonic forms of masculinity' (1997: 166). Certainly, this was the case for the *Real Geordies*, who encompassed many of the complex social class characteristics identified in the work of Raymond Williams: ' . . . the new generation responds in its own ways to the unique world it is inheriting, taking up many continuities, that can be traced, and reproducing many aspects of the organisation, which can be separately described, yet feeling its whole life in certain ways differently, and shaping its creative response into a new structure of feeling' (1973 [1961]:65). In this sense, the *Real Geordies* were managing a 'structure of feeling' that intersected with their educational aspirations, cultural values and leisure pursuits. For, as Roger Bromley has noted, 'If a "class" feels alien, or exiled from the *present*, it can superimpose upon the present the familiar and normative "ideals" of its "past". What matters is the memory, not the fact' (1988:142). The identification with a 'golden past' enabled the *Real Geordies* to cultivate a youthscape in which they are construed as the eternal 'backbone of the nation' – salt-of-the-earth natives who had failed to inherit an industrial heritage that was rightfully theirs.

19. Respondents also referred to a masculine cultural apprenticeship where initiation into drinking had taken place with grandfathers, fathers, elder brothers and cousins. They also recounted how season tickets were inherited from fathers and older male members who had occupied the same areas of the stadium until expansion had forced them to relocate.

In the absence of life-long labour, the *Real Geordies* appeared to be enacting the unspoken traces of a former occupational culture that was socially embedded in familial biographies and shared regional peer-group values. Thus, while the collapse of traditional apprentice schemes may have affected the *Real Geordies* most markedly in view of their familial labour histories, it had not dislodged their *investments* in an industrial lineage and the anatomy of labour.[20] Rather, these imaginary points of identification with manual, life-long occupational culture were foundational to the practice of a working-class identity. As the Regional Training and Development Co-ordinator for the North East micro-electronics industry recalled, 'There's very much a pit mentality in-bred into young people here.' In these circumstances the *Real Geordies* came to occupy the position of a 'residual' labouring culture (Williams, 1985 [1973]). Here, the long shadow of an industrial past that celebrated full employment, continuity and a strict sexual division of labour cast itself darkly upon the exaggerated performances of the *Real Geordies*.

Despite recent transformations, the participants exuded a self-righteous confidence in the face of the prevailing bleak economic situation. Indeed, the subculture was able to maintain the illusion of white masculine prowess despite the depletion of the manufacturing base by reconfiguring the anatomy of labour in other ways, as we saw primarily in relation to football, going-out rituals and the dismissal of other youth cultures. Loyalty to the region as expressed through the support of NUFC, and the perseverance of working-class manliness exhibited through drinking, fighting, humour and alleged sexual prowess, made this transition temporarily possible (Canaan, 1996; Nayak and Kehily, 2001). It was etched into the social landscape and embodied practices of the *Real Geordies*, as other post-industrial studies fleetingly reveal: ' . . . cultures originally associated with local workplaces (the cotton mill, the docks, the steel works, or the cutlery workshop) "escape" into the larger local culture generally and leave their indelible imprint or traces over time at several different levels within that local social formation' (Taylor *et al.*, 1996:34).

In effect, an imaginary set of identifications was taking place that engaged with recognized forms of industrial white masculinity. The empty space left by de-industrialization was thereby filled by the 'hereditary' promise of a white manhood that could be reiterated in other social arenas. Thus, the *Real Geordies* could embody the heroic elements of manual labour through an appeal to local culture and a corporeal enactment of white masculine excess. According to Cohen, white working-class males may 'live their class subjection through the proto-domestic

20. This contrasts with another local study, by Coffield *et al.* in the mid-eighties which declared: '. . . young adults who never have had a job have no occupational identity at all - they are not even an unemployed shop assistant or joiner, they are simply *unemployed*' (1986 [1985]:81). Instead, the *Real Geordies* culturally re-imagined a manual occupational identity which they embodied in daily rituals. For more recent local accounts see MacDonald (1999) and MacDonald *et al.* (2000).

features of their labour, but in such a way as to dissociate themselves from both by assuming imaginary positions of mastery linked to masculine "pride in place"' (1993 [1988]:82). That these relations may be an 'imaginative' reworking of a mythic version of working-class culture does not diminish their significance, nor does it alter the lived realities of growing up as working class in the 'global outpost' of Northeast England (Hudson, 2000). The fictitious relationship the *Real Geordies* had with the former world of manual labour meant that they were continually recasting the past as an 'imagined community' (Anderson, 1984 [1983]). That the subculture remained deeply nostalgic about a period they had never experienced did not lessen their sense of estrangement indeed, their actions continued to be encased in the mythical traditions of a former era. In the contemporary moment the *Real Geordies* were men out of time, the unreconstructed outsiders-within whose claim to regional authenticity remained forever symbolic.

Concluding Remarks

The ethnography indicates that in an increasingly globalized and 'shrinking' world, place-based identities continue to be of significance. The rich industrial traditions of the Northeast region are not easily dislodged from the socio-cultural economy of young lives, as the accelerated period of late modernity may lead us to suggest. Rather, the embodied practices of the *Real Geordies* would denote that young people are constructing a new sense of place from the rusting metal carnage of de-industrialization that at once draws upon, but imaginatively reconfigures, former traditions. At the same time, the creative reworking of local labouring traditions in an era of industrial inactivity has given way to the sublimation of a 'breadwinner' identity and its re-enactment through an exaggerated display of white industrial masculinity.

In dissecting the discursive practices of the *Real Geordies*, their subcultural responses must be understood as both the outcome of, and to some extent the precursor for, both resistance and accommodation to multifaceted local–global transformations. Here, young men were found to be making different life-choices that were negotiated through the local culture to varying degrees. Significantly, being a *Real Geordie* was no longer about economic production and the materiality of life-long labour, drudgery, 'craft' and 'graft'. Rather, 'Geordie' identity was anatomically retrieved through the art of consumption as enacted on the urban scene through the signs, symbols and the motifs of 'real' labour. Thus, the culture of manual labour was recuperated and refashioned in new, out-of-work spaces that resonated with the eerie echo of industrial prowess.

The study illustrates that while key debates in economic geography and youth studies may shed light upon how young lives are materially structured, they may be less sensitive to the contextual contingency of biographical life-paths and the subjective, and highly localized investments in corporeal labour, folklore, past-times and traditions.[21] The *Real Geordies* were, then, enmeshed in a complex spatial network of relations that drew upon kinship histories, peer-group culture, football-fandom, subcultural differentiation and leisure activities. Empirically grounded, sophisticated histories of the circuits of cultural production/consumption may now better enable us to capture the embodied spatial practices and seemingly 'irrational' desires that may come to underpin young people's emerging identities. This would suggest that as social relations become increasingly stretched over time and space, and places are drawn incommensurably closer together, locality and identity will continue to be of relevance in these changing times. With this in mind, we still appear some way off from witnessing the last of the *Real Geordies*.

21. According to Jackson,

> Cultural geographers should be concerned not just with tracing the effects of successive rounds of capital investment and disinvestment in particular regions and localities, accounting for their differences in terms of their distinctive histories and geographies. They should also begin to explore the diverse ways in which those processes are culturally encoded: how working-class history is appropriated and symbolically transformed in the course of urban development for example. [...] But so far these ideas have found few adherents in human geography. (1995 [1989]:185)

–5–

Charver Kids:
Community, Class and the Culture of Crime

Introduction

In recent times it has become fashionable to write about globalization, cultural hybridity and 'new ethnicities' in urban settings (Hall, 1993; Back, 1996; Mac an Ghaill, 1999; Bennett, 2000). This work has done much to extend current debates on race and ethnicity, whilst illustrating that popular youth culture is now a thoroughly chequered tapestry, liberally peppered with sustained legacies of black–white interaction. But what happens when global transformations impact unevenly upon nations, regions and localities, when people and places get 'left behind' and the landscape of youth becomes ever more divided? It is suggested that in between these fissures racism, crime and harassment can become ever more prominent as a 'way of life'. This chapter seeks, then, to shed light upon the 'dark side' of globalization and the youth cultures that have emerged in the penumbra of long-term unemployment, economic polarization, immigration and urban squalor.

The chapter begins with a brief overview of historical representations of the urban poor in late-Victorian and Edwardian Britain. The historiography suggests that the landscapes and bodies of the urban impoverished were frequently portrayed as dark and dangerous zones and that, moreover, these images continue to have a lasting appeal in 'new times'. Racial geographies of the inner city are displaced onto Nailton, the study site where research with a *Charver Kid* subculture was undertaken. The Nailton district is a multi-ethnic place where unemployment and the fear of crime perforate community relations. The research examines the multiple definitions and representations of *Charvers* through a case-study analysis of Tyneside's infamous 'Rat Boy'. It seeks to explore the role of race, place and global change in the lives of Nailton *Charver Kids*. The ethnography reveals how a number of lower working-class youth have become socially and spatially excluded by recent economic transformations. In response they have developed a highly stylized subculture of their own which is both feared and respected. By exploring the different life worlds of *Charver* respondents, the ethnography illuminates their illicit practices and participation in an 'informal' market economy. It is suggested that in the absence of work, street-crime is transformed into an occupational activity, a form of 'grafting' that is as oppressive as it is survivalist. Moreover, it is argued that the white status of *Charvers* is 'tainted' through their multi-ethnic residence, their poverty and their roots in a 'black' market economy. Race and class are seen as competing, conflicting and sometimes overlapping discourses in their lives.

The Racialization of the Urban Poor

Victorian and Edwardian historiography is littered with depictions of urban areas as 'dark', 'dirty' and 'dangerous' zones. Indeed, the sojourn to the English urban interior was directly compared with journeys into Central Africa, a theme Peter Keating (1976) exemplifies in his classic compilation, *Into Unknown England 1866–1913*. In *The Country and the City* Raymond Williams also reveals how 'Conditions in the East End were being described as "unknown" and "unexplored" . . . in the middle of the century, and by the 1880s and 1890s "Darkest London" was a conventional epithet' (1985 [1973]: 221). Elsewhere the cultural geographer Peter Jackson (1995 [1989]) remarks upon the popular circulation of texts such as William Booth's *In Darkest England* (1890) and Reverend Osborne Jay's similarly named *Life in Darkest London* (1891). We may also reflect on titles such as John Hollingshead's *Ragged London in 1861*, James Greenwood's *The Wilds of London* (1874) and George Gissing's *The Nether World* (1889), or his later edition, *New Grub Street* (1891), as further examples of the genre of 'slum literature'. Here, the bourgeois imperial gaze was turned towards and then writ large upon English urban centres and the bodies of the impoverished peoples who resided there.

In an introduction to John Hollingshead's *Ragged London in 1861*, Anthony Wohl makes a telling, if underdeveloped, observation about the depiction of slum dwellers in the urban study. The off-hand remark fleetingly alludes to the social construction of whiteness as a concept that was beyond the grasp of the industrial urban poor. It is alleged that 'the inhabitants of the slums are "swarthy", or "sallow", or have "yellow faces", or are blackened with soot, or possess "dark sinister faces" – any colour, it would seem, but white' (Wohl, 1986 [1861]:xix). A powerful observation indeed, but why were the faces and bodies of socially inferior classes never represented as white? It is suggested in this chapter that the urban poor, or casual 'residuum', have historically been positioned in a precarious and contingent relationship to whiteness. Thus, Jonathan Raban recalls: 'If the image of the native in the Africa of Empire was of a grinning black simpleton whose worst faults were his laziness and stupidity – or of a crazed Hottentot brandishing a wooden spear – the street people of London presented a face that was more inscrutably foreign, more complex, ultimately more menacing . . . '. (1975 [1974]: 95).

These complex, oscillating markers of race and class were projected onto the bodies of the urban poor in particular but also upon the lower echelons of the working population. Thus, Phil Cohen cites Lord Milner's remark during the Somme on seeing English soldiers bathing that revealed he 'never knew the working classes had such white skins' (1993 [1988]: 32). Furthermore, Victorian observers such as George R. Sims believed the working-classes were the embodiment of grime and that this was a symbol of their moral depravity. Sims complained, 'Dirtiness is ingrained in them, and if they had decent habitations provided for them tomorrow, they would no more live in them than a gipsy could settle down under any but a canvas roof' (cited in Keatings, 1976:79). Victorian commentators such as Samuel Smith were even more direct in their tirades against race and class. He compared the poor with the sewage floating in the Thames Estuary and wrote of the need to 'deoderize, so to speak, this foul humanity' (cited in Stedman Jones, 1984 [1971]:310). So, it is not social conditions that are to blame for grime, but poor people themselves. During this period lower-class peoples were most brutally espoused as the nation's Great Unwashed – an image which conjured up a teeming mass of blackened, sweating, toiling bodies. By contrast, lower middle-class workers from clerks to office personnel could always take solace that in the final analysis they were 'white-collar', 'clean-handed' workers who never dirtied themselves with industrial labour.

Significantly, the bodies of the lower labouring classes and the urban poor were seen to be anatomically different from those of the bourgeoisie. Moreover, this difference was not accorded to social factors such as living conditions, working environments or nutritional intake; it was seen to be *natural* to the 'species' of the lower orders. The imperial shadow this cast on sections of the urban poor was such that, like their colonized counterparts, the British lower classes were seen to require the civilizing light of bourgeois morality. This is evident in the urban literature described, and the organized forms of social control that were administered by way of religion, education and temperance movements. Iain Chambers explains how Victorians hoped to one day 'tame' the cities as 'Moral rearmament, in the form of religion, the temperance movement, schooling and education, was despatched to the "Hottentots" in the slums of "darkest England"' (1988 [1986]:23–4). Indeed, the working-class body was thought to be ingrained with dirt, diseased, wizened and decrepit. The social historian Harris goes on to remark upon an 1884 meeting of the Social Science Association, in which a spokesperson from the London Working Men's Association protested against the fashion for 'talking of the working class as though they were some new-found race or extinct animal' (1994 [1993]:236). Moreover, it was felt that the frail comportment of the urban impoverished reflected their weak moral character. Everything about their demeanour suggested that these denizens could never be proper, 'upstanding' members of society in the unforgiving eyes of the bourgeoisie.

More recently, discursive associations with 'deviancy' and 'juvenile delin-quency' have hastened the racial demarcation of particular youth subcultures as a 'race apart'. In an oral history analysis of working-class youth, Stephen Humphries (1981:175) remarks on the propensity for pre-war street gang members to be delegated labels such as 'savage hooligan', 'slum monkey' and 'street blackguard'. Such epithets served to demarcate between a 'rough' and 'respectable' working class while leaving unchecked the strong current of circulating racial undertones. Subsequently, Paul Gilroy refers to articles in *The Times* as late as 1958 in which 'Teddy boys and their urban community were described as a "race" in their own right' (1995 [1987]:81). Stanley Cohen echoes this view in his press analysis of Newcastle gangs, claiming, 'The teenager is given the same characteristics as the Negro' (1973 [1972]: 43), an issue intricately theorized by Dick Hebdige (1987 [1979]). We may also consider the remarks made by John Lydon of The Sex Pistols that 'Punks and Niggers are almost the same thing' (Young, 1977), a recognition of discrimination that may have stemmed from his own Anglo-Irish roots as documented in his autobiography, *Rotten: No Irish – No Blacks – No Dogs* (1994). For some youth writers this sense of estrangement may resonate with different forms of 'Othering'. '[T]here's something queer about all teen cults', declares Healy (1996:27); 'just like dirty homosexuals, they're dangerous, delinquent and demonized by the press.' Contemporary descriptions by politicians and the tabloid press of football fans, subcultures and working-class youth as 'yobs' and 'animals' is, then, a suitable *addendum* to a vocabulary that has frequently defined young people as 'beyond the pale'.

Ghost Town: Nailton in Northeast England

The number one track 'Ghost Town' by The Specials, written at the time of Thatcherism, mass youth unemployment and inner-city unrest, may seem an unusual point from which to embark upon an analysis of the contemporary urban environment. However, as we shall find, an emphasis on the magic of global change cannot disguise the more stubborn stains that continue to leave their mark in the restructuring of nation states. In particular, the geography of poverty, crime and unemployment are testimony to regional and sub-regional disparities. Thus, in 1991 the worst areas of nationally recorded crime show Northumbria (4,360) in the North East top the table in England and Wales, followed by Cleveland (4,271) and then Greater Manchester (4,001).[22] Within the county of Northumbria, the Nailton quarter of Tyneside had the highest local level of crime, yet the area also has the largest unemployment rate in the city. Between 1986 and 1991 the unemployment

---

22. Figures relate to offences per 100,000 population.

level of young men alone had quadrupled. It was this area that was most closely associated with *Charver Kids*. These place-bound representations of the subculture were consolidated by the 1991 uprisings that began in the outlying Meadowell estate and then encroached upon the urban quarter (see Campbell, 1993; Collier 1998 for discussion).

The Nailton district of Tyneside comprises a number of geographical wards with a total population estimated at 68,000. This urban quarter is made up of a band of old inner-city locales that were formerly designed to service armament workers at William Armstrong's plants. By the end of the nineteenth century over 25,000 people were employed in Nailton in the making of guns, armaments and battle-ships. Prior to this, the area had made hydraulic cranes before concentrating on shell-filling and fuse-making factories, employing men and women alike. Armstrong Whitworth was by some distance the largest employer in Tyneside, and by the end of the First World War some 78,000 people worked for the company. With its own blast furnaces it could produce iron and high-quality steel. Ships, guns and shells were the most prominent products developed in the quarter. However, factories around Nailton would later manufacture aircraft, tanks, loco-motives, engines, pneumatic tools, motorcars and vans.

Around the core armament industry sprung up lighter industries, including workshops and smaller stores selling nuts, screws, springs, barrels, bolts and engineering machinery. In its heyday Nailton contained a lead works and was also involved in the leather industry and the production of porcelain for bathroom suites. In the more recent post-war years Nailton has suffered economically for its over-reliance upon manufacturing industries. This was also to have a major impact upon jobs and the various secondary services throughout the district. Thus, by the end of the 1980s the production of armaments had diminished in Nailton to the extent that only around 700 people were engaged in this line of work, having gained contracts from the Ministry of Defence and the Nigerian Army (Robinson, 1988). Subsequently the area has continued to undergo a prolonged period of decline from better days when it once serviced many of the heavy industries in the region. Today, many of the white and multi-ethnic neighbourhoods in Nailton have the highest rates of unemployment and are amongst the poorest parts in Tyneside. This is testament not only to a more general North–South divide but also to the sharp socio-economic split that exists between different wards throughout the conurbation. In this respect Nailton is a 'ghost town' forever haunted by its industrial past.

Nailton contains a number of 1960s high-rise flats that were once the vision of the local councillor T. Dan Smith, who grandiosely believed these 'cities in the sky' would one day transform the area into the 'Brasilia of the North'. Time has not been kind to the exigencies of this vision. Beyond the run-down flats are to be found areas with long stretches of Victorian back-to-back terrace housing that is either council property, privately owned or rented, or, in many cases, boarded up. In what remains an ostensibly white region, multi-ethnic Nailton conjures up similar images to those inspired by the nineteenth-century urban explorers of East End London. The district is widely recognized as one of Britain's 'dangerous places' (Campbell, 1993), and many central parts of Nailton contain areas that are dilapidated with houses that have been burned and left as hollow shells of half-remembered lives. Thus, on one memorable journey through these districts a local Northeast taxi-driver compared Nailton to a 'shanty town', in a remark that at once collapsed poverty with multi-ethnic residential living. Although a number of neighbourhoods and estates in Nailton were subject to a racialized mythology, the material geographies of the district described were often overlooked.

During the research period I lived for three years on the Colmore estate in Nailton, which was a couple of miles away from Snowhill Comprehensive. In Colmore and other Nailton neighbourhoods the fear of crime was acute, with a number of insurance companies refusing to provide cover for the seemingly 'untouchable' civic dwellers. Burglary and street-crime, including threats, physical violence, drugs, car crime and robberies, was of particular concern. The fear of crime in these districts was well established in the minds of many young people.

[17 years]

Suzanne: I wouldn't walk through Colmore, there's no way I'd walk through Colmore.

John: Oh I've walked through Colmore.

Chris: [. . .] Y'know Mark Sager who lives by ours? He went through Colmore and someone held a nail to his throat. Took his shoes off him and his coat.

Suzanne: His father was Asian wasn't he, his mother's white?

Chris: He was adopted by her.

Suzanne: He's got three sisters that are white and he's Asian. He was walking through Colmore and he got pulled.

Chris: I dunno if it was anything to actually do with his colour, but you still wanna avoid those areas.

In many respects, Nailton was subject to a type of modern-day 'Orientalism' (Said, 1995 [1978]). For Edward Said, 'Orientalism' represents a hegemonic Western discourse that was applied to the East and its peoples during imperial times. However, this imagined geography was assembled from the tissues and fragments of Western imperial fantasy and a cultural inventory that would consistently produce the 'Orient' as 'Other'. It was precisely through these imaginative discursive tropes that the West – what Said terms the 'Occident' – was able to know itself. Like the 'Orient', Nailton can be viewed as a 'silent Other', defined by those living outside the district, who project their hatred of blackness and poverty onto the interior locality, and so constitute their own neighbourhoods as superior white hinterlands. Where once the Oriental and 'exotic' were 'out there', at a geographical remove, in global times we now find that the bodies of the once colonized are now pressed up under the very noses of the one-time colonizers. As a consequence of these social and economic changes, Nailton has been subject to processes of 'white flight' and suburban escapism. It is seen no longer as a land for workers but as a foreign zone complete with rampaging Street Arabs, who now form the outer skin of this projection.

Despite urban regeneration throughout many parts of the North East, Nailton has been left behind and continues to be associated with race, crime, poverty and irredeemable 'sink estates'.[23] As an 'imagined community' (Anderson, 1984 [1983]), it remains peripheral, out of reach, yet at once intriguingly unknowable outside the prevailing 'Orientalist' discourses which constitute it as Other. This perception is further compounded in comparisons with the war-torn Middle East as 'Britain's Little Beirut' (Campbell, 1995). By the end of the research period a number of places in the Nailton quarter had been recipient to an influx of refugees, notably from parts of Eastern Europe. In Nailton the number of reported racist incidents increased by 67 per cent (386 incidents) between 1999 and 2000. This trend is forecast to be increasing in the wake of the recent arrival of asylum seekers and the political destruction of the Twin Towers buildings in New York on 11th September, 2001. Discussions with youth and social workers in these areas reported how asylum seekers and Asians were subject to increasing abuse and the spraying of 'Taliban' on their doors, whether they were Islamic or not.

Charver Kids: Tyneside's Not-Quite-White

> Maybe, maybe it's the clothes we wear
> The tasteless bracelets and the dye in our hair,
> Maybe it's our kookiness
> Or maybe, maybe it's our nowhere towns
> Our nothing places and our cellophane sounds,
> Maybe it's our looseness,
> We're trash, you and me,
> We're the litter on the breeze
> We're the lovers on the street
>
> 'Trash', Suede, 1996

23. In certain parts of Nailton it was possible to purchase a two-up-two-down house for under £5,000. Unable to relocate, some residents had even left their properties behind in the belief that they could not be sold.

The period of Western late-modernity has given rise to a new social class stereo-type that depicts lower working-class groups as people with large families, satellite TV and pebble-dash terraced housing. Onslow, in the sitcom *Keeping Up Appearances*, 'The Kappa Slappers' in the comic *Viz* and comedian Harry Enfield's portrayal of Wayne and Waynetta Slob are all archetypes of this now identifiable lower-class stratum. *Charver Kids* were regarded as the offspring of these symbolic lower orders and the fulfilment of generational unemployment. The *Charver Kids* were a subculture identifiable to local youth throughout Tyneside. My first encounter with *Charvers* occurred in Emblevale School and the Nailton neigh-bourhood. *Charvers* were boys and girls who resided primarily in the Nailton district, were reputed to be burglars or 'joy-riders' and had developed a particular style of dress and body language. Renowned truants from school, the group were notoriously difficult to track down and interview over long periods as they had amongst the poorest school attendance records. However, my knowledge about *Charvers*, and the discourses that constituted them, also derived from local Tyne-side folklore and shared neighbourhood interactions. In certain respects *Charver Kids* are the living embodiment of urban mythology. Although the etymology of *Charver* is especially particular to the Nailton district of Tyneside, towards the end of the fieldwork period the term became more extensively applied to any young person of unemployed or lower-class background who exhibited a particular subcultural style.

The term '*Charver*' has various inflections, though its origins remain uncertain. One reading emphasizes that the term has Romany connections associated with travellers. Another suggests the word is derived from a hybrid combination of the allegedly archetypal lower-class names Sharon and Trevor (i.e. Shar/vor). In one case white youth elaborated on the term *Charver* to shout 'Charwallah' (a term that refers to Indian tea-servants) at another white student, thus providing the phrase with the additional derogatory value of a lower race and class status. Others still have suggested that regional variations of this phrase exist in other areas beyond the North East (e.g. Chavvy in the South of England) and can be compared with Liverpool 'Scallies' or Hull's 'Fila youth'. Regardless of the precise definition, *Charver* is defined across a shared discourse of lower working-class origins. *Charvers* were portrayed as a sullied urban 'underclass', and, for a variety of reasons, have become subject to a racialized discourse that constructs them as urban primitives. The cultural practices of the *Charvers* are seen as an alternative response to global change and de-industrialization. It is argued that in the absence of labour, *Charver Kids* have developed different strategies within the informal economy to sustain their livelihoods.

The discourses of race and class that have been encrypted onto the bodies of young people have been especially marked in the North East of England. In the wake of the 1991 uprisings in Tyneside, children, the very individuals who were said to need protection from crime, were assigned a new role as some of its worst perpetrators (Collier, 1998). More disconcertingly, this 'moral panic' centred not just on teenage youth, the typical targets of social outrage, but on children below the age of ten years.[24] In the North East, *Charver Kids* became synonymous with a 'spate' of uncontrollable neighbourhood 'crime sprees' that were especially related to motor vehicles, including joy-riding, TWOCing (Taking Without Owner's Consent) and ram-raiding – activities discussed at length in Beatrix Campbell's (1993) explosive account, *Goliath*. Having begun his criminal debut in spectacular fashion, crashing a Vauxhall into a neighbour's fence, Hartlepool's Gareth Brogden was soon to be widely commemorated in the national press as Britain's most notorious delinquent, 'Balaclava Boy'. Brogden received this inglorious tag, aged 11 years, following a BBC documentary in which he was shown donning a ski-mask and sticking up two fingers to the police.[25]

The image of the lawless *Charver Kid* was vividly in evidence in television and press-reportage of 'Rat Boy', 'a monster figure straight out of the steamy New York tenement blocks' (*The Sunday Times*, 28/2/93). In a detailed case study of the Rat Boy phenomenon, Richard Collier (1998) has considered the discursive construction of youthful, lower working-class masculinities through these 'hate figures'. He explains, 'The Rat Boy was so named because of the habit he had developed of hiding in a maze of ventilation shafts, tunnels and roof spaces in the Byker Wall Estate in the city of Newcastle upon Tyne, England, while trying to evade capture by the police' (p. 92). As Collier's criminological study reveals, Rat Boy was constructed as 'something very "UnBritish", once alien but now increasingly familiar' (p. 92). In this respect Rat Boy (aka Anthony Kennedy) was constituted as an anti-hero, a super-villain whose comic-strip pseudonym suggested his irredeemable evil. The discourse of the anti-hero as a scourge or plague on the community was further extended in the North East through press iconography of Spider Boy, Homing Pigeon Boy and the previously mentioned Balaclava Boy.

However, the depiction of poverty-stricken peoples through animalistic discourses associated with vermin is not in itself new. Consider C.F.G. Masterman's reflections on the growth of cities and the increased visibility of the urban poor.

24. Nation-wide fears concerning childhood symbolically crystallized around the murder of two-year-old James Bulger by two ten-year-old boys, Robert Thompson and Jon Venables, in Liverpool, 1993. As Blake Morrison (1997) has argued, this event, more than any other, came to signal the 'death' of childhood.

25. By the age of 18 years, Brogden would die of a heroin overdose. A press obituary revealed how the then Shadow Home Secretary Tony Blair equated the actions of Balaclava Boy with lawless children: 'This is behaviour that scars the very fabric of our society', he previously declared (*The Guardian*, 15/05/2000).

Our streets have suddenly become congested with a weird and uncanny people [. . .]
They have poured in as dense black masses from the eastern railways; they have
streamed across the bridges from the marshes and desolate place beyond the river; they
have been hurried up in incredible number through tubes sunk in the bowels of the earth,
emerging like rats from a drain, blinking in the sunshine [. . .] Whence did they all
come, these creatures with strange antics and manners, these denizens of another
universe of being? (cited in Keating, 1976:241–2).

The idea that poverty-stricken people 'poured' and 'streamed' into English cities
was later evoked in the 1980s with subsequent New Right discourses which
appealed to an imaginary sense of British decency to acknowledge that 'immigrants' were now 'swamping' the nation. As such, constructs of race and class may
be articulated through one another. Thus, in the above extract the urban poor are
seen as 'dense black masses' and vividly compared with rats, in what Masterman
believed to be the birth of a mutant and subhuman new race. The surreptitious
representation of the urban poor as alien, teeming hordes carrying all manner of
disease was secured in the hated symbol of the rat. Indeed, the rat can be said to
signify the defiled, 'polluted' Other which was ritually segregated from the
'purified' spaces of the bourgeoisie and marked as taboo (Douglas, 1992 [1966]).
More lately, David Sibley has recorded how 'The potency of the rat as an abject
symbol is heightened through its role as a carrier of disease, its occasional tendency
to violate boundaries by entering people's homes, and its prolific breeding' (1995:
28). It was precisely these aspects – disease, invasion and breeding – once reserved
for minority ethnic communities that were now virulently being applied to *Charver*
families in the North East. In this sense Rat Boy was the epitome of the lawless
Charver Kid, a monstrous alien 'Other' (half-rat, half-boy) who could be said to
embody the longstanding horror associated with the lower orders of over-breeding,
vermin and the spread of plague.[26]

A recurring theme in the ethnographic data concerning Nailton *Charvers* was
the way in which discourses of race and class could overlap with one another, as
Chambers has shown in descriptions of Victorian urban dwellers as 'slum monkeys' (1988 [1986]:26). The representation of poor urban areas is turned into a
fantasy space filled with marauding Rat Boys, *Charvers*, Ragamuffin Children,
Apes, Charwallahs, Street Arabs, Rogues and other semi-evolved mutations. The
animalistic portrayal of an urban residuum as 'slum monkeys', or its modern-day
equivalent, 'Rat Boys', says much about the repressed fears of contemporary

---

26. In the English imagination rats have long been associated with urban squalor (despite their
mainly rural habitation) and foreign disease (e.g. the Bubonic Plague, appropriately termed the Black
Death).

white, bourgeois, suburban culture. Collier explains how these corporeal fears are displaced onto working-class landscapes and bodies:

> The working-class city itself has, of course, like the working-class body, long been seen as a site of fear, desire, disgust and fascination from the perspective of the middle-class gaze. In a sense, the Rat Boy embodied some familiar fantasies around the corporeality of working-class urban poor. In contrast to 'cleaned up', fed and educated bourgeois children, proletariat youth appear as 'savage', their undisciplined bodies to be censured, disciplined and controlled, their very presence a 'plague' on the respectable streets. (1998:93)

The criminal, subhuman representations used to depict *Charver Kids* form a broader taxonomy deployed by young people, adults and press alike. The reference to 'savagery', 'apes' and 'slum monkeys' also hints at the underlying and connected historical racialization of these portrayals. Among young respondents the term '*Charver*' is also used to depict something that is rubbish or no good (e.g. 'It's complete Chava, mon!'). Of course, another word for rubbish is the Americanism 'trash', further compounding the association of *Charver* as 'white trash'. As rats reside amidst trash and rubbish dumps, the discursive connections between *Charvers*, Rat Boys, poverty and a tainted whiteness are drawn together.

The Alternative Youthscapes of Charverville

During my time spent observing, speaking to and living alongside *Charvers* it became increasingly evident that they occupied a different youthscape to that of other Tyneside young people. By this I mean that *Charvers* were geographically, materially and culturally estranged from many of the experiences and opportunities that were part and parcel of other young lives. As noted above, *Charver Kids* had amongst the poorest school attendance rates and on several occasions I spotted some of them carrying out casual labour or errands for their parents during school hours. For example, one so-called '*Charver* family' had briefly opened a local fruit and vegetables stall on the Colmore shopping parade and, unable to pay for workers, were forced to employ the children to help run the kiosk. On another occasion I witnessed two *Charver* brothers loading a shopping trolley with materials from the construction site of a multinational corporation. When I questioned their night-time activities in a school interview the following day it turned out that their father had actually asked them to collect up the timber for him to sell at a knock-down rate. In this way the 'scam' or illegal activity was a means of contributing to the household economy. In the absence of work the 'scam' represented a means of recuperating the material and symbolic value of labour through theft, risk and the culture of the street. In this respect the street 'scam' was a type of *cultural apprenticeship* through which children and especially young males developed the knowledge and skills required for a career in crime. Nailton youth explained to me how the 'scam' encompassed a range of activities from 'dodging' Metro fairs, 'blaggin'' (telling fibs to achieve a particular result) to theft and shoplifting. Within Nailton these actions were not unusual and demonstrated a survivalist response to the processes of globalization that had left many of these communities more localized and isolated than ever before (MacDonald, 1999).

Many residents on the estate lived by way of a 'hand-to-mouth' existence. Failure to pay gas and electricity bills had meant that many houses had switched to meter cards after becoming disconnected. These were bought from the post office, usually one at a time, in a prudent effort to control the bare necessities. Although a large supermarket existed nearby, this was seldom visited or used for the weekly shop. Instead, the local corner shop, which sold daily conveniences at a more expensive rate, was more readily used, for a number of reasons. Its proximity made it attractive, especially when many purchases such as a fizzy drink or cigarettes were required right away. Knowledge of the shopkeeper meant that in emergencies certain goods could be consumed but paid for later in the week when the Giro cheque was cashed. I observed many residents buying a single item (e.g. a can of strong lager) whilst the supermarket would only sell such items in four-packs. As money was scarce, the corner shop, though pricier, enabled residents to purchase whatever food items were required for their families according to their budget *at the time*, and so did not involve an element of planning and financial calculation. Women in particular would go without food for long periods especially when the 'lowy' (allowance) ran out; unsurprisingly, health and illness were major issues in the area.[27] However, as a consequence of social deprivation, *Charver Kids* were the qualified recipients of 'free dinners' from the school, though this inadvertently set them apart from other more affluent working-class youth.

In the course of the study a number of *Charver Kids* did admit to illicit activities, including petty theft, under-age drinking, the dealing and using of soft drugs, 'fencing' goods and TWOCing. For some young people these practices were seen as part of the 'culture of the estate', a social extension of their daily youthscapes. However, for others, these casual activities were embedded in deeper familial networks of crime and intimidation, with older males as 'ringleaders'. The power of the apprenticeship was evident when ringleaders would encourage even very small children to carry out illegal crimes, safe in the knowledge that they were

---

27. Along with the town of Gateshead, the Nailton ward had the highest premature rates of mortality and the highest incidence of permanent sickness. For a discussion of Tyneside's poverty and health differentials see Holohan, *et al.* (1988).

too young to be punished. In response to a long-term unemployment that had spanned a generation, some residents on the Colmore estate in Nailton had established a thriving informal economy. This included the buying and selling of cheap electrical goods, furniture and branded fashion items. It was an open secret that these commodities were either 'knock-off' (stolen), seconds or 'snides' (fake). The exchange of these commodities for cash took place in a local pub until its closure and demolition after a drug-raid. Subsequently much of the illegal business on the Colmore estate is now done door-to-door, in what is an older re-enactment of working-class traditions. The other serious crime that happened during my time on the estate was break-in and entry into the post office, which had occurred three times during my time in the area. This had resulted in the stealing of money, meter cards, licences and other potentially lucrative items that could then be re-sold. At the time of the research house burglaries were not especially high due to the closed nature of the community and the fact that most people knew one another. However, intimidation and ritual harassment were still reserved for 'grasses' (alleged police informants) and could also occur as a consequence of family or neighbourhood disputes. After the research period the estate also received a number of refugees and some of the more vulnerable have been subjected to house break-ins and racial terror. However, in an attempt tackle these persistent concerns the council is currently trying to deploy strategies that move perpetrators out rather than victims.

In his Los Angeles study *City of Quartz*, Mike Davis (1991) has written about what he terms the political economy of drugs. In the Colmore estate narcotics are also the key commodity of exchange, though in this case it is young white males who are the primary participants. However, it was often older men in their early thirties, some of whom were the fathers of *Charver Kids* I researched, who ran the drugs racket on the estate (see Winlow, 2001). The dealing took place in-house within the neighbourhood, with the buyers and sellers almost exclusively local. Heroin ('smack' or 'skag') was the most popular, addictive drug of 'choice' used by the older parental generation. However, amongst *Charver Kids* different combinations of cannabis, hemp and marijuana formed the preferred drug of choice and were referred to as 'pot', 'dope', 'grass', 'spliffs' or, most popularly, 'tack'. Other drugs, including 'whizz' (amphetamines) and 'E' (ecstasy), were sometimes taken, though they were more likely to be reserved for specific illegal music events that were staged in local squats and disused buildings throughout the conurbation. Attending some of these events enabled me to see how *Charver Kids* felt excluded from the night-time economy which involved smart dress codes and the additional expense of entrance fees, drinks, and so forth. Indeed, the after-hours drinking club WHQ, which promotes an explicit anti-racist attitude, advertises the venue as 'Friendly, multi-racial, and totally *Charver*-free'. The illegal Rave scene was then cheaper and more accessible in that it did not contain these restrictions. *Charver* youthscapes were spatially and temporally different to those of the *Real Geordies* and other young people. However, it should be noted that drugs were far from ubiquitous in either of the Tyneside schools I visited and it was only a minority of *Charver Kids* who resembled anything like regular drug-users. Indeed, the more protracted forms of drug use appeared in the parental generation and it was alcohol that was still the most popular drug of choice amongst *Charvers*. This would be bought from the local off-licence and drank either openly in the street or at home as a relatively cheap form of consumption.

More recently, the image of Nailton as a 'no-go' area of uncontrollable crime has subsided in the face of an organic community politics that is testament to the strength of the people in these neighbourhoods. Campbell (1993) has documented the pivotal role played especially by women in community-building exercises within impoverished estates, concentrating her account of urban spatial dynamics firmly within the field of gender relations. While there can be no denying the gendered formation of much criminal activity in urban spaces, young people's accounts seemed to suggest that certain girls were also involved in an audacious, intricate waltz with the law. Far from being shocking, these events broke up the humdrum boredom of 'doing nothing' (Corrigan, 1981 [1979]) and were even regarded as 'dead funny'.

> Nicola: There's this girl by wor's, she's 13 years and she drives her Dad's car. And she was driving roon the corner and she couldna' see o'er the steering wheel and she went smack bang into a bizzy [police] car. It wa' dead funny!
>
> *Anoop: You were watching this?*
>
> Nicola: Yeah. We wa gannin' ta go in wi' her, but we wa' on the kerb just watching her. She got done for stealing the car.

As the extract shows, crashing into a police car is a dramatic act of rule transgression, potent in symbolic value (Kehily and Nayak, 1997). *Charver* girls, then, did not necessarily nurse community relations. Furthermore, shortly after interviews were conducted, Nicola (12 years), a self-identified *Charver*, went missing from home for over week without contact. She had disappeared on another occasion but had turned up after a couple of days. Eventually she was found with a young man in his twenties in Blyth, an outer-city estate with a high level of social deprivation and drug taking. Teachers identified *Charver* girls such as Nicola as the ones most likely to become pregnant, and *Charver* boys as invariably the ones most likely to get sent to prison. Noticeably, Nicola's Nailton experiences appeared in marked contrast with other young people who lived in suburban quarters. Here, she performs her *Charver* identity in front of her school friends and myself:

|11–12 years|

Nicola: If you don't smoke and drink and other things you can't be in a gang.

James: Do you smoke?

Nicola: I smoke and drink.[28] If you wanna be in the gang you've gotta smoke, drink, etc. If I say, 'Mam go and get us a drink' she goes and gets it.

Michelle: My Mam wouldn't dare.

In this extract Nicola discursively places herself as a *Charver*. Her experience, like that of other *Charver Kids*, is located outside the youthscapes of most working- and middle-class childhoods. Rather like the eight-year-old watercress street-vendor Henry Mayhew famously encountered in the East End of London in 1851, who 'had entirely lost all childish ways, and was, indeed, in thoughts and manner, a woman' (1950:93), *Charver Kids* blurred the boundaries between childhood and adult status. They told tales of staying out late until the early hours of the morning and appeared to have first-hand experience of drug-use and alcohol consumption from an early age. At the same time, their experiences included taking on some 'adult' responsibilities. *Charver* girls were particularly called upon to take care of 'bairnes' and 'little'uns', and were sometimes responsible for organizing domestic chores, conducting shopping errands and occasionally helping out with the cooking. Teenage pregnancy also offered an early transition into motherhood and heterosexual adult status. As Skeggs reveals 'Responsibility provides respectability' (1997:61). However, many of these activities were viewed as 'beyond the pale' of accepted behaviour by the majority of students, and so compounded *Charver* status as inhuman, far from innocent, 'not-quite-white'. These experiences demonstrate the double-edged nature of the 'freedoms' and 'liberties' thought to be available to *Charver Kids*.

Subcultural Style and Cultural Representations

In the haughty condemnation of 'single mothers', 'absent fathers' and bricked-up Capris in estates, an accompanying accessory for moral rebuke has been the shell-suit, the favoured apparel of *Charver Kids*. Brightly coloured tracksuits, including brands such as Kappa or Adidas, were worn with Nike trainers and various sports accessories such as Morgan sweatshirts. However, these items may constitute more than an index of a lower-class status. In her study of inner-city black British masculinities Sally Westwood (1990) has suggested the dress style is no random costume, but is indicative of the micro-politics of the street. As such, the dress conveys sporting prowess, and doubles as the ideal clothing for a sharp get-away

28. The behaviour records showed that Nicola had been caught with cigarettes and a lighter in school. She also had a wider knowledge of drugs and drink than her peers.

from the police and other urban aggressors. Westwood recalls how 'Tracksuits and trainers were not just the whims of fashion, they express something about the nature of street life and the importance of physical fitness' (1990:65). Campbell similarly reflects how 'The poor have claimed for themselves the gear associated with striding, racing, jumping, climbing. [. . .] It is also about being hard, being survivalists in a brutalized, gendered, conservative culture . . . ' (1993:273). The dress styles of the streetwise *Charvers* should be read within this stylistic framework.

That *Charvers* sported clothes that were not dissimilar to many metropolitan black youth only served to further devalue their white status. The chunky trainers, garish tracksuits and peroxide hair set *Charver Kids* apart and provided a stark contrast with the understated fashions of the *Real Geordies*. For Connell (1995: 110), there is something 'frenzied and showy' about this particular style that can be equated with a 'protest masculinity'. Even so, the flash style was open to ridicule from other young people.

Michelle: They [*Charvers*] wear like Kappa.
James: I hate them.
Michelle: Adidas pants and Fila.
Sara: And big chunky trainers!

Charvers were also reputed to favour fake bronze tans achieved through visits to ultra-violet sun-beds and were said to wear chunky jewellery, including gold chains, heavy rings, ear-rings (worn by both sexes) and the occasional name-engraved bracelet. Multiple body-piercing was increasingly common. However, it was the *Charver* fringe that was especially distinctive.

Anoop: Are the Charvers lads or girls?
Sam: Both. They all wear Kappa.
Nicola: The boys do '*Charver*' their fringe, actually.
[. . .]
Sam: Aal the *Charvers* have a skinhead aal the way round, and they shave it with just the fringe left.

The *Charver* fringe hairstyle referred to was a peroxide, bleached-blonde look that could be added to the front end of the hairline or dyed all over. The overall appearance – fake tan, heavy jewellery, bleached hair – was interpreted by other youth as a signifier of 'bad taste' and a wilful display of lower-class credentials. And yet in boldly exhibiting their subcultural style the *Charvers* were also over-turning these negative inferences in what may be considered an act of 'symbolic creativity' (Willis *et al.*, 1990). In short, their stylistic activities were a celebratory statement of their 'underclass' identity and 'hardness'. *Charver Kids* such as Nicola resisted the assertion that the dress style necessarily concealed a lower-class stupidity and cast her and her friends as 'street louts'.

Michelle: They're all clueless, wearing these baggy pants.
Nicola: Don't say 'clueless'.
[...]
Michelle: They hang 'round shops and cars.
Nicola: We don't.

The resistance towards representations of *Charvers* as 'thick' (clueless) and thieving (hanging around shops and cars) reveals a struggle for working-class respectability that is occurring between and within class factions themselves. Here, it is worth reflecting upon Beverley Skeggs's (1997) engaging research on feminism, social class and young women. Although Skeggs focuses upon femininities and openly admits to her 'lack of responsibility for studying the category of race and paying it the same attention as I did class' (p. 36), the study is replete with fascinating observation. Skeggs shows how class values are materially processed through structural, institutional and discursive formations that are partially understood and then practised through a wider repertoire of 'respectability'. She illustrates how 'Respectability is thus an amalgam of signs, economics and practices, assessed from different positions within and outside of respectability' (p. 15). However, the codification of class is complex, contradictory and frequently marked by gender dissimulations. Subsequently, 'Representations . . . are not straightforwardly reproduced but are resisted and transfigured in their daily enactment' (p. 6). Nicola's willingness to embody a *Charver* identity, then, is nevertheless marked by a refusal to be seen as 'clueless', thieving and disrespectable. By portraying *Charver Kids* in this manner, *Real Geordies* and other local youth could purvey the illusion that by contrast they were implicitly respectable. However, such iterations only served to illustrate the role of ambivalence in the lives of many Northeast youth who were also regulated and governed by this 'emotional politics of class' (p. 162). As we shall go on to find, the discourse of respectability is not only underpinned by sexuality, gender and class, but is thoroughly intertwined with race and the formation of whiteness.

Thus, though the *Charver Kids* and the *Real Geordies* are both working-class subcultures, they did not share the same social histories. *Charvers* did not carry the industrial baggage of manual labour borne by the *Real Geordies*. Whereas the latter group had been part of an aspiring working-class tradition that sanctioned home ownership and 'white flight' from the inner city, the *Charvers* remained firmly entrenched in their urban environment, as the contemporary casual 'residuum', for, as E.P. Thompson has explained, 'class happens when some men [*sic*], as a result of common experiences (inherited or shared), feel and articulate the identity of their interests as between themselves, and as against other men [*sic*] whose interests are different from (and usually opposed to) theirs' (1982 [1968]:8–9). It is, then, not simply what *Charver Kids* say and do that is of consequence but equally *what is said and felt about them*; that is, how their actions are reported and discursively constituted through the matrices of race, class and urban youth. In the school context popular youth discourses about *Charvers* frequently centred upon their 'unkempt' appearance, 'tatty' uniform and the suggestion that they were 'dirty'. The depictions of desperate Nailton families with 'snotty-nosed', scream-ing kids elaborated older discourses of the poor as teeming, unclean hordes. Indeed, certain *Charver Kids* were singled out by their peers as carriers of infes-tation and were reported to have nits, fleas and be generally 'scabby'. This meant the most unpopular *Charvers* were identified as 'soap dodgers', and were renowned for being 'spotty' or having bad body odour.

The representations of *Charvers* echo a longstanding racialized discourse of disease that has equated ethnic minority groups with lack of hygiene, bad smells and disease. Thus, in a series of inflammatory articles entitled 'The Dark Millions', *The Times*, a primary contributor to the immigration debate in the mid-1960s, went on to make insidious connections between immigration, tuberculosis and the spread of venereal diseases (see Gilroy, 1995:84). In this reading, the *Charvers* come to make up the foreign bodies that constitute the internal colonial Other. Although poor social conditions and a lack of amenities may contribute to repre-sentations of migrants and *Charvers* as 'filthy', these ascriptions play an important role in young lives and reveal how youth cultures can be relationally defined through against one another. It was through the metaphors of 'dirt' that the *Real Geordies* could romantically construe themselves as true 'salt of the earth' natives in a bold show of their imaginary skilled, labouring credentials. In contrast, *Charver Kids*, on account of urban housing conditions and long-term familial unemployment, were the sullied flip-side, described to me as 'the scum of the earth' or 'a blot on the landscape'. In short, *Charvers* were modern-day urban primitives: their cleanliness and, by proxy, their white respectability had been called into question and they had been found wanting. The geographic location of *Charver Kids* within the multi-ethnic Nailton quarter made them appear closer to these migrant residents in the symbolic imagination and in turn acted as an effect-ive depreciation on their immediate claims to 'whiteness'.

Whereas the *Real Geordies* were predominately an all-male collective, *Charver Kids* could include young men and women who had become attuned to the rebellious street styles of Nailton.

Nicola: Wor street isn't posh cos there's loadsa *Charvers* round wor street.
Anoop: *Who are the Charvers?*
Michelle: Like, they're from Nailton like Nicky, with dyed bleached hur, like you
          [*laughs at Nicola*] and they aal wear Kappa and they've got hur really
          lacquered back and they talk [*affects deep voice*] 'like this mon'.

Nicola, who identified as *Charver* in certain situations, equates a dangerous metropolitan area with the subculture to provide evidence that her street 'isn't posh'. As we saw in a previous illustration, if Nicola was going to enact the subcultural *Charver* identity, she would do so only on her own terms. Even in school, where uniform was essential, Nicola could clearly be detected as a feisty *Charver Kid*, wearing numerous gold rings and adapting her dress and hairstyle. When I asked Michelle to identify feminine *Charver* school styles, she bluntly replied, 'Bleached blonde hair like Nicky. Short skirts like Nicky's. *Charver* fringe, like Nicky's.' Out of school this look was elaborated upon. With their pineapple ponytails, heavy jewellery, trainers and tracksuit-tops, *Charver* girls such as Nicola could negotiate new, urban femininities that made a mockery of the stereotype of the passive wallflower. Many were indeed loud, street-wise and capable of sticking up for themselves. 'I'd go up to anyone', asserted Ema, 'and say, "Giz a quid!"' Thus, Filo, a *Real Geordie*, told me about an altercation on the Tyneside Metro he recently had that stopped just short of outright violence. 'She was propa *Charver* girl. Y'kna, real fuckin' thick arms t'brey ye! [hit you]', he added. However, this apparent outspokenness came at a cost. In conversations with other young men and women, *Charver* girls are frequently derided as 'scrubbers', a phrase that suggests a certain sexual looseness and an implicit sense that they are 'unclean'. Moreover, in another link to the urban poor the sexual terminology replicates labels applied to Victorian washerwomen, dustwomen and female sweatshop workers. If existing local discourses are to be believed, *Charver* girls were hardened smokers, adept shop-lifters and highly likely to become young teenage mothers.

The excessive style of *Charvers* spilled over from fabrics to music. Many *Charver Kids* favoured Rave and Jungle music, sounds that were historically tied to the mutating patterns of cultural syncretism formed in British inner cities. Interestingly, some of the young people who had spoke disparagingly about *Charver* style in one context were willing to admit that they were 'a bit *Charver*' in their tastes towards music and certain elements of fashion. Thus, James admitted liking 'Rave, Coliseum kinda thing' and was willing to take on a *Charver* identity at certain moments. Furthermore, I witnessed some young people living on the Colmore estate in Nailton enact a much stronger sense of *Charver* identity (through fashion, body posture, peer group and even accent) in the neighbourhood than when at school. This indicates the geographical contingency of subcultural identities that could be 'toned down' or 'played up' according to time, place and context. The multi-site observations would support the arguments outlined in Chapter 2 that express a need to see youth formations as complex 'discursive clusters'. It also exposes the limits of writing unreflectively about *Charver* behaviour, actions and identity. The musical disposition of the *Charvers*, like their clothing, can be seen as related to the urban environment. I enquired about these musical preferences.

Sam: Ahh, they jus' like Rave.
Michelle: They just go around like in the car with the music pounding, the kinda stuff
          I like. The kinda stuff me and Nicky like.
James: Like some Americans who carry ghetto-blasters.

Charvers spoke to me about parties and musical events that they had attended, playing several dance tracks for me to listen to. Elements of this music led me to reflect upon my own involvement with Acid House and Techno in the late eighties and early nineties. The connections between music, de-industrialization and the urban environment were brutally evidenced in the repetitive, metallic sounds of Techno chillingly bashed out on silver decks by anonymous DJs in the smoke-filled, strobe-lit space of Northern factory warehouses. Though such cultural events were intrinsically hedonistic, they may have also symbolized an unarti-culated sense of post-industrial alienation. Remarking on a previous point of transition, the social historian Eric Hobsbawm notes how the Industrial Revolution in the 1840s came to 'mark the end of the era when folksong remained the major musical idiom of industrial workers' (1982 [1968]:91). Seen in this light, the musical tastes of *Charvers* may also tell us something about the changing worlds they inhabit. The uplifting Trance and deep Techno music they tended to favour draws closely on the contemporary urban environment of 'white noise', using samples from car alarms, push-button telephones, police sirens, breaking glass, barking dogs, computer video games, etc. It is a 'soundscape' comprised of exhilarating high-speed beats, pounding bass lines and repetitive syncopated loops: a 'homological' synthesis that is ideal for the hi-energy performance of car and driver. At the time this music was mutating into Hardcore or Hardhouse (dis-paraged as 'nosebleed' Techno by certain aficionados and carefully distinguished from 'intelligent' House) and the heavy bass line and 'ruff toastin' of Jungle. These subtle demarcations reveal the sophisticated properties of 'subcultural capital' in young people's worlds (Thornton, 1995).

Indeed, the popularity of Hardcore and Jungle in the North East had seen at least one local radio station provide extensive airtime to playing these tracks, with explicit references to the local environment. Independent record stores in the area also released various CDs aimed at this local market, including a compilation entitled *Charva Beats*. Throughout discussions with *Charver Kids*, Trance, Techno and Jungle music were an important means through which a *Charver* identity could be performed. Interestingly, Jungle is the product of Britain's inner cities and, as the music producer Chris Simon in *Face* magazine explains, it has particular meaning in these social environments: 'Jungle is our street sound. Just as hip hop became the sound of America's streets, jungle will take hold in every British city that's fucked up. That's why no one in the media wanted to touch it. It's a street thing. It's about enjoyment for people who might not have much to go for in life' (cited in Sewell, 1997:158). The emphasis on urban street culture, alienation and blocked opportunities enabled Jungle to become appropriated as a positive mode of identification by *Charver Kids*. I discovered that many Tyneside *Charvers* were embracing Jungle music with as much enthusiasm as the inner-city black British youth communities residing in London, Birmingham, Bristol and Manchester. Many *Charvers* and other impoverished youth were laying claim to the Jungle sound, which is essentially a mix of the heavy 'bass and toastin'' aspects associated with Reggae, set to the speed and technological 'soundscapes' of House and Techno music. The new production sound has spawned a series of hybrid, inter-related offshoots from Jungle, including Drum 'n' Bass, UK Garage and Ragga.

The homology between *Charver* style, music and the urban environment came to be articulated through the matrices of race and class. The term 'Ragga' itself derives from the older phrase 'ragamuffin', a word used to describe scruffy, dirty people in rags, and once again has a social immediacy for the poverty-stricken, not-quite-white identities of *Charver Kids*. As we saw above, British cities have long been constructed through racialized discourses as dark, dangerous jungles. Originally a Sanskrit word, the term 'Jungle' was 'brought home and applied to the "dark continents" of the working-class city. Urban jungles, concrete jungles, even blackboard jungles, where mobs of youth rampaged, and decent citizens feared to tread . . . ' (Cohen, 1993:80). The Jungle reference, then, combines the colonial appropriation of imaginary racial origins with the fear of urban, industrial unrest and the uncivilized bodies and activities of the poor. As an interior territory, Nailton too represents a 'concrete Jungle', a modern-day repository for the horrors Joseph Conrad (1994 [1902]) first encountered in heart-shaped Africa. As successive generations of migrant settlers develop their own lifestyles and infrastructures in Britain's run-down urban quarters, places like Nailton may become modern-day equivalents for a new 'heart of darkness' in global times.[29] Ultimately, lower working-class culture and the 'sound of the city' serve as an umbilical cord uniting *Charver Kids* unmistakably with the metropolis and a hidden history of multi-culturalism.

The association between *Charver* families, crime and 'trouble' was especially enduring. Long-term unemployment meant that *Charver* families were more likely to be depicted as 'lazy scroungers' and 'state spongers', rather than earnest would-be workers (Willott and Griffin, 1996). This discourse was frequently employed by adults and young people alike and was also extended to depict 'Makems' (people from Sunderland). Here, *Charver* families were regarded as the 'undeserving' poor who fretted away state entitlements. For many of the *Real Geordies*, the *Charvers* were a source of both amusement and moral concern. Lowly representations of

29. Certain neighbourhoods in Nailton were also prefixed to read colloquially, 'Darkest X' or 'Darkest Y'.

Charver families enabled the *Real Geordies* to display their 'superior' race–class credentials in a time when labour was a precarious zone for all young people.

Fat Mal:	It's like the Macauley's, a big *Charver* family reet. What reet have they got to expect everyone to help 'em?
Steve:	Macauley's a Netto family.
Sean:	A Nettie family?
All:	[*laughing*] A Nettie family!

The label 'Netto Shopper' had been sprayed on walls around the Colmore estate, implying that these families bought cheap food products from a down-market retailer. In local dialect the term 'nettie' means outdoor toilet and was used above by the *Real Geordies* to mock *Charver* families for their poverty-stricken lifestyles and make further associations with bad smells, faeces and sewerage. As in many British metropolitan districts, single-headed households are common: the 1991 census records over one in four families in Tyneside headed by lone parents. Instead of being seen as the victims of 'social exclusion', residents would remark upon the low age of *Charver* mothers and the size of certain older *Charver* families. The sexualized discourse maintained that *Charvers* 'bred like rabbits'. Some inhabitants went as far to imply that this was at one and the same time an indicator of sexual promiscuity and a calculated strategy to maximize state benefits. The undisciplined bodies of *Charver* families were a notable concern, and single mothers in particular were scapegoats for this moral rebuke (Campbell, 1993). They were frequently portrayed as 'bad mothers', women who 'canna control the bairns' and therefore should not be having children.

Consequently, *Charver Kids* were said to live with parents who held lax attitudes regarding drugs, crime and under-age drinking. Like other youth subcultures, *Charver Kids* were seen to be synonymous with trouble, and were a source of 'moral panic' amongst parents, teachers, children and residents in 'respectable' neighbourhoods. *Charvers* were associated with 'street-crime' and car crime in particular. 'Joy-riding', TWOCing, ram-raiding, stealing, 'ringing' and high-speed chases with the police were branded as '*Charver* crimes'. The displacement of a more general idea of street-crime or car crime into *Charver* crime followed similar discursive routes to those so painstakingly identified by Stuart Hall *et al.* (1979 [1978]) in *Policing the Crisis: Mugging, the State, and Law and Order*. Hall and his colleagues investigated how 'mugging' was imported from the American ghetto and applied as an explanatory term by media and popular discourse to account for British inner-city crime. In particular, 'mugging' was especially reserved for crimes where the victim was white and the perpetrator black. This racialized representation encouraged a 'moral panic' to emerge over the 'mugging' phenomenon and made it appear that certain actions, far from being race-neutral, were now the outcome of 'black crime'. The idea of crime as attributable to particular 'races' continued to be revisited in accounts of 'Steaming' in the late eighties, 'Yardie' violence in the nineties and, most recently, mobile phone thefts.[30] My argument is not to debate the existence of these activities or to imply that black youth are exonerated from these actions. Instead, my focus is the *racialization* of these practices and the point at which particular crimes become 'black crime' (or *Charver* crime), thus registering with the repertoire of youth mythology. Thus *Charver* identity is materially constituted, spatially located, discursively signified and, as we shall now see, physically embodied.

Race, Class and the Embodiment of Subculture

Popular discourses constructed *Charvers* as a retarded race with deep voices, hunched statures and aggressive, unpredictable attitudes. As a symbol of lower-class urban decline, the *Charvers* embodied the fears of a community: effectively they are Britain's equivalent to 'white trash'. Like the infamous Rat Boy, this degeneration was written on *Charver* bodies and felt to be intelligible to those who could read this corporeal schema. Their supposed body statures and immediate association with car theft and crime made *Charvers* the perfect receptacle for psuedo-scientific claims of a lawless, working-class body that had ultimately regressed in the squalid recess of the inner city.

The *Charver Kid* remains a discursive construction composed of an amalgam of fears now attributed to the new English urban underclass. The association between crime, *Charvers* and 'Radgies' (another name for the urban youth) meant they were frequently depicted as criminals with particular bodily traits. For many young people the *Charver* identity is equated with a 'gangsta' subculture geographically embedded in the 'hard' Nailton area and graphically embodied through the image of 'strutting lads' (McDowell, 2002b).

Michelle: They think they're dead hard.
Sam: Ya see them walking roon' the toon and everythin'.
Michelle: With their head down and with an arched back and they think they're dead good.
James: They think they're real gangstas.

30. These crimes were highlighted in the London *Evening Standard* before being further disseminated through the national newspapers. 'Steaming' was reported to be a particular danger in shops and on London tube stations, involving black gangs running through crowds and snatching chains, bags and money from passengers. 'Yardie' violence was a term used to refer to Jamaican drug culture and illegal activities. Mobile phone theft has also most recently been attributed to an alienated black masculine street culture.

The characteristic walks and styles of behaviour (disparaged in early Edwardian accounts of working-class youth enacting a 'monkey walk' or 'monkey run') continue to resonate with contemporary representations of poor youth bodies. Accordingly, *Charver*s were said to affect a loping stride and exaggerated, rough 'Geordie' accents. The *Charver* walk 'head down . . . with an arched back' was a sign of acting 'hard', and provided evidence of their subhuman, animalistic tendencies. The 'ape-like' walk was also parodied in other discussions and came to symbolize the stunted evolution of the 'knuckle-grazing' *Charver* youth. *Charver* males who embodied this identity through crime, violence and subcultural style were seen to be implicated in the learning of a 'Badfellas' masculinity of the type Winlow (2001) has identified in his study of organized crime in Sunderland.

While the postures of *Charver Kids* may have been pronounced, their vocal intonation also marked them out from other youth groups. It is difficult to express this in the written word, as only people familiar with the nuances of the region's distinctive, lilting dialect can interpret the different accents.

Sam: It's jus' like everyone goes round in big groups going, 'Ooooh trennnnndy' in deep voices.
James: 'Yaaaaar mon'.
[. . .]
Nicola: Yeah, they go, [*with emphasis*] 'Howay then ya little *Charver*' [. . .] They come up to you and say, [*sing-song intonation*] 'What-d'ya-think-ya-lookin'-at?'

Charvers were regarded as bodily distinct, with different accents, strange customs and mannerisms. In this way the language ascribed to *Charvers* took on a corporeal schema that elaborated the broader vocabulary of racism. The late-Victorian and Edwardian observers I drew upon earlier would no doubt have represented *Charver Kids* as society's 'Street Arabs'. This racialized concept was once deployed to depict children who attended 'Ragged Schools', institutions offering free education for youngsters from the poorest classes. Consequently, *Charver Kids* who received free school meals and state subsidies came to form part of the nation's modern urban underclass. They represented the darkened underclass, the new urban primitives of contemporary society. Like black youth, this lower working-class group were represented as 'gangstas', 'rogues', 'apes', society's evolutionary 'missing link' in the chain of human order.

A contemporary example of this double articulation of race and class occurred when I asked some of the *Real Geordies* if they would be attending the Hoppings (an annual open-air fair on Newcastle's Town Moor, alleged to be the largest in Europe). While they maintained that the event was a source of excitement ('Aye, they'll be loadsa lasses gannin'!') they also implied it was a place of danger, colonized by large groups of *Charver Kids* looking to harass and steal money ('It's

Charver country'). The *Real Geordies* went on to joke that the Hoppings was full of 'gypos' (Gypsies), a term that was ascribed to fairground workers and *Charvers* alike. This phrase had negative race/class connotations related to poverty and a Romany heritage that further embellished the not-quite-white status of these social groups.[31] Ultimately the *Charver Kids* were framed by a strikingly similar discourse to that attributed by bourgeois nineteenth-century writers of the urban poor. Thus, Nailton and its residents are portrayed in a near-identical manner to those in the East End part of London at the turn of the twentieth century: both were the retarded, not-quite-white of their social class milieu. In the final instance, then, the *Charvers* were 'slum monkeys' in the urban jungle.

The distinction between a 'rough' and 'respectable' working class is not a new phenomenon. Previously a considerable amount of historical evidence has demonstrated that urban residents in the West End of London were thought to be physically and morally superior to their counterparts in the East End of the city. Particular groups could be defined by their social class geography (e.g. Cockneys) or by their subcultural attachment (e.g. Teddy boys, Punks) as a 'race apart'. Similarly, *Charver Kids*, on account of being impoverished urban citizens *and* having formed a subculture of their own, were perceived as 'Other'. That Nailton was synonymous with *Charvers* symptomatically implied that these urban dwellers were racially distinct. As we have already seen, this perception was given credence by the suggestion that *Charver Kids* walked, spoke, dressed and behaved in a manner altogether different to other 'Geordie' youth. Overall, then, it is Britain's impoverished youth that have most noticeably found their white credentials called into question as 'moral panics' related to crime and deviancy have spread.

At the same time, those who did not identify as *Charver* remained cautious of these formidable Nailton youth and their 'gangsta' reputations.

Anoop: What's it mean if you're a Charver?
Michelle: It means you're from Nailton and you're a rogue.
[. . .]
Sam: My brother got jumped on by a load of *Charvers* outside the Regency Centre. These twelve kids jumped on him and kicked him in the mouth, he's got a big lip out here.

Tales of *Charver* violence were common amongst young people. The 'rogue' identities inhabited by the not-quite-white *Charvers* meant that they were labelled as trouble makers simply for 'hanging around' and having a visible street presence (Corrigan, 1981 [1979]). In popular discourse, the *Charver Kids* were street

---

31. Thus, the term 'Chavvy' is used in other English locales to denote children from travelling backgrounds. Here, Chavvy may also be a phrase to describe cheap, poor-quality items bought at market stalls.

urchins who were closely associated with the dangers thought to be inherent in Nailton. The extent to which *Charvers* were read as 'rogues' or 'gangstas' on the basis of their clothes, postures or accents meant that *Charver* style was seen to be embodied and emblematic of new articulations of race, class and gender identities.

As we have seen, there were a number of historically embedded urban myths about working-class life that have retained a contemporary significance. Alongside the common myths described, which equated *Charvers* with dirt and animals, ran other emphatically racialized legends. Throughout these narratives, the myth of a 'hard' black man was a familiar refrain, one utilized by James, who was at times identified as a *Charver Kid* – indicating the contingent, partial and open-ended affiliations with subculture.

> James: My friend was walking along the toon and this big paki kid goes, 'Crappa Kappa' cos [my friend] had a Kappa tracksuit on. He kept goin', 'That Kappa's a snide [fake] cos it's crappa Kappa' cos it had a rip under the arm.
>
> *Anoop: Who was saying this?*[32]
>
> James: This big paki kid. [. . .]
> He walked past him, grabbed him and said, 'Eeeh, that Kappa top's fake, all the things are blurry and that.' But it wasn't fake, it was real and he was goin' 'I hate the crappa Kappa tops.'

The symbolic value accorded to clothing can also not be underestimated in youth culture. Calling someone's items a 'snide' was a means of questioning another's masculine status and credentials. If the Kappa is 'Crappa', a fake, then the wearer is also a fraud. The image of a 'big paki' or a 'hard black man' also has resonance within popular youth culture, as will later be exemplified in a subcultural study of *White Wannabes*. Indeed, *Charver Kids* could evoke urban legends that concerned curious ethnic rituals. For example, they noted how black-coloured BMW cars would be termed 'Black Man's Willy' in a peculiar, colloquial reworking of the initials. This phrase drew upon popular urban folklore about Jamaican drug barons who were alleged to drive black BMWs. It was difficult to ascertain how meaningful these 'Northern myths' (Taylor *et al.*, 1996: 28) were, though their very production suggested much about the not-quite-white portrayal of *Charver* subculture, as we shall find below. Once again, the concept of an imaginary 'hard black man' was dramatically espoused.

> James: There's this thing called 'The Black Man's Convention' and you've gotta fight this dead hard black man to get in. Ya kna, you walk round pretending to be *Charvers* and that.

32. I purposefully repeated this question to James, a *Charver Kid*, as his use of the phrase 'paki' remained part of an unflinching rhetoric that he felt unselfconscious in expressing in front of me.

Anoop: *What do you mean, 'The Black Man's Convention'?*
Michelle: [*laughs*]
James: Just like a gang. A gang called, 'The Black Man's Convention'. Loadsa people all acting dead hard, they've gotta fight this big black person to be in 'The Black Man's Convention'.
Nicola: And other things they've gotta do – [*pointedly*] especially if you're a woman.
Anoop: *Have you got to be black to be in it?*
Nicola: No.
James: No.

According to the respondents 'The Black Man's Convention' was a crack, criminal unit comprised of 'hard' *Charver* types with established reputations for fighting and TWOCing. Despite its name, the outfit was said to contain white women and men who had passed certain tests. It was implied that these tests were sexual ones for women and aggressive, fighting ones for men. As such, *Charver* women and men were being asked to prove their 'blackness' through codes of sexuality and violence. For 'hard' *Charver* males, entry into 'The Black Man's Convention' was said to involve the ability to defeat a black Other in a fighting contest.

Anoop: *What you were saying last time about 'The Black Man's Convention', is that true?*
James: The 'Black Man's Convention'? It's true you've gotta fight the hardest black man.
Anoop: *But does it really exist?*
James: Yeah, it properly exists.
Anoop: *How do you know?*
Sam: Cos they go round in cars, about fifty cars.
James: Aye, I kna, wheel-spinning their cars and everythin'.
Anoop: *What do they do?*
Sam: They go round lookin' for people to chin [i.e. punch in the mouth].
James: They go round fightin' everyone, cos you've gotta fight this black man all the time to get in 'The Black Man's Convention'. Yer gotta be dead hard to be in it, they jus' go round chinnin' people and everythin'.

In this extract, the mental image of a 'hard black man' was the defining Other which *Charvers* had to negotiate. Proof of their own 'hardness' was provided in evidence that they truly were not-quite-white if they could successfully 'chin' and tame the primitive black man. This would allow them to inhabit the prestigious status of a 'hard' black masculinity and develop mannerisms of black speech, posture and gait with less obvious contradiction.

However, we would be mistaken in believing that all pretensions to whiteness were forgone. Rather like the immigrants Ignatiev records in *How the Irish Became White* (1995), who used the performance of blackface and minstrelsy to ridicule

Southern American negroes, these acts were also a means of asserting one's own whiteness, however precarious this may appear. Thus, for all their 'not-quite-whiteness' the *Charvers* were never completely black, as regular racist assaults upon Asian families in Nailton served to testify. A number of *Charver Kids* expressed little hesitation in referring to 'the paki-shop', whilst some mentioned first-hand acts of racist violence. Like other *Charvers* in the school, Nicola was reputed to have a large number of relatives, many of whom were alleged criminal associates. During the research, her father, whose biography had been punctuated by a series of prison sentences, was arrested after a violent brawl with Indian male workers outside a Nailton take-away.[33] The fight was alleged to concern a business dispute, but there had been a previous history of racist altercations involving family members. According to Nicola, the fight involved, 'Sticks with metal chains on them', and on enquiring about the outcome I was told, 'Me Dar and them lot started at them with the metal bars an' that and when the police came he got lifted.' Such struggles happened on a daily basis and there remained a widespread feeling amongst many Nailton families that public monies such as New Deal initiatives were benefiting 'pakis and asylum seekers' at the expense of white communities. However inaccurate such perceptions may be, they remain informative of a deeper sense of white injustice. In an area where resources are scarce and competition fierce, racist antagonism is an uneasy resolution that does little to conceal the stark inequalities wrought by urban regeneration, unemployment and global change.

Concluding Remarks

Charles Booth, in his encyclopaedic report of urban life, displayed an early sensitivity to the numerous sub-divisions that existed within this highly marked social category 'working class'. Richard Hoggart encapsulates this internal variety when he reminds us of 'the great number of differences, the subtle shades, the class distinctions, within the working-classes themselves' (1966 [1957]:21). It was these 'subtle shades' that effectively produced *Charver Kids* as Tyneside's not-quite-white in schooling, city-centre and neighbourhood locations. This distinction between 'ordinary' white Tyneside dwellers (working- and middle-class) and Nailton *Charvers* is apparent in dusky descriptions of the latter as a 'blot on the landscape', 'an alien breed', a 'cancer', 'dirt', 'filth' and, as one student memorably added, 'scum'. In short, the *Charvers* can never be *Real Geordies*, distinguished carriers of an archetypal industrial whiteness; somehow their youthscapes are altogether too 'unclean'. *Charvers* are at the centre of a curious

---

33. In 2003 it was estimated that around 1 in 15 school students in Britain has a parent who is in prison.

triangulation of circumstances that means they are forever placed at the borders of whiteness as the socially excluded, the economically redundant.

Firstly, *Charver Kids* are undeniably impoverished and occupy amongst the lowest strata of (non-) working-class life. By exploring the discursive construction of *Charver Kids* in media reports and popular discourse it is clear that they are seldom viewed as 'victims' and invariably seen as 'trouble'. The subcultural values attributed to *Charver* style are indicative of the racialization of a lower working-class corpus as dirt-ridden, smelly and ragged. Moreover, *Charver* parents are seen as state parasites who purposely have large families in what is regarded as both an expression of their unrestrained sexual libido and a calculated attempt to claim extra child benefits. In this sense, a dichotomy between *Real Geordies* and *Charver Kids* is enacted, a split that separates the 'rough' from the 'respectable' echelons of the working class. The 'moral panic' concerning *Charver Kids* associates them with theft, robbery, car crime, disease, dirt and over-breeding. These social indicators of 'deviancy' are seen to have an historical resonance that draws upon a Victorian fear of and fascination for the city and the peoples who inhabit these central zones. However, for many *Charver* families these are lived responses to the uneven nature of globalization and inter-generation unemployment.

Secondly, *Charvers* particularly reside in and around Nailton, an area that is subject to numerous cultural fantasies and racialized projections. Here, it can be seen that while place shapes the fabric of youth subculture, these cultures in turn shape the local environment. The place-bound complexities of 'local' cultures are, then, integral to understanding young people's place within the global economy. The subcultural style adopted by the *Charvers* is itself a mediation of contemporary urban form expressed in dress style, haircut, accent, body posture and musical preferences. Ultimately, the *Charvers* are treated as urban untouchables, families who have colonized this zone of the city and made it their own. A third circumstance which makes it difficult for *Charvers* to lay claim to the mantle of whiteness is that they reside in the same locality as Tyneside's main, non-white ethnic minority populace, South Asians. By dint of inhabiting the same social space, using the same public facilities, breathing the same polluted air, *Charver* claims to whiteness and the badge of white citizenship are all the more precarious. Unlike other more mobile working-class factions, *Charver* families had not made the magical leap required for a 'white flight' to the suburbs. Worse still, the reputation of *Charver Kids* is 'blackened' by their associations with urban crime, the 'black' economy, law and disorder. It is this contingent, mobile combination of factors – geography, poverty, migration and subcultural embodiment – which leads to the establishment of *Charvers* as 'tainted' whites, twilight residents of Tyneside's urban, shadowy recesses.

–6–

Wiggers, Wannabes and White Negroes: Emerging Ethnicities and Cultural Fusion

Introduction

By focusing upon the material aspects of globalization and the spread of capital, goods and trade across time and space, economic geographers have provided important understandings of production and uneven development in what is an increasingly global economy (see Harvey, 1990 [1989]; Bryson *et al.*, 1999). At the same time the global marketplace has been characterized by technological innovation and new patterns of consumption that have encouraged a growth in service sector economies. Importantly, these changes have been occurring within particular places that have themselves been subject to change, not least through deindustrialization, but also as a consequence of new diasporic flows, migrations and settlements (Brah, 1996; Robins, 1991). To this extent it is imperative that we now engage with the cultural transformations in young lives to understand how youth identities are shaped by interactions with global processes and the creation of new world markets.

Unsurprisingly, urban districts housing relatively large multi-ethnic communities have tended to be the primary site for examining ethnicity and changing youth cultures in Britain (Hewitt, 1986; Jones, 1988; Wulff, 1995; Back, 1996). In contrast there is little research on youth cultural identities in predominantly 'white areas', including new towns, 'Middle England' and suburban quarters (see Watt, 1998; McGuinness, 2000; Nayak, 1999b, respectively). Much contemporary work on 'new ethnicities' (Hall, 1993) is characterized by what Paul Watt identifies as a 'hegemonic discourse in relation to race and space' (1998:688). This spatialized discourse has tended to ignore ostensibly white regions in favour of vibrant, cosmopolitan inner-city areas found especially in the South. This chapter aims to displace this hegemony by considering global change and emerging ethnicities in the North East of England (see Bennett, 2000). The ethnography suggests that a more detailed treatment of race and place is needed which extends to predominantly white preserves and those zones beyond the metropolis (Bonnett and Nayak, 2003).

The assumption that young people in peripheral white locales are untouched by multicultural influences is increasingly unfounded. As people and places are drawn seemingly closer together, local cultures are no longer immune from international cross-fertilization. Mass communication systems and changing patterns of consumption – including the development of youth, niche and lifestyle markets – have broadened the range of youth identities available in a global marketplace. This has meant that even in a mainly white area such as the North East it is possible for some young people to draw upon the signs and symbols of multiculture to re-fashion their ethnicities beyond the spatial limits of the local. For some, cross-cultural interaction can be a tentative, brief affair. For others, the enactment has longer-lasting implications that may come to leave a deeper impression upon their ethnic habitation and styles of behaviour. Either way, these performances are evidence of young people's emerging ethnicities and their engagement with globalization, hybridity and new styles of consumption. Through a local analysis of 'race traitors', including *B-Boyz*, *Wiggers*, *Wannabes* and *White Negroes*, the chapter will demonstrate how young people are creating new youthscapes within the changing global economy.

B-Boyz: The Discursive Production of a Term

> Mis-shapes, mistakes, misfits,
> We'd like to go to town but we can't risk it, oh
> 'Cause they just want to keep us out.
> You could end up with a smack in the mouth
> Just for standing out.
> Oh really.

> 'Mis-shapes' – Pulp, 1995

In the principally white district of Tyneside evidence of the influence of multi-culture upon the identities of white youth is, on the surface, relatively marginal. This contrasts sharply with other British centres such as Birmingham, Manchester and London, where a new black urban style can be vividly detected in the inter-meshing youth cultures of African-Caribbean, Asian and white youth. In the absence of a substantial, visible minority community in the North East, a cluster of white youth known as the *B-Boyz* were establishing a subculture of their own which was directly implicated in the transatlantic, global circuit of cultural production. The *B-Boyz* comprise a diverse group of males including members from various middle- and working-class backgrounds. Such variation is less apparent in the subcultures of the *Real Geordies* and *Charver Kids*, where class culture was found to be a source of conflict. The term 'B-Boy' is a negotiated construct that holds multiple and contingent meaning. I was informed that the phrase emerged from the subculture's association with basketball, so could be a shorthand term for (B)asketball-Boys. Other members said it was musically derived and drew upon US Hip-Hop and dance culture, where the 'B' could stand for break-dancing, BeBop or even the Bronx. Some subcultural members claimed it meant they were 'Bad' (or Bad-ass Boyz), an inverted Americanism which implied the linguistic opposite (i.e. they were 'cool', dangerously 'hard').

However, the term was also subject to a number of competing definitions and is frequently deployed in a derogatory manner. Thus, the *Real Geordies* insisted that the label is used because the group are 'wannabes', that is, white youth who 'want-to-be' black, hence (wanna)Bee-Boyz. Another insinuation by the *Real Geordies* – the ever-present arbiters of ethnicity – is that the *B-Boyz* are aptly named since they represent that most controversial of social groups, *Black Boyz*. Once again, there is the assertion from the football-playing subculture that they are the 'Real' carriers of white ethnicity and it is the *B-Boyz* who lack the moral certainty of whiteness so deeply imbricated in 'Geordie' identity. In view of these negative inferences some members of the basketball subculture wished to disassociate themselves from the *B-Boyz* label. However, nearing the culmination of the ethnography, a number of youth had taken up the symbolic marker with pride, in what may be adequately seen as a struggle for the sign. Transforming the negative epithet *B-Boyz* into a positive signifier of identity offers a means through which the subculture can re-define themselves against other social groups and establish a strong collective identity. The political appropriation and re-signification of terms such as 'Black', 'Queer' and, most recently, 'Nigga' in particular North American contexts are examples of this inverted encoding.

The most popular term used by *Real Geordies* to describe the cultural syncretism of the *B-Boyz* is the Americanism 'Wigger', which implies that the basketball-playing subculture are, literally, 'white niggers'. One is reminded here of Norman Mailer's famous essay 'The White Negro' (1970 [1957]) and Jack Kerouac's description of white longing in the beatnik novel *On the Road* (2003 [1958]). It is this definition of *'Wigger'* as a white-on-white epithet that *Real Geordies* seek to invoke when disparaging the *B-Boyz*, whom they see as 'race traitors', people who have relinquished their white heritage in favour of more global, emergent ethnicities. At the expense of the global, the *Real Geordies* were far more interested in local identities: Geordies and Makums, Northerners and Southerners, who is 'Real' and who is a *'Wannabe'*. These differences transpire at corporeal levels through the consumption of fashion, haircuts, music and sport. At the bodily scale these are key zones for youth experimentation and the making of a new cultural heritage, and so shall be explored in detail.

Corporeal Consumption #1: B-Boyz, Sport and Basketball

... basketball is more than a sport; it is a cultural practice ... its symbols and myths are deeply racialized. Images of basketball become a site for understanding relations between the black and white races [*sic*] between the city and the suburbs.

Mathew Brown, 'Basketball, Rodney King, Simi Valley' (1997).

Brown's quotation above draws attention to the racialization of basketball and how this interconnects spatially. This section examines how the sport became a cultural signifier of blackness in a mainly white locale, and the effects this process of racialization has upon the lives of Tyneside's expressive *B-Boyz*. Indeed, in both Emblevale and Snowhill Comprehensive basketball is something more than a sport; it is also a wider 'cultural practice' to be lived out on the social landscape and the loaded surfaces of the body as 'style'. In this sense, the sporting affiliations of the *B-Boyz* become an arena for the complex interplay of numerous racialized and masculinized engagements. In Emblevale School the first remark made to me by students questioned whether I played basketball. At Snowhill Comprehensive, I quickly became aware of a form of spatial jousting taking place on the playground as the *B-Boyz* jostled for space with the *Real Geordies*, who had hitherto occupied the central spaces for football games. These dynamics can also be traced in the wider community, filtering into a range of other 'meeting places' (Massey, 1995). If the *Real Geordies*, as dispossessed working-class youth, represent a 'residual culture', then the *B-Boyz* with their global outlook and new forms of cultural expression embody an 'emergent culture', performing a *Wigger* identity as part of a new mode of being (Williams, 1971 [1958]).

Notwithstanding the occasional brief conflict, by the end of my time at Snowhill Comprehensive the *B-Boyz* managed to lay claim to particular spaces of the playground which at one time would have been seen as the sole territory of the 'lads', footballers and other *Real Geordies*. The *Boyz* were quick to remark upon the increased participation in the sport, which was now flourishing amongst younger students. However, they saw themselves as early pioneers of this 'minority sport'.

[16–17 years]
John: Our Year's probably the best Year for basketball the school's ever had.
Chris: We got to the semi-finals of the Northern Pool International Cup. It was just a fluke how there was so many people like in one Year who like the same thing. And it was still a minority sport but at least you could see it.

Where basketball had been a minority interest, relegated to the outskirts of the street and playground, its popularity was now extending into other leisure spaces and could be detected in a range of sportswear and street fashions, as we shall go on to see. Chris, whom we heard from above, had been an exceptional player and was previously involved in Tyneside's Under-17s team. After developing a career-ending knee injury he was forced to retire from the game, but basketball had nevertheless provided him with the opportunity to form new alliances. Chris told me how living in Tyneside and attending Snowhill Comprehensive with its massive white majority meant he had never really come into contact with black people. This situation had altered as his interest in basketball mushroomed. I asked him if there were any black players in the squad and he informed me that most of the team were black:

> Chris: I was like Under-17s and that. But most of the professional team was black. The best players on it was black, and like my coach was black! So I associated with them, and all.

Basketball offered Chris his first prolonged contact with black youth. It opened a passageway towards meeting other black players and allowed him to develop multi-ethnic bonds in the otherwise white highlands of the city. As his confidence grew, Chris developed other tastes in dress style and music, becoming more acquainted with the global branding of black style. He reported how he 'used to be a basketball fan and like try and wear the same type of baggy shorts the players wear and same kind of cool trainers'. In this respect the sport of basketball opened up Chris's social world to new experiences and cultural practices beyond the immediate local environment as he travelled to games with the team and met other black players from different cities. The sport encouraged him to become increasingly aware of his conservative 'white' dress style as he gradually began to adjust it in accordance with his new-found multi-ethnic peer group. This self-conscious attempt to grapple with white 'self-hood' provides a revealing insight into how, why and where the boundaries of whiteness are constructed and regulated (Frankenberg, 1994). Thus, it was through an engagement with blackness that white youth like Chris came to understand the meaning of whiteness in their social lives.

However, negotiating these changes could be problematic without the support of an influential multi-ethnic friendship group at school or in the local neighbourhood. This meant the *B-Boyz* risked being abused as 'race traitors'.

> John: You got a bit of prejudice if you were one of the basketball players.
>
> Chris: And you'd get stick cos you didn't like footbaal as much.
>
> *Anoop: What got said?*
>
> John: Are you one of these B-ballers and that. They just couldn't understand reely. They'd say, 'I hate that' and they reely can't even see how you can like that.
>
> Chris: Like they don't like basketball so they can't see how anyone can . . . and anyone who does like it must be a bit of a fool.

In the relative absence of a significant black population the *B-Boyz* became easy targets for assuming the role of a racialized Other. In the white peripheries of the North East the multi-ethnic style of the *Boyz* singled them out as select repositories for racial intolerance. As the above extract reveals, the language of race was surreptitiously inscribed in both the treatment of, and responses from, the *B-Boyz*. Depicted as *Wiggers*, the *B-Boyz* explained to me how they were subjected to 'prejudice' from *Real Geordies*, a term that implied some form of racist discrimination. The *Boyz* claim they receive 'stick' and are 'discriminated against' because they choose to wear different clothes and adopt an alternative repertoire of style to the 'mainstream' of 'Geordie' youth. Some even reported that this resulted in them being chased, harassed and beaten up by other young people. However, the growth of the subculture also meant that more youth were now taking an interest in the sport and the style was gaining an increasing visibility.

The *B-Boyz* saw basketball as a rapidly expanding sport and enthused about the increased coverage being given at the time by Channel 4, satellite TV and other international media. They seemed acutely attentive to the 'inheritance' claims of the *Real Geordies* discussed previously and consciously wanted to subvert the legacy of their social standing.

> Chris: The thing I would like to do would be teach my son basketball.
> John: Yeah!
> Chris: I could play against him and I could teach him what I know, and get him going so he could be one of the top in the sport. I've had me injuries so I can't play anymore.

By imagining they were teaching their future offspring basketball, the *B-Boyz* are toying with notions of a new, masculine cultural inheritance. While the new ethnicities adopted by the *B-Boyz* stood in stark contrast to the parochial identities of the *Real Geordies*, each subculture can be seen to be designing their own future utopias. Moreover, the differences between the two groups extended well beyond their emphatic sporting allegiances. Of particular interest, then, is the process by which basketball develops from being simply a sport to becoming a *subcultural practice*. Chris explains how playing the sport is cultivated over time into a broader subcultural activity encompassing musical styles:

> Chris: I played it for the school and liked it, I watched it a couple of times and thought it was good. There was a few people into it, there's loads [now], we all got together and started listening to the music that seemed to fit with the sport.
> *Anoop: What music was associated with the sport?*
> Chris: Well Rap music, I suppose, with basketball. I dunno why but it just does, it just *seems* right. And it's also black culture, in basketball there's a lot of black culture. The best players are black in general.

According to Chris there appears a 'fit', or what Willis (1978) terms an 'homo-logy', between basketball, Hip-Hop and black culture that the *B-Boyz* could be said to subscribe to. The organic development of this stylistic repertoire through music, dress, attitudes and behaviour is implicit, 'it just *seems* right'. As we shall now find, the 'fit' or homology extends from basketball to Hip-Hop, particular hairstyles and fashions.

Corporeal Consumption #2: Dress and Fashion

The symbolic challenge offered by the *B-Boyz* to the *Real Geordies* is, then, not merely about preferring basketball to football. There is a sense that each group has an opposing philosophic ethos that is implicitly ethnically divergent. Crucially, each subculture is accentuating different aspects of the local–global dichotomy, with the *Real Geordies* prioritizing locality while the *B-Boyz* practised trans-nationalism. These nuances are seen in a multitude of stylistic references. *B-Boyz* favour Hip-Hop over Brit-pop, basketball over football, baggy American street-wear over smart casual designer labels. To gain deeper insight into this stylistic homology, I enquired about the preferred fashions of basketball-playing youth:

[11–12 years]
Sam: There's normally baggy clothes for Hip-Hop. I normally wear baggy clothes and caps and everythin'. Basketball tops and jeans, big jackets and everythin'.
Anoop: And that's the stuff you wear?
Sam: Yeah. It's big and baggy.
James: I normally wear the fashion stuff, like Adidas pants and that.
Nicola: Nike.

That the clothes of these youth were 'big and baggy', unlike the tailored, Modish appearance favoured by the *Real Geordies*, is not itself inconsequential. The *B-Boyz* are not simply taking on an imported version of American youth culture, as may be presumed, but are also arranging their identities through and against the parochial values of the *Real Geordies* and the lower-class exhibitionism of the *Charvers* at a local scale. In this respect the *Boyz* invoke a dialectical relationship between global and local cultures (Massey, 1998). These 'style wars' need to be understood not just through processes of Americanization but in the internal configurations that arise in particular places amongst different youth groups themselves.

The *B-Boyz* had a global outlook that stretched across the Atlantic for its points of reference: basketball, Hip-Hop, black urban culture. The dress code is also symbolically expansive ('big and baggy') and transnational, looking beyond the locality and stretching the boundaries of identity. Out of school the *Boyz* wore long t-shirts and baseball caps with motifs relating to American basketball teams. This represented a switch away from the obligatory NUFC insignia favoured by the *Real Geordies*. Furthermore, the transatlantic dress code of the group is seen by the *Real Geordies* as global not local and deemed to be essentially 'UnBritish'. Paradoxically the fabric of *B-Boyz* subculture could be used to knit the group together, bonding them against the hostilities they were made to endure from others who saw them as 'race traitors'. Even so, this did not deter white Hip-Hop followers, *B-Boyz* and other white renegades from expressing their subcultural allegiances through style.

> *Anoop: Is there a link between basketball and Hip-Hop then?*
> Sam: Well it's American.
> James: It is. It's like American and basketball's baggy stuff and dead long t-shirts.
> Sam: Cos everyone that plays basketball listens to Hip-Hop.
> *Anoop: Do you?*
> Sam: Yeah ... Me big brother plays for the Under-15s Newcastle team, the Newcastle Sparrowhawks.

The subcultural homology between 'baggy' gear, 'long t-shirts', basketball and Hip-Hop music is transformed into a uniting anthem for the *B-Boyz*. A subcultural identity is realized through a combination of sport, fashion, music and a seemingly shared value system. At the same time, it is necessary to look beyond the masculine matrices of sport and subculture to understand how young women articulate changing ethnicities in global times.

Only a few young women in the region were comfortable enacting a so-called *Wigger* identity. For many, the black–white assemblage is felt to be in danger of undercutting a desirable, white heterosexual femininity. Helena was a white, working-class, 17-year-old student who had a Norwegian mother and an English father from Tyneside. She had spent nearly all her life in Norway but was living with her grandmother in the North East at the time I got to know her. She had long, blonde hair and blue eyes and was strongly influenced by black music. Helena liked listening to artists such as The Fugees, LL Cool J, Missy Elliot and Mary J Blige, recalling, 'Hip-Hop, Rap and Swing, I like R 'n' B Swing'. She wore 'baggy' gear and would immerse herself in the full blazonry of black cultural style. At various moments Helena perceived herself to 'be' black, or at least made firm identifications with black ethnicity. 'I feel at *home* in this style cos I'm one of this myself,' she recounted. Helena consciously wore baggy clothes, trainers and hooded sweatshirts. She indicated how these items had a unisex status that many Tyneside women tended to avoid. For Helena, 'baggy' style was a form of self-expression that transgressed the rigidly ascribed boundaries of white femininity.

Anoop: *Are there others that wear the same as you?*

Helena: Mmmm. The lads, not the lasses. Just the lads and one of me black friends, Beverley. Me and Beverley wear all the same clothes and everything, and the lads.

Anoop: *Why is it mainly lads?*

Helena: Cos like basketball maybe, skate-boards, skating.

Participation in black culture, may, then, offer opportunities for meeting black youth and developing multi-ethnic friendships in white locales. It may also enable critical reflection. Fern (10 years) pointed out how 'Coloured people think their clothes are special,' and Alistair (10 years) added that this was cos it's got a culture behind it.' In so doing, these engagements can also rupture the conventional strictures of white femininity, which, not unlike a symbolic corset, are tightly laced through conservative ideals. In her study of multi-ethnic friendships among teen-age girls in South London, Wulff concludes that in the process of ethnic experimentation young white women internalize 'ethnic equality with their femininity through bodily consumption of youth styles and music' (1995:77). However, in Tyneside the performance of 'sporting femininities' through a dress code that had real or symbolic attachments to basketball, skate-boarding or roller-blading is not necessarily seen as desirable. In one interview Helena explained how she would later be going out in the evening to a school dinner-dance at a hotel, where she would be dressed differently to her white female friends. She proudly revealed, 'I'm the only one that's gonna wear pants. Everyone's going posh and everything in dresses and I'm gonna wear like me pants.' For Angela McRobbie, black culture can provide templates for a 'changing mode of femininity' (1997:36), but in the predominantly white area of the North East most young women favoured short skirts, high-heels and figure-hugging evening attire.

Corporeal Consumption #3: Hairstyles

If basketball offered a masculine arena for the negotiation of white ethnicity, it appeared that music, fashion and dance were more inclusive points of iden-tification for girls and young women. For many, the body was a 'corporeal canvas' upon which global fashions and hybrid haircuts could be practised

[12 years]

Michelle: I want my hair beaded

Nicola: I want my hair beaded

Anoop: *Beaded?*

Sara: It takes about seven hours to do.

Michelle: And then you get little beads and you plait them.

Sara:	It takes ages to do it and when you take it out it rips all your hair.
Anoop:	*So who wants it?*
Sara, Michelle, Nicola:	[*together*] I want it!
James:	My sista's got her's done like that, about forty of them.
Sam:	You have tiny little plaits and then you put beads in it.
Anoop:	*So what kinda style is that?*
Sam:	It's called braids. Braids.
Nicola:	It's plaited and you can get fake hair and they plait it to there [*demonstrates length*].

Although hair braiding involves intense bodily labour and a certain amount of pain, young women were not put off by the idea. In an inversion of the racist sentiment that all black people look the same, some youth reflected on the multiple possibilities embodied in black cultural style as opposed to the seeming homogeneity of whiteness:

Helena: I think I love the hair. It sounds so stupid, but look at this hair! [*grabs her long, blonde strands*] I can't do nowt! It's just like straight. They can have curls, it can stand up straight, or have it really Afro. Not only the hair but they can hide everything, like do things with their body, with special shades [i.e. sunglasses] and stuff. It's like everything – everything's attractive.

The explicit longing attributed towards particular ethnic signifiers of style such as hair, clothes and music is largely concerned with the *symbolic* aspects of blackness. For many it does not signify a reconfiguration of values beyond the level of style, as it has done for certain members of the *B-Boyz* who had formed lasting friendships with black youth as a consequence of direct multi-ethnic contact. If girls fantasized about tightly plaited hair with beads, boys too spoke of having various patterns or insignia shaved into their head.

[12 years]
James: I like the bricks me. You get all of it shaved off to a No. 2 or 3 or something, then you get a step shaved in a No. 1. Y'kna bricks.
Anoop: Bricks?
James: Aye, like little rectangles shaved in with a step.
Michelle: With lines.

Hairstyles in this vein include shaving zig-zags into the scalp, or even etching labels such as the global brands 'Nike' or 'No Fear'. Clearly, many of these cuts are stylistic appropriations of black culture by white youth. Indeed, Hebdige has compared this reconfiguration of white ethnicity to a 'phantom history of race relations' (Hebdige, 1987 [1979]:44–5) in which the subtle traces of multiculture are silently inscribed, over time, upon the loaded surfaces of post-war British youth cultures. However, for a section of Tyneside youth, these hybridized spaces also offer possibilities for new forms of ethnic experimentation to take place. Here, some white youth openly acknowledge their identifications with black culture:

[16–17 years]

Anoop: What do you mean when you say you're into 'black style'?

Helena: Like the clothes style, the style of going out, music style . . . yeah, the hairstyles and everything.

Anoop: So what are those styles?

Helena: It's African things. All strange styles, cos here in Europe it's like all boring hairstyles.

Jolene: And the black Americans, it's like the hair, they do so much with it and we canna do anything like that.

Discussions concerning style offer a partial glimpse into white dissatisfaction. At such moments, whiteness is constructed as 'boring', monolithic and bland. However, it would be wrong to read these sentiments as anything other than a selective appreciation for black culture within a particular youth context. Most interviewees had little connection with Tyneside's main visible minority, South Asians, implying that a number of white youth do not want to 'be' black as such; rather, they want what is culturally ascribed to versions of blackness in popular youth culture. Thus, James, who had previously mentioned that his sister wore African-style braids, later revealed, 'My sista does kna like black fellas, she'd ravver 'ave a white fella than a black fella.' Such accounts flag up the limits of cultural hybridity, where racism can still be used to mark boundaries between Self and Other, despite the presence of channels of dialogic exchange and incorporation.[34] As such, the overarching whiteness of the Tyneside conurbation and the absence of a variety of recognizable black street styles is socially prohibitive of wider ethnic experimentation. Moreover, where creative multicultural dialogues do occur through subcultural style, they are likely to remain short-lived.

Some students such as Sam (12 years) also saw beneath the superficial dialogues with black culture attempted by some whites. Sam is an avid fan of Hip-Hop and Reggae music and had a particular appreciation of Bob Marley, himself a pivotal figure in the global take-up of Reggae music. Throughout the fieldwork period Sam and I shared lengthy conversations about Marley's life and music. Sam would frequently defend his preference for Bob Marley over newer artists such as

---

34. Wulff's (1995) study of white adolescent girls who had formed black friendships in the multi-ethnic district of South London draws a more positive conclusion. The author claims, 'it is likely that the idea of ethnic equality will stay with them as they grow up to be young women' (p. 17), indicating the meaningfulness of direct black–white interaction.

The Fugees, who he pointed out were 'copyin' him'. His allegiance to the 'cult of Bob' was such that in one interview he boldly stated, 'I would like to live in Jamaica and be a Rasta!' At this point I made the mistake of presuming Sam wished to be black, yet this was not what he had said, as for him there was no contradiction in being white and Rastafarian (see Jones, 1988). Indeed, Sam's identification with Bob Marley encouraged him to consider getting dreadlocks in his hair at a time when most *B-Boyz* and fetishists of black style wanted to shave patterns or tram-lines into their scalps. His comments go on to reveal how ethnic experimentation is often likely to be a solitary pursuit in mainly white areas.

[12 years]
Sam: I'm gettin' dreadlocks, me mam says I can get them if I have the money.
Anoop: Isn't your hair too short Sam?
Sam: I'm getting it done in the last three weeks of the Summer holidays, or the last.
Nicola: You can get 'em done short.
Anoop: Has anyone else got dreadlocks in the school?
Sam: Naa.
Anoop: Then why do you want them?
Nicola: Cos it means you're different.
Sam: Yeah, it's different. But I like Bob Marley music as well, I like Reggae music and Hip-Hop. I'd like it done, it's different.

In many cases it is difficult to know whether the embodied desire for intercultural exchange would be effected. However, disclosing desires for braids or dreadlocks in front of friends is a means by which these ideas can be 'tried out' in the immediate peer-group to see whether such practices are approved of or opposed. For Sam, as long as the identification with Bob Marley and Reggae was consistent, the *fantasy* of 'crossing over' and becoming a Rasta remained. Kobena Mercer (1994) has written extensively about the political signification carried by black hairstyles at particular moments. He argues that dreadlocks are not the 'natural' black style they may purport to be but are 'stylistically *cultivated* and politically *constructed* in a particular historical moment as part of a strategic contestation of white dominance and the cultural power of whiteness' (p. 108).[35] The wearing of dreadlocks by white youth, amidst the ever-popular shaven-headed styles in the locality, can also contest whiteness, albeit in differing circumstances.[36] However, in a

35. In his study of the Rasta Heads in *Young, Gifted and Black* Mac an Ghaill (1988) found that this type of black style could be used by young men as a form of resistance to schooling authorities. See also Dick Hebdige's paper 'Reggae, Rastas and Rudies' (1977).

36. In contemporary British street culture, white youth with dreadlocks are frequently identified as 'Crusties', associated with travellers, New Age and Green politics. Social stereotypes of the subculture portray Crusties as unkempt cider-drinkers who rarely wash, have dogs on strings and enjoy living in squalor.

multi-ethnic context Jones (1988) found that many white youth with black friends had been through adolescent phases of having dreadlocks, but only those with a more thoughtout ideological position maintained this look through their later teenage years. Sam's comments should be read cautiously in the light of this knowledge, but we should not forget the pressure to conform to whiteness in the absence of an immediate black peer group in the Tyneside setting.

Corporeal Consumption #4: Music and Dance

One of the most important arenas for young people to experiment with global change and hybrid ethnic affiliations is through the consumption of music and dance. Helena had only recently joined Snowhill Comprehensive but had quickly become best friends with Beverley, one of the few black students in the school. She recalled, 'When I came to [Tyneside] this Autumn I was like [*excited tone*], "Ah, Beverley!" She loves my music.' Helena emphasized how she felt much more comfortable around black people, adding, 'Like [with] Beverley, we're really close about music and we talk about it for hours and hours and hours.' In-depth discussion reveals that Beverley and Helena participate in what has been described as a 'culture of the bedroom' (McRobbie and Garber, 1977 [1975]:213), which offers girls an intimate space to chat and 'hang out', as well as to experiment with singing, rapping and dancing. In many respects, for the young women concerned, the bedroom represents a paradoxical space. On the one hand it is place of control and confinement, while on the other it is a zone for freedom of expression, a space in which to live out fantasies of the 'self'. For McRobbie these inbetween spaces can yield 'different, youthful subjectivities' (1997:36). When asked what occurs in these shared yet private spaces, Helena remarked how Beverley and herself, 'Like rap to each other', whimsically adding, 'we can do anything'. The 'bedroom rap' they refer to is literally a form of rapport that also encompasses rhymes, songs and daily chat. In the context of an ostensibly white region, the bedroom becomes a 'safe space' for intercultural dialogue and the elaboration of a black vernacular.

The learning of a new vernacular is an issue open to ridicule. Although the majority of young people spoke of an inability to understand certain Rap or Reggae terms, others, such as Sam, claimed to have an elementary understanding of patois and Creole phrases.

[12 years]
Michelle: It doesn't make sense, 'No Woman, No Cry' [A Bob Marley song] what's that mean?
Sam: It does.
[...]

Anoop: *So, do you understand what they say on Rap or Reggae records?*
All [except Sam]: Naa.
Sam: Aye. [*To the rest of the group*] It's jus' cos you don't listen!

Whereas most of the young people felt that Bob Marley's lyrics were somewhat opaque, Sam had spent time listening to, and interpreting, the meanings of black music. In a sense, Sam's challenge to the claim that Reggae is impenetrable and his assertion that white youth did not listen to black experiences is a challenge to conventional white wisdom (Carby, 1982; Amos and Parmar, 1984). Sam's fascination with black culture stemmed from a passion for music, an emerging interest in black politics, and a desire to be 'different'. Furthermore, Sam expressed strongly egalitarian sentiments and would directly reprimand other students when on occasion they slipped into racist discourses.

For a select number of white youth who had developed a deeper race consciousness, and those who sustained contact with black friends, a more sensitive appreciation of the politics of race, ethnicity and nationhood could yet be achieved. Students such as Helena spoke directly about political issues concerned with social class, racism and discrimination. She was especially critical of young people who celebrated aspects of black culture at the level of consumption, but retained an overall posture of white chauvinism.

Helena: One of my friends is like, 'I'd love to be black, *but* . . . ,' and they're okay about
          it. Some of them are racist, I'm talking to them and everything, saying, 'I really
          like you as a friend but don't like that opinion.'
Anoop: *They're racist even thought they're into black music?*
Helena: Yeah, black music but not black anything else! They wear some Hip-Hop
          clothes. They go on about how the government spend the money on black
          people and everything, rather than on white. They don't say it in front of me cos
          I'll cut their head off in me words, with me arguments.

Helena's identification with blackness extended into music, dress and complex forms of body management (engaging in 'black' forms of dancing, invoking stylized gestures or expressions, even attempting to 'turn black' through the daily use of a sun-bed). Moreover, Helena's Norwegian–Geordie dialect is inflected with a lexicon of cultural phrases derived from her previous multi-ethnic friendship group and then further elaborated by listening to Rap and Swing records. I went on to ask Helena if it was possible to like black music but still be racist, and she was in little doubt, 'Yeah, it's so stupid, aye it is mon.'

While not all students showed a commitment to black culture *and* anti-racism, some did emphasize the political aspects of black cultural style. In such statements whiteness is viewed as an empty category that is somehow 'cultureless'. By contrast, black culture is made to appear profoundly political.

[10–11 years]

Alistair: I like The Fugees and Coolio.

Anoop: *What's good about The Fugees then?*

Andrew: Well, they've got good songs, songs like *'Bounty Killer'* and it's really good.

Alistair: They've got other things as well, like singing about Africa and the refugees as well.

Anoop: *Is that important?*

Andrew: Yeah, cos it gets a message across, cos people listen to loads of music.

Andrew's favourite musical artists were Public Enemy and The Fugees. He emphasized the political messages carried by these groups and claimed that they had encouraged him to reflect more on issues of social concern. The discussion of black music implicitly critiqued the 'hollowness' of whiteness.

Alistair: The songs 'ave got *life* in them.

Andrew: Cos it sounds like they're actually gonna do something. Y'kna', like the singin' and tha'? It sounds like they've got something to say, and they've got something to do. And we just sing for the fun of it. You hear all these new things, like 911 comin' in, like Boyzone an' it's all about love stuff and tha'. All this rap like Tupac[37], most of the songs, they're saying stuff what's happened [...] They're not actually sayin', 'We need help' but in the songs it's there [...] England's slightly borin' cos you've got everythin' an' you've done it all, you're jus' waitin' to get older [...] They [blacks] actually sing about wha's happenin', and we sing about love songs and tha'. We're not tellin' anyone anythin'! They do. People understand them.

Andrew's sentiment that people relate to the message of black music reveals his own subjective identifications. The responses indicate that black music has 'life' in it, it is trying to 'do' something and is grounded in the material 'reality' of daily life. By contrast, we can suggest that the norm against which this form is judged, 'white' music, is lifeless, passive and unexciting. In classroom cultures, the epitome of this is said to be 'boy bands' and upper-class 'white' music styles, especially classical. The replies reveal much about broader perceptions of whiteness.

[9–10 years]

Anoop: *Why don't you like classical?*

Jane: It's jus' borin'.

Andrew: Too squeaky.

Kirsty: It's got violins and trumpets and things like that, piano.

37. Tupac Shakur was a controversial 'gangsta rapper' signed to the American label Deathrow. In 1996 he was shot dead at the age of 25.

Andrew: It's got no beat! Jus' [*starts humming*].
Fern: It's jus' all plain and borin'.
Kirsty: It's like Victorian.

For particular white youth, blackness is felt to offer more exciting possibilities than the arid, encrusted remains of whiteness. Students describe Western music (including 'boy bands') as squeaky-clean, 'plain and borin'', somewhat staid, and, in the case of classical music, even 'Victorian'! The starched lifelessness of 'white' music ('it's got no (heart)beat') compares unfavourably with the energy and exuberance felt to be embedded in black cultural style. Such representations of whiteness as deathly and lifeless are similar to those expressed by Richard Dyer (1997) in his analysis of film. In contrast, Andrew explains, 'People, like, into Rap will appear like Ravers, real mad people – people like myself.' Black music, according to Andrew, captures the active dynamism of urban US street-life. His imaginative identifications across time and place suggest possibilities for reconstituting his own life. By and large it is precisely at the points where blackness holds high prestige in youth culture by way of music, sport, language, street-style and 'attitude' that it appears most deliriously attractive. Such representations are highly informative of the unspoken identifications that lie across the other side of the racial binary divide, namely whiteness. In view of the imagined sterility of whiteness, when juxtaposed against the youthful verve of black culture, some young people extended their identifications with blackness into new forms of ethnicity. As we shall now discover, for these white youth black culture offered new possibilities for reconstituting white ethnicity altogether.

White Negroes in the North East of England: The Possibilities and Constraints of Cultural Hybridity

Throughout the research, black culture appears as the silent screen upon which white youth could project their darkest fantasies of racial cross-over. For some, these experiments were little more than cultural voyeurism, a symbolic tour through the shadowy recesses of an imagined Other, but for others, the act could entail a deeper race consciousness and, at times, a flickering recognition of their own whiteness. The diverse subject positions that arise from these encounters indicate that a more thorough treatment of the possibilities/constraints of cultural hybridity is now required if we are to begin to understand contemporary racisms and ethnicities. In the absence of an established black population it appears that accelerated, global mass media images of black American 'cool' have become desirable models for many young people to follow. Helena's comment that some white youth were into 'black music but not black anything else' and James' reference to his sister who wore beads in her hair but 'does kna like black fellas' are reminders of the dangers of confusing a wish to 'be' black with the meaning of blackness as it is culturally represented in youth peer-groups. To investigate these issues further I will begin by exploring some of the limits of cultural hybridity to show how longing for the 'exotic' can consolidate essentialist notions of race. Drawing on alternative youth accounts, I will then reveal how cultural mixing can be politically useful and enable a fresh reconsideration of race, class and gender identities.

Hybrid Constraints: White Men Can't Jump?

In recent post-colonial literature cultural hybridity has been celebrated for its radical potential to disturb established racial polarities between black/white, East/ West or colonizer/colonized. It has been argued that subaltern peoples who are subjected to colonial rule may enact new forms of resistance through acts of 'mimicry' that translate and thereby alter the inscriptions of power (Spivak, 1990; Said, 1993; Bhabha, 1994). As Robert Young (1995) has noted, colonial desire is always underpinned by the threat of hybridity and so is a highly ambivalent zone where race, sexuality and fantasy intermingle. Furthermore, for Homi Bhabha cultural hybridity is even a productive force that offers a new terrain for resistance and negotiation, a 'third space which enables other positions to emerge' (1990: 211). Debates on hybridity and new ethnicities have offered insightful ways of understanding globalization and cultural cross-over in young lives. Here, the practices of the *B-Boyz* may be seen as postcolonial forms of mimicry that subvert, parody and reconfigure whiteness, race and nationhood, setting it free from any *a priori* sense of biological origins. Unsettling the racialized inscriptions that are culturally encoded in basketball, Hip-Hop, beads or braids is one way of displacing the signifiers of race from the wider grammar of racism.

Despite an evident flowering of research on post-colonialism, new ethnicities and cultural hybridity, the proliferation of transnational ethnicities has not gone hand in hand with the end of racism (Bonnett and Nayak, 2003). In particular we may remain cautious about the limitations of hybridity as a model for contemporary analysis when removed from its historical–geographic axis of nineteenth-century anxieties over inter-breeding (R. Young, 1995). Notwithstanding the multiple possibilities for racial transgression available in hybrid styles of ethnicity, it is perhaps timely 'to ask about the *limits* of cultural hybridity' (Werber, 1997:1). This liminal space, at the cross-roads of colonial encounters, has been conceptualized as a site of 'inbetweenness' (Katz, 1994; Nast, 1994) and, more combatively, as a 'contact zone' (Pratt, 1992). For Mary Louise Pratt the term '"Contact zone" is an attempt to invoke the spatial and temporal co-presence of subjects

previously separated by geographic and historical disjunctures, and whose trajectories now intersect' (1992: 6–7). However, the contact zone is not a neutral
space, but imbued with 'conditions of coercion, radical inequality and intractable
conflict' (ibid.). As Jan Nederveen Pieterse states, 'what is not clarified are the
terms under which cultural interplay and crossover take place . . . what is missing
is acknowledgement of the actual unevenness, asymmetry and inequality in global
relations' (1995:54). Thus, in the North East the desire to 'be' black is by no means
unproblematic and remains only one, rather utopian solution to the inexplicable
issue of white, English ethnicity (see Nayak 1999a).

Consequently, though a number of white peers may consider *B-Boyz* and
Girlz as 'race traitors', it would be an exaggeration to portray them as exemplars of
anti-racist practice. Their performances creatively reworked stereotypical images of
the Geordie 'lad' or 'lass' but could also reveal an adherence to a bodily discourse
of racism. To gain a more clear-eyed view regarding why certain white youth wanted
to be black, I asked the *B-Boyz* if there were any advantages to blackness.

[16–17 years]

Chris: Well from an athletics point of view I think that there are. They're good at
          most sports [. . .]. When it comes to sprinters, stuff like that, blacks seem
          more powerful.
John: There's more power thrusting you see.
Chris: The black basketball players can jump higher than the white basketballers. I
          dunno why, maybe they've got more explosive legs or something. Sprinting,
          jumping both things – explosive legs!
Suzanne: Then there are blacks who aren't that athletic at all, same as whites.
Chris: Yeah, but when you look at the athletic whites and the athletic blacks, the
          blacks are more athletic than the athletic whites.

Although the *B-Boyz* celebrate some aspects of cultural fusion, there continues
to remain a belief in a fundamental, corporeal difference between black and white
bodies. As such, their comments reveal how the complex constitution of whiteness
is reliant upon racialized Others. In an interesting historical shift, the contemporary
belief in black athletic superiority is less about seeing blacks as subhuman and
more about conveying them as superhuman. These discourses exemplify the ideas
expressed in Fanon's (1970 [1952]) *fear/desire* couplet, where whites may simultaneously project longing and loathing onto the black body by way of 'doubling'.
Both discourses converge around biological notions of bodily difference, only in
this reading it is blacks who appear the most physically evolved specimens in the
Great Chain of Being. It seems that in these accounts, the only means of interpreting black sporting achievement is through recourse to essentialism, the idea
that blacks are 'naturally' endowed with superior physical qualities on account of
their genetic capability. These differences are thought to be *embodied* by black

subjects, who are described as having explosive, power-thrusting legs which make them into majestic jumpers and lightning runners.

The silent underside of these beliefs is the fiction that 'white men can't jump', a racialized mythology which Dyer (1997) suggests has masculine reproductive connotations, related to leaping spermatozoa. Chris's earlier comments, then, resonate with a sexual envy for the mythical black body as 'hypersexual', or, in his words, 'explosive'. A belief in excessive black sporting superiority spilled into the accounts of white youth.

[9–10 years]

Andrew: If you're black you'd be like Michael Jordan, and Shaquil O'Neil and Grant Hill at the same time, cos they're coloured. Coloured people have more athletic ability. Carl Lewis was black, Michael Jordan is black, Donavon Bailey [. . .] Colin Jackson, Chris Akabusi as well. [. . .]

Fern: Black people 'ave got more skill.

Andrew: More athletic ability [. . .] They've got more flexibility, They've got the clothes as well. They've got better athletics ability, I dunno . . .

Fern: They're jus' better!

In a peculiar twist upon earlier models of racism, the claim is less about whether blacks are equal to whites but rather centres upon an imagined superior black physique. Bodily racial differences are foregrounded to suggest that black people have more skill, greater flexibility, a higher level of athleticism and, at least in this respect, are conclusively 'better' than their white counterparts. What we find in these readings is not a stable notion of white superiority, but a much more complex interplay of sexual anxieties and desires. Stuart Hall explains the ambivalent articulation of race and sexuality and its ensuing uncertainties:

> The play of identity and difference which constructs racism is powered not only by the positioning of blacks as the inferior species but also, and at the same time, by an inexpressible envy and desire; and this is something the recognition of which fundamentally *displaces* many of our hitherto stable political categories, since it implies a process of identification and otherness which is more complex than hitherto imagined. (1993:255)

It is these complex styles of racism that are most prevalent amongst contemporary youth in global times. The *Boyz* are fixated with the black body as a 'hypersexual' source of difference, displaced in awe-struck remarks concerning superior athleticism. The dangers embedded in this discourse become apparent when strategic, racialized splits are made between mind/body. The ensuing conversation concerns a discussion about the Olympic world record in long and triple jump. At the time, the long jump record was held by the American black athlete

Colin Powell and the triple jump record was held by Britain's Jonathan Edwards, a white man. Sport is seen here as an arena for the interplay of racial difference.

[16–17 years]
Chris: Well the long jump's a black man, the triple jump's a white man. The triple jump's a lot to do with technique [. . .] Depends on what you need for the sport. Long jump is just a burst, one burst of power to push yourself. But triple jump you've got to have balance and er . . .
John: You've got to measure your jump so you don't do big jumps, and then you can't do a massive one.

Even amongst the *B-Boyz*, the assertion of black superiority in certain sporting arenas is a partial, tenuous and often contradictory discourse. For the subculture, there is a clear distinction demarcating the *types* of masculine sporting prowess which blacks can be endowed with. Black sporting success is immediately related to physical differences, the muscular ability to make explosive leaps or bounds. However, white sporting success is imputed to arise because of superior 'technique' that prevails over raw power in certain situations. Furthermore, where qualities such as balance or other functions associated with the mind are required, white superiority wins out. Thus, the need to 'measure' jumps is seen to place the black athlete at a strategic disadvantage when s/he can no longer rely on a primitive 'burst of power' but has to calculate the point of departure. The idea that blacks embody athleticism on the basketball court or sports track is, then, an ambivalent attribute to be burdened with. The corollary implies that they rely upon natural brute savagery, unable to cultivate their mental skills or hone their talents. Black athletes are continually read through a bodily schema, and this may mean that their sporting success is rarely attributed to hard work, strategy, technique or timing – the mind-zone of the white man.

White youth frequently read sporting ability from the racialized body in a deterministic manner that freezes the black individual out of subjective existence. White fantasies about the black body envisioned it as a site of excess, capable of supernatural physical feats.

[16–17 yrs]
Ema: Tell you what I hate about coloured people, they're always good dancers aren't they? It really annoys me that.
Paul: I'd like to jump as high as 'em in basket-ball, it'd be great. I could jump into the hoop.
Ema: They 'ave springs.

Although there remains a general appreciation of spring-heeled black sporting ability, this success did not extend to all sports. A self-procalimed member of the

B-Boyz graphically graphically demonstrates the bodily boundaries he feels exist between black and white athletes:

Chris: I heard somewhere that black people aren't as good swimmers for reasons
(17 years) like the legs I was saying, with the jump. It's all to do with jumping. I'll tell
            you what it is right [*puts foot on desk and rolls up trouser leg*]. The twitch
            muscles or whatever they are on the bottom of your legs, just below your calf
            muscle if you can jump higher then they're more explosive, they react
            quicker to what you wanna do so maybe it's like that. If you've got explosive
            muscles down here, then you haven't got as much flexibility in yer leg as
            well. You can't kick as well, can't swim as well.

The so-called 'twitch' muscles that Chris describes and demonstrates in detail are seen as 'evidence' of an anatomical difference that suggests that blacks have 'springs' in their feet. The accounts of young students indicate that these perceived differences are double-edged. If basketball and athletics are regarded as sexualized zones of black expertise, dance and music are also seen as the cultural preserve of black people. A similar variant of the statement 'white men can't jump' is the equally familiar refrain, 'white men can't dance'. This again is a source of displaced envy for many white youth. For example, Paul (17 years), an established *B-Boy* and an ardent Hip-Hop fan, added, 'D'ya kna what I really hayut about blacks? They're all such good dancers!' That Paul and Ema should 'hate' or envy blacks, however ironically, for their reputation as 'good dancers' hints at the insecurities of whiteness and also alludes to the way these emotions collapse into one another. Here, blacks are 'hated', desired, envied and disparaged within a complex web of white anxiety. The view that black people are good dancers and more adept musically than whites is a theme echoed by young people of different ages.

[9–10 years]
Fern: Another thing is, is black peoples 'ave got more rave than English
                    people.
Anoop: *What d'you mean? You mean black people themselves or the
                    music?*
Fern: Like both. They've got more rave and that than the English people.
[. . .]
Andrew: Coloured people *look* better.
Anoop: *What d'you mean 'look better'?*
Andrew [*giggling*]: I dunno. When they're talkin' and doin' rap, they jus' *look* better!
[. . .]
Fern: I think English are like quiet and coloured people are more like
                    groovy and loud. [. . .] It's like a 'gift' thing.

It is believed that black subjects embody the magical properties of blackness in the form of a natural 'gift'. They are seen as essentially 'groovy', and able to embody 'rave' in a way that whites cannot. For anti-racist scholars and practitioners it is imperative to realize that these opinions are pervasive amongst a number of white youth, including many who did not identify as racist and would justifiably have been offended to be categorized as such. These imaginary corporeal differences also have a bearing on the constitution of whiteness. By over-investing in an imagined black lifestyle, white existence, by contrast, is seen as mundane, boring, empty. This partly explains the imaginative practices of the *B-Boyz*, who wanted to 'escape' whiteness, however fleetingly, in a symbolic journey towards a high-tan future.

Hybrid Possibilities: Re-articulating Race and Class

> White riot – I wanna riot
> White riot – a riot of my own

> 'White Riot', The Clash, 1977

In the above accounts it becomes necessary to distinguish the desire to 'be' black (which may have little to do with black subjectivity) from what is culturally ascribed to blackness as a social category. Indeed, there were a number of different versions of blackness elicited that could oscillate between a changing repertoire of African, African-American, Jamaican and Black-British styles of identity. More-over, these moments of affiliation were also classed, gendered and sexualized in particular, often unspoken, ways. Understanding claims made by white youth to 'be' black as a culturally constituted set of desires may, then, move us beyond what, at least on the surface, appears an implausible identification. The fantasy of getting into the skin of the Other is most explicitly referred to by Helena (17 years). She revealed, 'I've always had my little dream since I was like a little kid, like "Dad, why can't you be black?" Even if I'd be bullied I've always wanted the black colour and everything.' Helena went on to compare her younger self to an inverse image of the singer Michael Jackson, admitting, 'I do everything, like Michael Jackson who tries to be white, I try to be black!' Like a photographic negative, Helena sought to superimpose a reverse image of blackness upon her white self. In Helena's case the desire to 'be' black, and embody the meanings carried by this racial signifier, became so extreme it led her to remark, 'Oh, I would love being black . . . I always feel I'm not Norwegian, I'm not English. I feel like I've more in common with the black people.' Indeed, 'becoming' black had been turned into an embodied life-time project when she disclosed, 'I'm not saying I'm a black person in a white man's [*sic*] body but I wish, and I always have, that I was more tanned'.

– 126 –

Helena is especially conscious of her white pigmentation: 'I'm so white', she informed me, 'what am I gonna do?' She went on to reveal, 'I spent loads of money last year. All my money goes on sun-beds, but not now. For example: sun-beds, creams, stuff and everything.' During interview Helena identifies her desire to be black as a type of compulsive 'sickness'; it had governed her life and now she was attempting gradually to gain control over the obsession.

> Helena: My white friends in Norway, I started it off, and now they think, 'I need more tan.' I started it off and now I feel so sorry cos they're still doing it. They're lying in the sun-bed even more than me mon, they're lying there and one of my friends came with a pure black stomach and I was like, 'Woah! You're too black now, you look sickly black. No, that's not you.' I want a golden skin, like your [Anoop's] colour, but I know I'm never, ever going to get that colour, the golden thingy.

Extensive tanning under artificial ultra-violet rays is one way in which white bodies can take on the semblance of the 'exotic'. Given the time, expense and risks involved from skin cancers, this bodily regime cannot be taken lightly.

> Helena: |*Adamantly*| I want to have a colour. I want to have some tan.
> *Anoop: It's quite important to you?*
> Helena: Yeah, I think you can relax more. I can relax more when I look tanned Otherwise I think, 'Oh look at my white legs!' I can't go out without tights that have colour. |*With embarrassment*| I feel so stupid mon! [...]
> I would love to be black and have black skin. I don't wanna change my personality at all. I want to have darker skin, I would love that. It's always been my dream to have like a mixed colour.

Having moved through early-adolescent forms of experimentation, Helena now drew upon black culture in a more self-conscious, politically aware manner. This now entails locating the politics of race through an experiential understanding of social class oppression. This process involves firstly 'decoding' the attendant meaning of race as it is understood in popular youth culture. Secondly, these values have to be skilfully 'encoded' through a critically informed white working-class consciousness. This process enables white youth to negotiate new cultural references that allow them to participate in the language of oppression and resistance found in black culture and Hip-Hop music. Helena felt the messages employed in Hip-Hop and Rap had increased her class-consciousness: 'If you get in an argument with one of these Conservative people', she warned, 'you learn to stand up for your rights.' In this way, Helena sees Hip-Hop as a movement that articulates the anger and frustration of the socially and economically disenfranchised, including certain white Europeans. She had signed up to the Labour Youth Party and saw

Hip-Hop and politics as interrelated. Other white students had also thought about 'being' black, and a few had even considered the cost of racism, as we saw above. These students are not completely naive about the effects of racism, but in global times, when national or regional ties may be eroded, a disparaged identity can offer a new site for solidarity.

For example, when Andrew (10 years) asserted, 'I'd just preferred to be coloured,' I felt compelled to enquire further.

> *Anoop:* *But do you think there would be any problems with that?*
> Andrew: No, I'd like to be coloured cos if I was an' people started takin' the mick I'd jus', like, stand up for it an' not take it. Like if my friends were all coloured I'd like tell 'em [*stands up*] 'Stand up for it!'

In the coolness of academic prose it is difficult to capture the sense of passion in the above statements. When Andrew excitedly talked about 'standing up' for black rights, it seemed as if he could momentarily inhabit a black identity. When Sam declared that he wanted to be a Rasta and live in Jamaica, he appeared deadly serious, as did Helena when she challenged the casual racism of white peers. A minority of white students, then, reckoned with the consequences of racism and still professed a desire to 'be' black.

> Sam [12 years]: I'd like to be black cos [. . .] I'd like to see what the black people 'ave suffered See what I mean? Everyone says that they're h'ways bein' caal names so I'd like a'see what it was like to be black.

Although these opinions may no doubt change throughout young people's coming-of-age, it would be most disingenuous to dismiss them as insignificant phases in their lives. Consequently, the initial interest in basketball and black street-culture held by students like Chris extended into black friendships and a fuller understanding of ethnic minority experiences. Similarly Sam's fascination with Bob Marley had encouraged him to gain a certain amount of fluency in patois and black 'speak'. This had enabled him to reflect on the social messages delivered in various sound tracks. It also provided a cultural forum for learning about particular black experiences and the consequences of racism. Helena, too, believed that music and black friendships had helped her to develop a politicized race awareness so that she was critical of white appropriators who 'dissed' (disrespected) black people. This suggests that transcultural dialogues may provide young people with a looking glass with which to reflect back upon their own whiteness in a critically conscious manner.

Over a period of successive interviews in which I grew to know Helena, the apparently superficial attraction to blackness she expressed was found to have a deeper meaning than may at first be imagined. She continually reiterated how she felt 'at home' in the company of black people, and in the context of a white school and locale the shared intimacy with her best friend Beverley, a black student, stood out. This sense of comfort in black circles had been developed over a sustained period of her childhood. It also chimed with the ethos of the tight-knit working-class family set in contradistinction to bourgeois, aloof 'snobs'. I went on to enquire if Helena felt comfortable in white circles, and gained an insight into the emplacement of blackness through class.

> Helena: No. I don't feel comfortable at all. In black circles they haven't got this thing with snobs. They've got snobs, but they're more straightforward. Like snobs always look down on you. I like black circles better, in Norway I've got black friends. I would love being black.

Helena's mother worked as a nurse and her father was a school caretaker. She was bold in her social class affiliations, stating, 'I'm a working-class girl, I come from a working-class family.' 'I was in Labour Youth,' she continued, 'and I stand up for me rights in Norway, it's the same as here [the North East], we are really, really working class – it's good!' She went on to reflect, 'If it wasn't for Labour Youth I wouldn't have come here to see my working-class background.' This working-class sense of 'belonging' is, then, a critical element within her youthful biography.

> Helena: What I like about [the North East] is they're really working class. It's economic. It's like ordinary people not like snobs or anything. In Norway we got loads of snobs in the town, everyone tries to be snobs, have the most beautiful house – really nice inside – and the best clothes for a hundred pounds for example and everything. I'm working class and I show everyone I'm lower working class.

Helena was able to demonstrate a fierce working-class pride through the adoption of local culture and an appreciation of black musical style. Many of the lyrics she listened to had a particular meaning for her as a working-class young woman with a migrant history. Her experiences enabled her to draw links between racial and social class oppression. She described Hip-Hop as the style of the 'underclass', prompting me to question what she meant by this.

> Helena: Cos it's like the text in it, the words. If something was bad its about going to shoot off his head and everything, but if you look under the text at the lyrics it's about the underclass. That's how I see it anyhow.

Helena is thus involved in a creative reconstruction of black music: she decodes its political meanings and applies them to certain aspects of white, working-class identity. As a 'foreigner' coming from Norway, Helena has a peculiar status in

Britain as a type of white-outsider-within. When discussing her tattoo, it is evident that identity is a central issue to her.

> Helena: [*Lifting up shirt top to reveal Chinese motif on lower back*] Here! It means happiness. That's what I want. They saw my belly-button and five minutes later they all had it pierced and tattoos done. It's funny like cos I'm a foreigner and suddenly everyone's taking my style! It's strange mon. […]
>
> *Anoop: What made you choose that particular tattoo?*
>
> Helena: I was thinking of a dolphin cos that's my sign of freedom and I wanted it on me ankle but thought, 'That's gonna kill, that.' Then I thought, 'I don't want a dolphin up there' [*on her back*] cos that would be stupid, like Mark in Take That [a defunct 'boy band']. Then I thought I'd have a Chinese sign of something I really care about. That's what it means in my head. It's quite deep.

In the same way that Helena can read 'beneath' the lyrics of Hip-Hop to access a 'deeper text' related to social justice, she likewise sees her tattoo as more than just a fashion symbol. The Chinese motif signifies her multi-ethnic affiliations, sense of mystery and philosophical outlook on life. It is something she personally feels strongly about and recognizes to be 'quite deep'. The ability to go 'beneath' the surface of whiteness and explore hidden depths – a form of critical youth deconstruction – is a theme that emerges at various points in Helena's narratives. When discussing her upbringing and the pervasive attitudes towards racism, she rhapsodized, 'I look *behind* colour, that's the way my family brought me up.'

By reading race and class through one another, Helena is able to identify with black people and utilize the language of the oppressed. Moreover, she is critical of middle-class white youth who selectively appropriate what she now understands to be 'her' black street-style.

> Helena: I had me own music and now the posh ones are into it, it's horrible. They never liked it before and said, 'I hate Hip-Hop, it's an underclass thing.' I was like mad, really, really mad. They were stealing *my* style, *my* music and everything – it was *nothing* to do with them! That's what I thought anyway.

Helena is able to align herself with black expressive styles through her identification as working class. By locating herself within a broader notion of an 'underclass' she can thereby lay earnest claim to Hip-Hop and Swing culture as part of her own culture, 'my style, my music'. Her rejection of 'posh ones' gaining access to black culture is a direct criticism of a commercially driven (white) desire to appropriate the Other through global marketing. Helena is not interested in the superficial consumption of black music. For her it represents a 'lived' style that she inhabits in her outward dress code and inner value system. She is particularly critical of white youth who appropriate the surface skin of black culture without looking 'under the text' at the deeper political meanings carried. Helena has transformed herself into a moral guardian against the cultural theft of black style, a politic that extends from music and clothes onto the dance floor.

> Helena: Before, they [white youth] were talking behind me back about me clothes style and now everyone's wearing it and have started to hear me music. When I went on the dance floor – I like dance 'black' or whatever you wanna call it, like butterflies and everything – and they'd say, 'What the hell is she doing?' And they've now started copying my style. Everything I do, they do. I don't like that.
>
> Anoop: *But might there be black kids who are saying, 'All these white kids are stealing our style'?*
>
> [. . .]
>
> Helena: They do say that . . . If you say like you like football here [the North East], lads say, 'That's a man's thing to do,' it's the same: you have to *prove* you like it.

Helena demonstrates a commitment to black culture that extended beyond the exterior gloss of contemporary fashion. She has earned her spurs by regularly attending black cultural events, often on her own, and slowly making friends with people there. At the start she encountered scepticism from black youth for her initial forays into Hip-Hop and Swing, but now she feels more at home in these circles. While she maintains that she is totally comfortable at black cultural events, it would appear that this level of ease has been acquired through a gradual process of acceptance. She describes her early experience of attending predominantly black venues.

> Helena: They [black people] started . . . saying, 'White woman, white woman, white sheep'. It gets to you sometimes. When you don't know anyone you feel always alone.

By demonstrating a commitment to black culture, Helena has overcome black suspicion. It is to her credit that her persistence has earned her a degree of respect and acceptance from black youth, and that she is recognized as someone other than a 'white impostor'. Furthermore, as noted previously, she did not hesitate to counter the white racism of her peers. At times this means making a direct stance against complicit white bonding, especially when she is in the company of black friends.

> Helena: I always get assumptions like from the lads who say, 'The lass is trying to be cool like.' They say, 'Why are you talking to her, she's black?', in my home in Norway. I'm like, 'Sharrup!' I don't talk to him, so I'm like never ever talk to 'em mon. When they're sitting there, I look ugly at 'em and just never talk to him so he never talks to me.

Helena is able to use black language, postures and gestures to resist the racism of white peers. At such moments she is able to vacate a concept of white identity that draws on an allegiance to nationalism and racism, and take up an alternative subject position located in the making of new ethnicities. As a 'race traitor' she has proved that she is unprepared to take up the baton of whiteness that is held out to her by a group of white, young men. Her refusal to do this, and the vernacular response 'Sharrup!', culminates in a proud statement, 'I look ugly at 'em!'.

Here, cultural hybridity can allow for 'the possibility of new, positive ethnic anti-racist identity fusions' (Werbner, 1997:16). These may be lived out on the surfaces of the body and enacted in stylized gestures and performances, but may also be understood through a deeper, critical race consciousness. By using her body as a type of 'corporeal canvas', Helena could express a multicultural identity invoked through belly-button piercing and tattooing. 'I've got a Chinese tattoo on us,' she revealed, 'I think its cool, Chinese signs and everything. I used to wear some Chinese clothes that were silky.' As we have seen, there exists a subtle delineation demarcating sensitive forms of acceptable multicultural participation from the unbridled practices of white seizure. It appears that white youth who have been involved in aspects of black cultural identification for a longer period of time are more likely to view themselves as defenders against potential white appropriators.

> Helena: I like the music and everyone's like [*derogatory tone*], 'Ugh, she likes Hip-Hop.' There was no one else that likes it. And a couple of years ago some started to say [*positive tone*], 'Oh, she likes Hip-Hop, wow, it's cool. She likes baggy clothes, maybe I'll wear it.' And they started wearing it.

In contrast to participants of youth ethnic commodification, Helena views cultural syncretism as an embodied politics that could be practised in everyday life. She sees the fusion of style as a way of breaking down barriers and a means of creating new, hitherto unexplored identities. This is evident in her description of a recent Swing concert she attended.

> Helena: There was this Asian rapper who was swinging and she had also Asian tones on the top. She was rapping, swinging a bit, she had this Asian thing too. She was brilliant! I think it's cool – it's a mixture of each culture. That's what I want, a mixture.

It would appear that contemporary artists such as Apache Indian, Talvin Singh, Asian Dub Foundation, Nitan Sawney, Cornershop, Punjabi MC and Fun Da Mental are creating new zones of cultural inquiry in the 'third space' of British Asian culture (Bhabha, 1990, 1994). These musicians are moving beyond black/

white racial dualisms by drawing on a spectrum of multi-ethnic influences. Despite the celebration of syncreticism witnessed above, Helena remained sceptical of white appropriators who 'stole' black style and a friend whose sun-tan she described as an excessive, 'sickly black'. She was equally scathing about the status of many white rap artists. 'The white rappers in Norway for example, they're shite!' she affirmed.[38] Indeed, in the predominantly black arena of Hip-Hop, whiteness, for once, is brought out into the open. Here, white identities are made aware of their ethnic particularity so that the norm of whiteness is disrupted. Thus, white rappers have frequently deployed an appellation that alludes to whiteness, as can be seen in the street names of white artists such as Vanilla Ice and Snow. The recent credibility bestowed upon white rappers such as Eminem is indicative of new identities and more recent possibilities for articulating white injustice through a Southern American poor, rural, 'trailer park trash' subjectivity.

Helena also utilized the radical potential of a politics of race and class based on inter-mixture. She explained her multicultural perspective on the nation, remarking, 'I would say like that England is a big mixture of loads of cultures combined.' Indeed, her own subjectivity is informed by a series of partial identifications, including notions of blackness, working-classness, 'Geordie' and Norwegian identity. Moreover, this is not a point of cultural confusion but a mark of achievement – 'That's what I want, a mixture' – that comes to inform a conscious, hybrid politics of subversion.

Anoop: Is that what you're living out, a mixture?
Helena: Yeah, that's what I'm trying. I mix culture and everything. I think it's ridiculous, there's all different cultures and we should learn about each other . . . I'm living it out, I'm a mixture! I'm not just saying it in my words and all, I'm *doing* it.

In Helena's experience, culture is not pretentious or abstract, but something that you 'live out' and 'do'. She makes a distinction between cultural syncretism as a form of benign appropriation, and syncretism as a politically informed way of being. 'Doing' cultural identity in this manner can be a troubling prospect for sacred governors of whiteness such as the *Real Geordies*. Helena's style is a conscious celebration of syncretism and blends different cultural forms to produce new meanings and points of identification. Rather than interpret these exchanges as simple forms of incorporation, it has been suggested that these exchanges may,

38. In a study of 30 middle-aged white women involved in the African-American jazz scene Patricia Sunderland (1997) identified a similar type of discourse. This led her to 'take seriously the possibility that for these European American women, all that was African signified positive and desirable, and all that was non-African did not' (p. 36).

at times, produce radical moments of disruption in the broader signifying chain of representation. Recounting Helena's musical 'mix-'n'-match' interests in these terms, we find no 'original' point of production; rather, a polyglot process of global influences drawn from America, Jamaica, Africa, Britain, China, Norway, etc. Even so, Helena's distrust of white youth who pilfer black culture is well founded and she herself is sensitive to the historical 'traces' which inform her own cultural practice. By mixing styles, Helena disturbs notions of cultures as hermetically sealed categories. In a sense, the boundaries between Us/Other were disrupted in a radical blurring of social categories.

Moreover, this is a culturally aware politics of transgression performed through dress, language and gesture.

> Anoop: *Are your going-out clothes a 'black' style?*
> Helena: I would say mix. It's like [*gesturing with hand*] mix-mix-mix! [...] I usually like going white-skinned carrying my belly-button pierce, with me tattoos. I was the first one, now all the lasses wear it in the school. It's Chinese style.

Unsettling whiteness through culturally hybrid youth styles is, then, one way of reforming white identities in the present post-imperial moment. The personal costs involved mean that derogatory labels can be incurred from both sides of the cultural divide, where the individual may be labelled a *Wigger*, a *Wannabe* or 'white sheep'. However, 'crossing-over' still retains subversive potential for contemporary postcolonial critics who claim that cultural hybridity may yet 'turn the gaze from the discriminated back upon the eye of power' (Bhabha, 1984:97).

Concluding Remarks

The *White Wannabes* occupy different, but no less complex youthscapes to those mapped by the *Real Geordies* and *Charver Kids*. Evidently they are sited, and position themselves, differently in relation to local–global change, flaunting their new ethnicities in a bid to escape parochial forms of whiteness. Their cultural attachments to basketball, Hip-Hop music and baggy clothes are seen by other youth as evidence that they are modern society's contemporary *White Negroes*. In many respects the young people whose lives are discussed in this chapter can be seen as white mavericks, individuals who subvert the acceptable boundaries of white, English ethnicity through hybrid interactions with global cultures. At the local level the cost of this transgression can result in prejudice and verbal abuse from peers. These renegade youth had once been described to me as Albino Kings: white youth who could reign over the symbolic values of black culture in the absence of a prominent black population. This void enables the subculture to distinguish themselves as the cutting-edge pioneers of cultural syncretism.

Although many are content with living in the region, a number expressed a desire to move abroad or relocate to multi-ethnic cities where it was felt more jobs and excitement are on offer. The discussion reveals that a sustained engagement with black culture through the medium of dance or basketball can open up rare avenues through which white youth may come to meet other black acquaintances in Tyneside. Where such liaisons have occurred there is the possibility of forming lasting friendships with black peers as white youth gradually became educated in the learning of new urban dialogues. At the same time some Albino Kings held highly contradictory attitudes to black people in which the body was transformed into a site of fetishization, projection and longing. For many *Wannabes* their own bodies are zones for pleasure and adornment. These nuances indicate the variety of subject positions taken up by white youth in relation to the production of blackness in the global marketplace. Furthermore, they illustrate the fragile nature of multi-ethnic relations in a predominantly white area wherein young people may or may not move beyond racially loaded understandings through syncretic youth styles. This implies a lack of equivalence between cultural hybridity and anti-racism in the lives of young people. Despite these limitations there is evidence that young people can yet 'decode' the grammar of race and tear it from the wider vocabulary of racism. The signifier can then be 'encoded' and given a new personal meaning through the 'twisting' of race and class. The making of a new cultural heritage is at stake in this complex negotiation of white ethnicity and global change in the post-industrial city.

Part III
Coming Times

–7–

Contemporary Racisms and Ethnicities: Rethinking Racial Binaries

Introduction

What does it mean to be young and white in the present post-imperial moment? Until relatively recently few anti-racist scholars or practitioners would have concerned themselves with such a thorny issue. Thus a cursory review of the extant literature on race and ethnicity boasts a number of important studies focusing on the schooling experience of visible minorities (particularly those identified as black or Asian) in multi-ethnic institutions (Fuller, 1982; Mac an Ghaill, 1988; Gillborn, 1990; Sewell, 1997; Connolly, 1998) with little meaningful discussion of whiteness. While this work has continued apace, the striking contradiction is that we now seem to know far less about the racialized identities of the ethnic majority (notably English whites) and who they are in the present post-imperial moment. The 'burden of representation' endured by visible minorities has unwittingly implied that they have an ethnicity or a culture whilst others, in particular the white English, have not. This has led to an over-racialization of visible minorities at the expense of a de-racialization of ethnic majorities. A pressing question for race and ethnic scholars may now centre on the identities of the hitherto under-researched white-Anglo majority – who they are and who they may yet 'become'.

To date there have been very few race studies which have explored the ethnicities of white youth in any sufficient detail. Moore's (1994) study of Skinheads in Perth and Bell's (1990) account of youth marching bands in Ulster each offer valuable insights into how a sense of white English ethnicity could be re-constituted and celebrated in the context of Australia and Northern Ireland alike. Excellent ethnographies by Hewitt (1986), Jones (1988), Back (1996) and Cohen (1997) also go some way to shedding light upon new ethnicities and black–white cross-cultural interaction in urban spaces. Even so, there has been a distinct geography marking much of this work. The thick creolization that occurs in the multicultural crucible of the British inner city has enabled these spaces to become the primary sites of investigation. At the same time there is a tendency to explore the extremities of whiteness – white Rastafarians, National Front supporters, Skinheads, Loyalists or white youth who wish to present as black.

So what about the majority of white youth whose lives do not register with these categories and the extremities of whiteness? For, as Diana Jeater observes, most white Anglo-youth 'don't feel they have an "ethnicity", or if they do, that it's not one they feel too good about' (1992:107).[39] Far harder, then, to engage with the normalcy of whiteness as ordinary, monotonous or humdrum. Indeed, the sub-cultural analysis of *Real Geordies* and *Charvers* provides more mundane portraits of whiteness that are subtly textured by class, locality, gender and generation. The more difficult challenge is now to investigate the power and invisibility of white-ness in daily settings to illustrate how these relations structure a myriad of youth encounters. As such, there is a paucity of detailed, qualitative research concerning why young white people may view their racial identities as problematic; and even less regarding the issue of what can be done about this. In support of this, I provocatively asked some older students I knew to provide me with the stereotype of a white person. The reply below illustrates the way white racial identities can become straitjacketed by association with extreme racism.

|16–17 years|

John: You've got like the blonde bimbo; you've got like the Skinhead. You think, 'Oh God.'

Chris: You think like racist, Nazi kind of stuff, Skinheads.

Henry Giroux asks the pertinent question, 'What subjectivities or points of identification become available to white students who can imagine white experience only as monolithic, self-contained, and deeply racist?' (1997b:310). This view has hardly softened in wake of the acquittal of the 'prime suspects' involved in the trial against the murder of the young black British teenager Stephen Lawrence (see MacPherson, 1999). In the post-colonial moment of population movements, new settlements and the resurgence of nationalism, understanding the contingency of white, English ethnicity and the multiple, fragmented forms of identity young people come to inhabit remains paramount. A failure to engage with this issue may bolster the image of white masculinities and femininities as, respectively, the 'Skinhead' or 'Blonde bimbo'. To develop new subject positions, this chapter seeks to address the question of white-Anglo ethnicities at theoretical, empirical and political levels. The objective is certainly not to revitalize whiteness by arguing for an inclusive multiculturalism that celebrates 'white heritage' through such curious rituals as Morris dancing, queuing and afternoon tea: there is enough 'white pride' already. Instead, the theory-led discussion draws upon recent insights in the field

39. The need to understand white identity is signalled in a study by Ann Phoenix (1997) of 248 young Londoners (14–18 years). She found 92 per cent of black youth and 77 per cent of mixed-heritage youth claimed to be proud of their colour, while only 34 per cent of whites shared this feeling.

of race and ethnic studies developed from post-structuralist and psychoanalytic paradigms. This is allied with a critical ethnography that accesses the perspectives of white youth in order to develop a place-specific and culturally meaningful anti-racist pedagogy for 'new times'.

Rethinking the Black/White Binary: Post-structuralist and Psychoanalytical Interventions

> My involvement with radical politics on the left had taught me to disavow the racial exclusivity of white ethnicity, but never to analyse or try and understand it. [...]. The problem with intellectually disowning English ethnicity was that the left never got around to working out what it was, and what our own emotional connections to it were ...
>
> Jonathan Rutherford, *Forever England* (1997).

For Rutherford's Leftist-generation depicted above, white, English ethnicity was a landscape long given over to the Right, and as such had become an unknown continent to be disowned or disavowed. The problem with expelling ethnicity in this manner is that the projected form continues to return in other, less visible guises, rather like a white phantom in serious need of an exorcism. The failure to engage with white, English ethnicity was made acutely apparent in a poignant study of Burnage High School, Manchester, which followed the fatal stabbing of an Asian youth, Ahmed Iqbal Ullah, by a white male, Darren Coulburn, in 1986. The team-led inquiry into the reasons behind the 'murder in the playground' (MacDonald *et al.*, 1989) produced a comprehensive account of student race relations in what was to become known as the Burnage Report. The Report highlighted the lack of attention paid by anti-racist initiatives to the needs and perspectives of white (especially working-class) students, who were treated as 'cultureless', wandering spirits.[40] The gravity of this omission meant that 'many of the students, especially those in the "English" category, had little or no notion of their own ethnicity and were agitated and made insecure by their confusion or else showed anger and resentment . . .' (MacDonald *et al.*, 1989:392). In short, the school's attempt to disavow white, English ethnicity did not make it magically disappear altogether; instead, these emotional investments fatally returned in the

40. The Report was later hijacked by sections of the press to make the spurious claim that the school's anti-racist policy led to the murder of Ahmed. This, of course, had been a misreading of the findings proposed by the inquiry, which had stated almost the reverse: anti-racism needed to be *extended* to incorporate white youth rather than retracted (see Rattansi, 1993, for more details). To avoid further confusion, I would like to state at the outset that any criticism of anti-racism made in this chapter is to be carefully placed within this caveat.

guise of a racist murder. It was not the institution's anti-racist policies that were to blame, but rather the limited extent to which these initiatives touched the everyday lives of students. For these reasons, this chapter seeks to address how whiteness, Englishness and ethnicity are experienced by white youth in school-based cultures.[41] By focusing on whiteness and Englishness in student cultures, I aim to expose the varied, ambivalent connections to race and nationhood undertaken by the dominant ethnic majority.

Although some writers have provided compelling post-structuralist analyses which deconstruct the 'making' of white youthful identities in school, few have indicated how (if at all) oppressive styles of whiteness can be challenged, resisted or transformed. This chapter seeks to understand the meaning of whiteness in young people's lives by exploring how white racial identity is 'lived out' in classroom contexts. Moreover, it argues for an engagement with white, English ethnicities and outlines how this task was undertaken in Tyneside schools. The research points to the need for the development of critical projects on whiteness which may take their lead from post-structuralist accounts, and so move beyond what Henry Giroux describes as 'the jaundiced view of Whiteness as simply a trope of domination' (1997a:302). Instead, I want to suggest that we need to reconceptualize what it is to be white and English in the current post-colonial period.

Recent post-structuralist approaches in the area of ethnicity have begun to challenge the fixity of black/white models of race and racism. For example, contemporary cultural theorists have indicated that racism is not something that is inherent amongst white youth as a consequence of racial privilege, but, rather, all ethnicities are 'suffused with elements of sexual and class difference and therefore fractured and criss-crossed around a number of axes and identities' (Rattansi, 1993:37). This approach has called for the need to further develop anti-oppressive models of identity politics that were formerly concerned with the social exclusion of minority groups and how relations of power constructed these subjectivities as subordinate. In this reading, whites and blacks, for instance, are inherently located in a respective power dynamic of dominance and subordinance. It is the social inequalities of racism that mark out the terrain upon which black and white actors are located. Here, power is a dangerous, determining force that benefits white citizens at the expense of oppressing their black counterparts.

Such a rationalist account of the effects of power, and how it is lived out, has been most thoroughly critiqued by the French analyst Michel Foucault (1980, 1988). For Foucault, power is not uniformly experienced, nor is it a wholly

---

41. Elsewhere I have discussed how whiteness is variously negotitated by Asian, African-Caribbean, Jewish and mixed-heritage people (of Irish/Asian and Anglo/Asian descent) in educational arenas (Nayak, 1997).

negating activity. Instead, it is conceptualized as *productive* since it 'doesn't only weigh on us as a force that says no . . . it induces pleasure, forms of knowledge, produces discourses' (1980:119). Here, power relations are continually produced and reproduced in often unpredictable ways as the contours of oppression and resistance shift and intertwine. Rather than seeing power as a simple matter of closed binaries – white/black, men/women, straight/gay, bourgeoisie/proletariat – where the former categories come to dominate and subsume the latter elements of the dichotomous equation, post-structuralist analyses investigate the multiple interconnections between race, gender, sexuality and social class, to ask how these processes can be seen to interact, and so inflect one another.

More lately, some writers have used psychoanalytical approaches to avoid overly rational, simplistic conceptions of young people's social power relationships. In so doing they have pointed towards unconscious investments, unspeakable fears and desires, complex structures of feeling (Walkerdine, 1990; Cohen, 1993; Hall, 1993; Henriques *et al.*, 1998 [1984]). Psychoanalytical responses mark a crucial step forward in the movement from a fascination with black subjectivity, towards a renewed interrogation of whiteness. As such, accepted discourses of racism are turned upside-down, or, to be more accurate, 'inside-out'. It is within the internal landscape of subjectivity, then, that racial identities come to be given deeper meaning and expression. As the writings of the French-Martinque psychiatrist Frantz Fanon (1967 [1952]) have shown, the construction of one particular racial or cultural identity (black, white, racist or anti-racist) is relationally dependent on the displacement of another, unspoken, often less desirable identity. So this process of rejection is not a neat, clinical method of expulsion. Like a shadow cast by a moving figure, the sublimated identity is ever present in the act of subjectivity, operating in the dark margins of the unconscious. This inability to truly escape the shadow of whiteness means that the Negro that is the subject of Fanon's inquiry 'is forever in combat with his own image' (p. 136) as the split between Self/Other comes to rupture essentialist notions of black subjectivity.

In psychoanalytic understandings of subjecthood, then, identity must be understood as a perpetual process of symbolic interplay and recurring ambivalence. The established racial polarities that come to make up the black/white binary then dissolve in the knowledge that they are each partially constituted by – and come to embody – the inner configurations of the Other, albeit as image or imago. For as Fanon so lucidly reveals, it is not just a question of external interactions (black skin/white skin), but rather a dynamic that now encompasses inner compulsions, better encapsulated as 'black skin'/white masks'. In this example, it is the suppressed emotional connections to whiteness that continue to cause anxiety to the Negro long after the process of de-colonization has taken place. Small wonder that Frantz Fanon, in his typically forensic analysis, compares his own encounters with

whites in terms of a fractured epidermal schema that evokes corporeal metaphors
of psychic scarring, splitting and internal rupture.

As such, the post-structuralist and psychoanalytically informed arguments have
produced refined understandings of young people's lives that may be of primary
relevance to anti-racist and feminist practitioners alike. Thus, in their landmark
study of school anti-racism, the authors of the Burnage Report (MacDonald *et al.*,
1989) found they could no longer view the death of Ahmed Iqbal Ullah as simply
a matter of white power (although this dynamic informed the attack). Instead, they
were led to consider, 'Did Ahmed Ullah die at the cross-roads where the power of
masculinity, male dominance, violence and racism intersect?' (p. 143). Here, issues
of gender and power form part of the cultural nexus through which racist violence
can be understood, where epithets such as 'paki' may be shot through with 'feminine' or 'homosexual' connotations. On the other hand, teachers and pupils repre-
senting blackness as dangerous, physically aggressive and sexually alluring may
encode certain black masculinities in a stridently 'phallic' manner (Mac an Ghaill,
1997 [1994]; Sewell, 1997). However, this phallic assemblage occurs in the realm
of the imaginary and is only articulated beyond the level of the symbolic order
through tropes, motifs and the mythologies that come to surround black masculinity. The silent underside of this psychic manifestation is the construction of
whiteness as simply absence or 'lack', an issue that will become apparent in the
empirical sections. Extrapolating from Fanon, then, it may not only be the negro
that is now in conflict with his or her own image, but the post-imperial generation
of white English youth who are struggling to fashion a new sense of place and
identity in changing global times.

Significantly, such critical readings on gender and ethnicity can furnish anti-
racist and feminist scholars or practitioners with new theoretical perspectives to
interpret the cultural identities of young people. In particular, the post-structuralist
and psychoanalytical appreciation of ambivalence in the face of a deterministic
rationalism can inform us of how young people may express a fetishistic fascination toward selective aspects of black popular culture while retaining an unbridled
investment in white chauvinism (Hebdige, 1987 [1979]). Seeing whiteness as a
discursive formation – and a most contradictory one at that – can then widen the
aperture of race analysis. In such readings young people's racist expressions can
be understood as 'situated responses', further articulated through the discursive
matrices of gender and sexuality. Here, issues of context, power and subject
positionality come to complicate any 'simple' understandings that invoke a
racial binary. The issue of 'positionality' now remains central, where 'a thorough
"pedagogy of positionality" must entail an excavation of Whiteness in its many
dimensions and complexities' (Maher and Tetreault, 1997:322).

Recently, a number of writers have expressed dissatisfaction with black/white
models of racism. A key proponent in the UK remains Tariq Modood, who offers

a robust challenge of the common usage of the term 'black' (or, more conventionally, 'Black'), indicating that policy debates within this frame occlude the diverse experiences of South Asian peoples in particular (see especially Modood, 1988). Here, the multicultural and anti-racist factions that conveniently came to congregate beneath the shared umbrella of a black/white dichotomy are now finding that such assumptions are increasingly strained at the level of theory, political practice and cultural identity formation.

In particular, recent work on 'new ethnicities' and global change has offered a not wholly unproblematic challenge to these earlier models of race and racism. This research has been more attentive to emerging forms of cultural syncretism, hybridity and a new urban ecology (Hall, 1993; Back, 1996; Cohen, 1999). Notably, 'new ethnicities' studies have sparked a post-structuralist clamour to do away with 'the innocent notion of the essential black subject' (Hall, 1993:254). But if this line is to be pursued, by the same token is there not now a need to do away with essentialist notions of white youthful subjects as either 'anti-racist angels' or 'racist demons'? Such questions point to a move away from binary relations of racism (black/white) towards composite forms of discrimination and internal gradations within the categories 'white' and 'black'. By deconstructing whiteness in this way one may allude to inter-ethnic nuances such as the tainted status of the 'bogus' Eastern European asylum seeker or those white minority groups whose cultural experiences do not chime easily with the ideological harmonies adhered to by the Anglo ethnic majority. Here, established types of racism may continue but they have also fragmented and multiplied into new, sometimes contradictory, expressions of hostility, as we shall go on to discover (Cohen, 1993; Rattansi, 1993; Back, 1996; Gillborn, 1996).

Classroom Cultures and Racist Name-Calling: Ethnic Majority Perspectives

> The celebratory language of multi-culturalism has tended to reproduce Asian and black British people as Other simply because it never took white English ethnicity as problematic. Similarly white anti-racism in its disavowal of whiteness and English ethnicity ignored or denigrated white people's emotional attachments to their ethnicity. Neither strategy provided the space to analyse whiteness and English ethnicity and make it a subject of debate.
>
> Jonathan Rutherford, *Forever England* (1997)

Schools are agencies for the production of racial identities via the curricula, beliefs, values and attitudes propagated. In this sense, they cannot be regarded as institutions which passively reflect or mechanically reproduce social relations of race. There already exists an extensive literature on how school authorities use racist labels to interpret the experiences of black youth, and how teacher typologies and classroom cultures differently affect the behaviour and performance of these students (Coard, 1982; Driver, 1982; Fuller, 1982; Mac an Ghaill, 1988; Sewell, 1997). Moreover, ethnic identities are continually negotiated through student/teacher interactions, and the complex interplay of student cultures themselves.

The old assumption that schools in majority-white preserves are free from racism has now been rendered problematic (Gaine, 1987, 1995; Tomlinson, 1990; Short and Carrington, 1992; Troyna and Hatcher, 1992a). Indeed, this research indicates that anti-racism may be of more import in all-but-white locales, a view supported by the Swann Committee: 'Whilst most people would accept that there may be a degree of inter-racial tension between groups in schools with substantial ethnic minority populations, it might generally be felt that racist attitudes and behaviour would be less common in schools with few or no ethnic minority pupils . . . we believe this is far from the case' (Department of Education and Science, 1985:36).

In Emblevale School white students were at times critical of the existing anti-racist policy, though few indicated that it should be done away with. Many believed racism should be challenged, yet were scathing of the current institutional structure of anti-racism that viewed them as inherently privileged (Gillborn, 1996). Instead, they saw the occasional 'special' session on multiculturalism as evidence of a 'bias' towards minority pupils (Jeffcoate, 1982). For example, during the fieldwork period an announcement was made over the school tannoy asking all Asian students who were interested in Indian cooking to go to the school hall, where a demonstration was in progress. Asian children were frequently racialized in this manner as exotically, unalterably different when it came to daily social routines. Similarly, there was an assumption that white children were only concerned with what lay directly within 'their' cultural realm of experience. I later spoke with a teacher who mentioned having white students in her class who were very interested in the session, and resented what they perceived to be a form of white social exclusion. Thankfully, the teacher ignored the assumptions embedded in the statement (that only Asian children are interested in Indian food) and sent a mixed cohort of willing pupils.

In her own pedagogic practice Christine Sleeter (1993) found that such forms of multiculturalism all too readily failed to engage with whiteness. She recalls, 'When teachers told me about "multicultural lessons" or "multicultural bulletin boards", what they usually drew my attention to was the flat representations of people of colour that had been added; multidimentional representations of whiteness throughout the school were treated as a neutral background not requiring comment' (1993:166–77). Here, whiteness is construed as normative, the blank canvas of experience, or what Alastair Bonnett has termed, 'the Other of ethnicity' (1993b: 175–6). The perception that some teachers had was that white working-class students had no culture, yet this was in direct contrast to how young people experienced 'Geordie' identity within the locality. In contrast, young people continually stressed local ties and a genuine pride in being 'Geordies'. Moreover, these students felt that their black peers were strategically advantaged when it came to interracial conflict.

|11–12 years|

Anoop: *Are there any advantages to being white in this school?*

Nicola: Well, no.

Michelle: Cos coloured people can call us |names|.

James: It's not fair reely cos they can call us like 'milk-bottles' and that, but us can't call them.

Sam: The thing is in this school, is like if you're racist you get expelled or something, but they [blacks] can call us names and the teachers don't tek any notice of it.

James: They tek no notice.

The school's sensitivity to racist harassment appeared to bolster white injustice among respondents, and create a feeling that such forms of 'moral' anti-racism were 'not fair' (see also MacDonald *et al.* 1989; Hewitt, 1996). That teachers were said to ignore claims of name-calling made by black students, yet expel white students for using racist taunts, affirmed a sense of white defensiveness. These feelings may be more pronounced in multiracial locations and ethnically diverse schools. Certainly, while researching in the West Midlands, white students made it clear to me that black males were often the most feared, respected and visible youth group within inner-city schools, encouraging white peers to state, 'How can they be victims?' At its most extreme, a disillusioned white student (16 years) in a large, urban, multiracial school in Birmingham responded to my question if he thought the school was racist, by claiming, 'Yeah, it is – this school's racist against its own kind!' Where a large number of black students exist, this may not be an unusual sentiment. David Gillborn describes a similar feeling amongst white students in London provinces:

In particular, white students pinpointed a shift in power that seemed to privilege minority perspectives and deny legitimacy to whites' experiences. This issue . . . arises from the multiple locations inhabited by white students as class, race, gender and sexual subjects: the assertion that whiteness ultimately defines them as powerful oppressors simply does not accord with the lived experience of many working-class white students. (1996:170)

However, even in the white locales of Tyneside some youth maintained that black students were given preferential treatment deemed 'unfair'. Furthermore, it was said that they could even exploit this situation when it came to name-calling.

Anoop:	*So what do the name-callers say?*
Michelle:	Things like 'milk-bottle'.
James:	And 'whitey'.
Michelle:	And 'milky way' and things.

Alongside the opinion that anti-racism was 'unfair' to the needs of white youth ran an overwhelming feeling that black students had an identifiable culture that they could draw on which was denied to English whites. Moreover, the positive expression of black ethnicities could be experienced by sceptical white youth as a broader exclusionary device.

Sam:	What I don't like is all the Pakistani people all talk in their language an' you dunno what they're talkin' about. Used to be this lad in our class, Shaheed, he would talk to his mate Abdul, half in English, half in another language.
Nicola:	If they wanna talk about you they can talk in another language.
Michelle:	If we wanna talk about them, they know what we're sayin'.

Again, the implication is that it is white youth who are culturally impaired in exchanges with their black counterparts. This is a reversal of older academic assumptions that it is black students who are compromised, 'caught between two cultures'. Instead, as globalization takes hold and cultures dynamically cross-fertilize, white youth in Emblevale were keen to emphasize the advantages of being bilingual and the classroom benefits of being construed as the potential victims of racist harassment. Troyna and Hatcher (1992a) also found that positive assertions of black identity were frequently viewed by white children as an attempt at dominance. However, the choice for minority students within the predominantly white region appeared to be 'act white' or 'return' to Tyneside's multi-ethnic urban interior.

Emblevale students were keen to make a careful distinction between racism as a discourse of power available to them through regimes of representation (in language, speech, metaphors and imagery); and racism as a 'chosen' subject position that was explicitly ideological and practised in daily, vehement exchanges. Whereas the former stance offered a latent potential for racist enactment, triggered only at certain moments, the latter position was more readily condemned as explicitly racist and wholly unegalitarian. It is this 'unevenness' of racism in young people's lives that we need to be attentive to. The grainy line separating what white students said to their black peers in certain situations, and how they felt towards them more generally, became a source of tension when episodes of racism surfaced in classroom contexts. Most specifically, in fraught, personal exchanges between students, racist name-calling offered an inviting mode of redress for whites.

Sam: We canna sey anythin' cos they [black students] can get us annoyed and it's hard
not calling them a racist name or somethin'. I never bin racist cos I don't think it's
right but some people jus' think it's hard to not call them a racist name if an
argument starts.

The student responses listed here signal a confusion regarding the issue of why
white racial epithets such as 'whitey', 'milk-bottle' or 'milky way' are not construed as forms of racist name-calling. As other researchers have implied the
meanings carried in white derogatory terms rarely carry the same weight as anti-
black racist terminology (Back, 1990; Troyna and Hatcher, 1992a). Troyna and
Hatcher (1992a, 1992b) argue that racial insults such as 'white duck' or 'ice-cream'
must be carefully distinguished from terms such as 'paki', which are saturated with
racist power: 'Black children wanting to call racial names back faced several
problems. First, the white racist vocabulary was much richer, as many children
recognized. . . . Second, white children knew that there was no social sanction
against white skin. . . . The third problem concerns the issue of "nation". There was
no reverse equivalent to the racist name-calling of "Paki". . .' (1992a:158). In
Troyna and Hatcher's (1992a, 1992b) definition, it is precisely because black and
white students occupy different structural positions of dominance and subordinance in race relations that white epithets are considered 'racial' name-calling
forms and black epithets are viewed as 'racist' name-calling terms. Here, there is
no equivalence between black and white name-calling, as ultimately, 'Racist
attacks (by whites on blacks) are part of a coherent ideology of oppression which
is not true when blacks attack whites, or indeed, when there is conflict between
members of different ethnic minority groups' (1992b:495). However, this anti-
oppressive model reifies race, and may have less import at a global level, where it
is subject to alternative forms of racism and differing relations of power. A further
concern remains with how identity is deterministically conceptualized in this
paradigm, since 'Within an anti-oppressive problematic, an individual's subjectivity is conceptualised as coherent and rationally fixed' (Mac an Ghaill and
Haywood, 1997:24).

Because of the striking manner in which young children in Emblevale perceived
racism and anti-racism, I was curious as to how older students, who had a life-time
of schooling experience under Conservative leadership, would respond. Snowhill
Comprehensive was an enormous, all-but-white school in Tyneside (see Appendix
2). The Lower Sixth students I interviewed indicated that the predominance of
white students was beneficial to the extent that inter-ethnic struggles were avoided.
Blaming black people rather than white antagonism was a common discursive
mode of analysis (Gilroy, 1995 [1987]). There was a sense that if the school
merged with a mixed, local establishment, black students would compartmentalize
into ethnic groups; there was no recognition that ethnic majorities were themselves

engaged in forms of 'white bonding'. Moreover, many white working-class students felt that black students were as culpable as their white peers when it came to racism.

[16–17 years]
Anoop: Do you think that blacks can be as racist as whites?
Lucy: I think it works both ways.
Chris: More, I would say.
Anoop: More racist?
Chris: Er, they're like bitter against the way they've been treated like slavery and that. They feel like somehow they've been hard done by.
Lucy: It works both ways.

The idea that blacks are 'bitter' against whites and feel 'hard done by' draws on a familiar schema which portrays ethnic minority groups as having a 'chip on the shoulder'. As with younger Emblevale students, there was a belief that racism 'works both ways', it is something that blacks and whites commit alike. Chris, whom we heard from above, went on to describe the 'reverse racism' he perceived in multiracial districts:

Chris: There's a lot of racism but it's like different, it's from the blacks against the whites, you know what I mean? Me dad went into a bar y'kna in Leicester and it was like blacks everywhere. And he went in and it was like, 'Oh white boy' and all this.
Anoop: What kinda things were being said?
Chris: Jus like, y'kna how some fools may call 'em 'Niggers' and stuff? It was like, 'You white honky', and all this kinda crap, mon. It was like 'What you doing here?' and all this, 'Get back to where you come from.' [...] And now that it is more equal, like the equal rights and stuff, they want to get their own back on whites.

The geographical location of Leicester in the Midlands and Tyneside in the North East is strikingly different, which in turn has a bearing on race relations in these parts (Bonnett, 1993c). Since many Tyneside students operated with a parallel model of racism which equated the term 'black nigger' with that of 'white honky', their cynicism towards anti-racism became clearer to understand. However, other white, working-class students refuted the parallel model of racism and emphasized the privileged position of whiteness in name-calling interactions. Here, Ema, who is Anglo-Irish, elucidates on the difference between terms such as 'black bastard' and 'white trash':

Ema [16 years]: If I was arguing with a coloured person and I said something that wasn't needed to be said and they said it to me and went into [the Deputy Head's] office and I said, 'I called him a black whatever' and said, 'but

> he called me "white trash"', he'd think, 'How's that gonna harm you?'
> I may have been called a name like that but it wouldn't bother me.
> [...]
> If someone come to me and says, 'She just called me a black b,' I'd say
> something and get 'em done, if I was a teacher. But if someone says,
> 'She's just called me "white trash"', I'd say, 'And what's wrong with
> that?'
> I'd probably think, 'Well maybe it would hurt them, but to me it wouldn't
> be anything to say "white".' I'd be proud of it.

Ema makes a qualitative distinction between the use of a black or white racial epithet before an insult. She indicates that white has a neutral, even positive, signification that cannot be easily overturned ('I'd be proud of it'). As Troyna and Hatcher (1992b) would have it, the prefix 'white' does not draw on an historical, 'coherent ideology of racism' (slavery, imperialism, apartheid, discrimination, xenophobia, nationalism) in the ways that a term 'black bastard' might. When I questioned Ema about black people's right to be in the country and use public resources, her response was particularly eloquent as she recognized that black people were invited to Britain as part of the post-war rebuilding process.

> Ema: That's like someone inviting you to help with a party and ten minutes before it
> starts saying, 'I don't want you anymore.' After you've put all the food out and
> .helped with the preparation, but on a much bigger scale. They were invited over
> here so you can't just kick them out cos of a lack of jobs or anything. Everyone's
> got a right to work. It should be the government that sorts it all out.

Although awareness of the qualitatively different racialized experiences of black and white youth remains pertinent, contemporary definitions of racism have been further extended. While Troyna and Hatcher's definition foregrounds the 'asymmetrical power relations' (1992b:495) between blacks and whites and is a welcome improvement on liberal, power-evasive models of racism, there remain potential shortcomings with the anti-oppressive framework. To begin with, there is an immediate reification of race as an insurmountable point of difference that too readily equates whiteness with oppression and blackness with victimhood. Moreover, whites are endowed with the privilege of being the central architects of history, and the key agents of social change. The multiple positions that blacks and whites may come to occupy, and how these subjective locations are nuanced by class, gender, sexuality and generation, are subsequently condensed into a racial dichotomy of power/powerless. Furthermore, the tendency to construe racism across a black/white binary may in turn occlude other examples of racist hostility such as anti-Semitism; 'ethnic cleansing' in Eastern Europe; and the ritual persecution of the Irish. Indeed, an engagement with whiteness beyond racial polarities may allude to a complex understanding of racism that may invoke aspects of nationhood or religion as further points of discrimination.

Recently, other writers have pursued this line of inquiry. Connolly, for example, has remarked how 'We cannot assume that racism will always be associated with beliefs about racial inferiority; that it will always be signified by skin colour; that it will be only White people who can be racist; or that racism will always be the most significant factor in the experience of minority ethnic groups' (1998:10). As such, the exercise of power is subject to context and situation, and can come to mean different things at different moments. David Gillborn extends this differ-entialist reading of racism to incorporate black students as potential aggressors:

> Hence, while black and Asian people – as a group – can be said to be *relatively* powerless in Britain, in certain situations black and Asian individuals clearly exercise power; therefore, they have the potential to act in ways that are racist. This would apply to the school situation, for example, where black and Asian students may enjoy power through peer relations (1996:170).

In the two schools I visited, the overwhelming whiteness of the Tyneside conurbation (Bonnett, 1993c) meant that minority ethnic students rarely shared the peer-group power that some black youth may enact in inner-city, multiracial locales. However, while conducting research with a colleague, Les Back, investi-gating the perpetrators of racist violence in the English West Midlands, we found evidence of racist involvement by mixed-heritage youth (with African-Caribbean fathers and English mothers) against Asian peoples. Similarly, Phil Cohen (1993) has persuasively written about ethnic alliances between white working-class youth and African-Caribbean young people against Asian communities in urban Britain. These examples point to a move away from binary relations of racism (black/ white) towards composite forms of discrimination; we may consider this shift in the emergence of a plural concept of *racisms* (see Miles, 1995, for discussion).

This points towards a need for anti-racist practitioners in majority-white schools to engage with the salience of whiteness, or otherwise, in young people's cultures and discuss the social meaning of these terms with students. A failure to engender the perspectives of white students only serves to encourage confusion, and the claims of unfairness we have witnessed. Notably, many of the students who voiced these grievances did not identify as racist, nor were they vehemently opposed to anti-oppressive school policies. Their points of resistance had less to do with a rejection of anti-racism as a democratic strategy; rather, they appeared more concerned with perceptions of being 'left out'. Thus 'special' multicultural sessions designed for minority students in dance, art or cookery had a tendency to suture white defensiveness (Roman, 1993). Similarly, the bilingual skills of some students were frowned upon as a conscious attempt at white exclusion. These feelings were further compounded by a belief that school rules on name-calling indirectly 'favoured' minority students over ethnic majorities.

As the Burnage Report (MacDonald *et al.*, 1989) signalled, young people need clear guidelines about discriminatory practices, but these policies must be formed more closely with all students whose lives are directly touched by these actions.[42] This would indicate a need for interventionist strategies that are more sensitive to the varied cultures of young people. Tyneside responses appeared to indicate that many students were inconsistent in their use of racist language; certain youth may be regularly targeted while others were not; context, situation and circumstance all appeared to affect the emergence of a racist vocabulary in young people's social interactions. This does not detract from the pernicious aspects of racism but provides careful insight into the problems of imposing an insensitive and pro-scriptive anti-racist policy. However, as we shall now see, white students were themselves highly ambivalent about the value of anti-racist practice in school institutions. While initial interviews appear to suggest that students hold egalitarian values when it comes to issues of race and ethnicity, more penetrative, long-term ethnographic investigation revealed that a number of 'unspoken' white grievances could simultaneously be harboured beneath the surface.

'White Backlash' at National and Local Levels

The anti-racist backlash (anti-anti-racism) was most viciously pursued in tabloid newspapers in the late eighties and early nineties during the pomp of New Right ideology. Somewhat surprisingly, vivid traces of these events were recalled in much detail by a generation who would have been toddlers at the time of these affairs. The students in Emblevale had a skewed interpretation of these incidents, no doubt drawn from older members in the white community, who saw the incriminating representation of these events as evidence of the curtailing of white ethnicity. Significantly the provocative tabloid headlines had been developed as an attack on English Southern Left-wing councils, including Brent, Haringey and the Inner-London Education Authority (ILEA). The phobic attack on an imagined anti-racist 'political correctness' (PC) has been widely documented by other writers in the area (see, for example, Barker 1981; Gordon and Klug, 1986; Epstein, 1993). Ali Rattansi succinctly sums up the Right-wing hysteria of the period as a series of 'moral panics ... orchestrated around "loony-left councils" supposedly banning black dustbin liners, insisting on renaming black coffee "coffee without milk", and

---

42. These rules may also be of use in other institutions. For example, in his youth club research Les Back found that the proscriptive anti-racism policies available 'took no account of the lived cultures of the young people who were subject to these rules' (1990:15).

banning "Ba-ba black sheep" from the classroom – scares which turned out to rest on complete fabrications (Media Research Group, 1987)' (1993:13).

However, while many of the above events were taken out of context, exaggerated or simply invented, this did not seem to detract from a 'common-sense' understanding of anti-racism and multiculturalism as an attack on white cultural practices.

[11–12 years]

Nicola: I've got this book from when I was little, it's called *Little Black Sambo*. It's got Black Mumbo and Black [*giggles*] Jumbo.

Sam: Oh, I had that, I used to 'ave that.

Michelle: It's been banned You're not allowed to say, 'Baa Baa Blacksheep' [a nursery rhyme].

Nicola: And you're not allowed to ask for a black coffee.

Michelle: Aye.

Anoop: *Who says?*

Michelle: On the news.

Sam: So we go round singin', 'Baa Baa Multicoloured Sheep!'

I was surprised to find that despite the young age of the children and their particular geographic situation, this did not detract from them having an intimate knowledge of media representations of anti-racism. These debates appear to have left a deep scar on the psyche of white, working-class subjects to date, in economic outposts as far removed from the English capital as the North East, where extensive evidence of 'lashing back' was found.[43]

The notion of whites as under surveillance, where literature is 'banned', and seemingly innocent tasks such as ordering a coffee are open to an imagined scrutiny, was taken a step further. It was even thought that legislation existed which censored white behaviour.

Nicola: And there's these dolls that you're not allowed to 'ave.

Sam: Gollywogs.

Nicola: Aye. And on the news now |it says| every child has gotta have a black doll.

Anoop: *Hold on, are you saying that every child by law has got to have a black doll?*

Nicola: Yeah, so they grow to accept black people.

Sam: Y'kna how they've started making black Sindys and that, and Barbies? |female dolls]

James: And black Action Man |male doll|.

Michelle: Aye, black Action Man!

43. According to Alastair Bonnett (1993c), anti-racist practitioners on Tyneside are permanently wary of a backlash and so opt for a 'softly-softly' or 'gentle' approach to anti-racism, favouring a concern with 'local sensitivity'. This feeling, however constraining it may be, is not overly paranoid. Some three years after the Right-wing media 'bashing' of London city councils, local papers carried the headline 'Baa Baa Pinksheep' as the lead for one of their stories.

The language used in student descriptions of anti-racist practice suggests they interpret it as a largely proscriptive, often negative, set of values. Students continually refer to items that have been 'banned', symbols that you have 'gotta have' and things you are 'not allowed' to say or do. In essence, anti-racism and multi-culturalism are reproduced as part of a 'discourse of derision' within the social peer-groups of white youth. The feeling among these students was that white ethnicity had to be regulated and that British anti-racism was a somewhat arbitrary mode of 'policing'. At best, anti-racism was random and nit-picking in its choice of execution (black dolls, gollywogs, coffee, nursery rhymes, dustbin liners, etc.); at worst it was downright 'unfair', and even prejudice against whites!

James: They don't go on about 'Baa Baa Whitesheep'.
Nicola: That's even more racist.
James: Them [blacks] could be banned for buyin' white milk.
Michelle: [*laughing*] Well ya can't buy black milk!

White students appeared acutely sensitive to any semblance of preferential treatment, and at times saw the school's anti-racist policy as a form of institutional discrimination against themselves. Roger Hewitt discusses perceived 'unfairness' by white youth as a major obstacle for anti-racism as it functions as 'a screen which filters out the possibility of some whites fully understanding the meaning of racial harassment, and generates an almost impermeable defensiveness' (1996:57). In the context of the Tyneside conurbation, a more meaningful approach may be to ally the experience of working-class students with the local culture, to include discussions on 'Geordie' identity, for example, or the precarious position 'Englishness' holds within the region. Understanding the different types of anti-racism required in various locales remains of key significance. Specifically, Bonnett (1993a, 1993c) has argued for the recognition of spatial complexities, because forms of anti-racist practice which may be successful in London cannot be surgically transplanted into Tyneside, where the ethnic composition is sharply different. Indeed, the 'radical' practitioners he interviewed advocate a response that engages with the interstices of race and class, and have a contextual meaning of the local populace. This would mitigate against a 'best practice' model involving the standardization of anti-racism.

New Ethnicities

We still have a great deal of work to do to *decouple* ethnicity, as it functions in the dominant discourse, from its equivalence with nationalism, imperialism, racism and the state, which are the points of attachment around which a distinctive British or, more accurately, English ethnicity have been constructed.

Stuart Hall, 'New Ethnicities' (1993)

Throughout my time spent in the North East I became aware of how 'Geordie' identity was almost akin to a form of overriding ethnicity. 'Geordies' appeared to have their own tight-knit communities bound by culture, language, humour, ritualised practices and numerous other points of identification. Yet how can we reconcile the tacit rejection of an assumed Englishness with the take-up of racism in the local Tyneside context? As Stuart Hall indicates above, separating ethnicity from nationalism is a complicated task. In my own research I found that attachments to Englishness, Britishness and whiteness were often tenuous and could not be explained through an anti-oppressive stance that identified these subject positions as permanently embedded in an imperialist past. Rather, this past, while shaping contemporary white experience to date, could not account for the feelings of white injustice and anxiety voiced in certain youth studies (Gillborn, 1996; Mac an Ghaill, [1997] 1994).

A further complexity when discussing whiteness was that in the predominantly white preserves of Tyneside, the majority of youth felt white privilege amounted to relatively little. By speaking about white ethnicities, I am aware that the term 'ethnicity', so often used as a by-word for race, cannot be taken lightly. This was most apparent in Martin Barker's (1981) seminal British study of media presentations of race, where fixed notions of ethnicity all too quickly could become transformed into a 'new racism'. For example, in 1978 Margaret Thatcher, then leader of the Conservative oppostion, was able to argue that there was something 'natural' to the British way of life (i.e. an 'intrinsic' ethnicity) which was opposed to being 'swamped' by immigrant peoples. However, what was perceived as a 'natural' British desire to 'stay with your own kind' transposed into a deep-seated resentment when the issue of ethnic bonding between minority groups was discussed. Speaking in 1991, the Conservative MP Norman Tebbit used the gauge of a 'cricket test' (as an indicator of which team migrants chose to support in international test matches) as 'evidence' of what he saw as the immobile structure of ethnicity amongst settler communities. That in cricket matches against England many minority groups may have shown loyalty to their former heritages by supporting India, Pakistan, Sri Lanka or the West Indies (countries that second- and third-generation settlers may never have visited) was condemned by Tebbit as a wholly 'unBritish' sentiment. Consequently, it was the ethnicity of minority groups that was laid open for inspection, and their alleged inability to come to terms with a perceived British 'way of life'. It was never suggested that ethnic pride and British racist hostility had inadvertently encouraged minorities to adopt the heritage of their ancestors. Nor was it evident that individuals could forge multiple affiliations and a shifting, ambivalent sense of beloning.

In the ideologies of the New Right, ethnicity was removed from a fluid interpretation, evoking various cultural patterns of ritualized belonging formed over time, particular to specific cultures, regions, religions or generations, for example.

Paradoxically, English ethnicity was translated into something that was inherent, yet at once in need of protection, via stricter immigration laws, Right-wing press propaganda, the attack on multicultural education strategies, and so forth. In contrast, academics on the Left such as Stuart Hall asserted the need for a 'renewed contestation over the meaning of the term "ethnicity" itself' (1993:256) that did away with the confusing notion that implies ethnicity is essentially unchanging. Hall explains, 'The term ethnicity acknowledges the place of identity, as well as the fact that all discourse is placed, positioned, situated, and all knowledge is contextual' (p. 257). The placing and positioning of whiteness is now a crucial part of race relations if we are achieve a genuinely anti-essentialist anti-racism.

The 'Honorary English'

Because of the uncertain relationship many Tyneside students had with Englishness, the majority claimed to use this reference (often with a tinge of embarrassment) only when outside of Britain, favouring the local identity 'Geordie' (Colls and Lancaster, 1992). As many local students were selective in their use of the label of Englishness, they saw no reason why black people could not have a similar, slippery purchase on the term. Thus, although the North East as a whole cannot be described as a cosmopolitan area, the issues of nationhood and 'New Ethnicities' continue to inspire meaning. However, this process of acceptance is negotiated over time and involves a certain amount of reciprocity. Here, we see the emergence of these new cross-cultural dialogues:

> Fern [10 years]: I think that English people are becomin' more like black people and black people are becomin' more like English people | . . . | I think tha' black people are becomin' more into white people and white people are becomin' more into black people.

In this reading it is not simply a case of black youth assimilating themselves into a white 'host' culture, but a dual process that is as much about the negotiation of new, white, English ethnicities. The making of new ethnicities is, as Fern explains, a process of 'becomin'' for all groups. However, the fluidity of ethnic identities could always be curtailed by racist expression. Accordingly, some students, like Alistair, were aware of the privilege of whiteness, remarking, 'I'd ravva be white cos you wouldn't get as much hassle in England.' He lived in a multi-ethnic district of the Nailton quarter and was willing to stick up for Asian friends he knew, considering them to be 'English'.

> Alistair | 10 years|: Where I live there's loadsa coloured people in |name of place|. Me and my brother went out and saw kids throwing stones [at an Asian home] and we said, 'Why d'ya do that?' an' they said, 'Cos *they*

don't belong here.' And we said – ya kna like how some coloured
people are English – we said, 'Yeah they do!' and walked off.

The feeling that 'some coloured people are English' and thereby form an integrated
part of the local community is a feature Les Back (1996) describes as 'neighbourhood nationalism'. This expression of multiracial belonging may exist in
multi-ethnic pockets of Nailton where close, longstanding relationships have been
forged. These relationships were always struggled over, as Campbell (1993) has
shown in her study of Newcastle, Oxford, Coventry, Cardiff and Bristol, demonstrating that some white families supported their black neighbours while young
men took to the streets. This indicates that whilst working-class neighbourhoods
may well be sites for the production of racism, they are also spaces in which more
complex ideas of multiculturalism are worked out. Although such dynamics meant
certain black youth could acquire the status of the 'honorary English', limited
identification with black communities could also lead to forms of stereotyping in
the absence of social intimacy. In Emblevale many black students had developed
friendships with their white peers through a slow process of daily interaction. This
did not mean that racism evaporated; rather, chosen black students became accepted
as select individuals, even 'honorary whites', while more general hostile attitudes
persisted. Troyna and Hatcher describe the strategy of including occasional black
friends in otherwise white peer groups as a form of 'refencing' (1992a: 101), in
which the boundaries of race are reconstructed but generalized racist perspectives
continue unabated. Sam (12 years) was an acute observer of white suspicion
and hypocrisy in schooling culture and commented on this practice of cultural
'refencing'.

Sam: This new kid, he's Pakistani, they didn't like him before they ever knew him.
         They made up their minds that he wasn't gonna be their friend, and then they
         started playin' with him.
Anoop: Was that cos of his colour or cos they didn't know him?
Sam: Cos he was a different colour. And also they didn't know him.

This extract informs us about some of the most pervasive ways whiteness was seen
to operate in children's social worlds, not through overt racist language and
actions, but through a covert suspicion and distancing. These attitudes could alter
as white students became more acquainted with their black peers, but this did not
stop them resurfacing with ethnic minority pupils who were less well known.
Moreover, even in well-established relationships markers of racialized difference
could unexpectedly appear.

[11 years]
Carl: [*accusatory tone to Aisha*] You were born in Africa.
Aisha: Yeah, I was.

Paul: And she saw a lion, and the lion came forrer and she hopped on the Metro and
          said, 'Take me to Newcastle!'
All: [*laughter*]
Anoop: [*sternly*] *Hey, I don't think that's what happened.*

However, some students on Tyneside were open-minded in their appreciation of
black experiences and even extended notions of Englishness to incorporate black
peers, in a rebuttal of a Right-wing dogma that asserted ethnicity as fixed and
static. I asked if black students could occupy an English ethnicity.

|12 years|
Danielle: Uh-huh.
Alan: Jus' like Americans.
Lucy: We'd normally classify 'em as English anyway, cos some of 'em, people
          like Michael 'Chopper', we went through school with 'em. We'd classify them
          as English.
Danielle: It's jus' his dad that's not.

Michael 'Chopper' had an Asian father and English mother. His nickname 'Chopper' was derived from an anglicized version of his surname, Chopal, and signified
his complete immersion into the peer group as an 'honorary Englishman'. The
erasure of his surname blanks out the partial Asian heritage of the student and at
the same time 'whitens' his identity in the peer-group context. Even so, the
inclusion and 'refencing' of black friends within white peer groups can at times sit
uneasily with the New Right race theories which have marked education up to the
contemporary period. New Right doctrines drew notably on the ideas of Enoch
Powell, who continually insisted that although black people may reside in Britain
as UK citizens, they do not belong here (see Barker, 1981; Centre for Contemporary Cultural Studies, 1982; Gordon and Klug, 1986; Rutherford, 1997). In
Eastbourne on 16th November 1968, Powell remarked that simply because a West
Indian or Asian was born in England, he did not become an 'Englishman': 'in fact
he is a West Indian or an Asian still' (cited in Wood, 1972). Because New Right
thinking conflated the cultural aspects of ethnicity with nature, biological forms of
racism could give way to notions of fixed cultural difference, the 'new racism'
(Barker, 1981). Thus, there was the sense that Enoch Powell was merely voicing
'common-sense' opinion in proposing that black people, 'by the very nature of
things have lost one country without gaining another, lost one nationality without
acquiring a new one' (cited in Wood, 1972). In contrast, the youth responses
indicate that minority identities *can* be interwoven into both the region and a more
inclusive notion of Englishness.

To this extent, today's visible minorities are no longer the 'dark strangers' Sheila
Patterson (1965 [1963]) once recorded in an early study of West Indians in
London. They can no longer be considered 'colonial immigrants in a British city',

as Rex and Tomlinson (1979) later reported, but are now fashioning new ethnicities that at times collapse blackness, Britishness and, as we have seen on occasion, even Englishness (Gilroy, 1995 [1987]; Solomos and Back, 1995). Nevertheless, within Tyneside I collected various anecdotes about black youth some of whom it was said identified with the extremities of whiteness. A teacher at Emblevale informed me about a black student in her class who used derogatory racist language to impress his white peer group. One young woman reported knowing an Asian youth who used to assume the symbols of Nazi regalia in her Northeast home town. Other students spoke of individuals who evoked racism to consciously 'whiten' their identities. Such tales were particularly prevalent in the white establishment of Snowhill Comprehensive.

> John [17 years]: Like in this school where there's only like a couple of blacks and all whites. Well, shallow people like Balbir Singh he was like racist against blacks, 'cos he'd been with whites all his life.
>
> *Anoop:* *What do you mean by that?*
>
> John: Well if he saw a black person, like if he was arguing with someone who was black, he'd just shout abuse saying all this racist stuff to them.

For Balbir Singh, who was described as a 'bit of an outcast', this social standing may have fuelled a tendency to over-compensate for his perceived difference through a fierce alignment with whiteness. Racist humour, in this case, may be a symbolic gesture of white bonding, a display of loyalty towards white friends ('I'm like you') and statement against a presumed association with other black youth ('I'm not like you'). The case of Balbir Singh offers a vivid illustration of points of racial identification and dis-identification.

> [16–17 years]
> Jolene: Yeah, he'd shout all this racist stuff to them [black youth].
> Chris: Even though he was the same colour. He probably felt that he was white.
> Jolene: He'd say, 'Go back to where you come from!' and all that.
> *Anoop: He thought he was white?*
> Chris: Yeah.

In today's multicultural societies where positive models of blackness exist, accounts of black youth identifying as 'white' are relatively sparse. This has not always been the case. Early psychological studies using black and white dolls found nearly all children showed a greater propensity to choose white dolls, regardless of their racial identity (Clarke and Clarke, 1939, 1947). In another classroom study, Coard (1982 [1971]) found that white pupils in his class refused to paint their black friends with dark skin tones and that self-portraits by black children also construed themselves as 'white'. No doubt these dynamics are historically contingent.

More recently, France Widdance Twine (1996) has explored the under-researched case of middle-class 'brown skinned white girls' in American suburban communities; that is, black women who have been 'raised white' and enjoy the material privileges of whiteness to the extent that they self-identify as 'white'. However, the phenomenon of black people who identify as 'white' is best exemplified by Frantz Fanon (1967 [1952]), through a complex, psychic interaction he terms 'black skin/white masks', the title of his ground-breaking analysis. The French-Martinique writer describes a personal ambivalence to whiteness: 'as I begin to recognize that the Negro is the symbol of sin, I catch myself hating the Negro. But then I recognise that I am a Negro . . . I have unthinkingly conceded that the black man is the colour of evil' (p. 140). By constructing a 'white mask' of racist intolerance, it is possible that students like Balbir Singh are able to temporally relinquish the 'colour of evil' and attach themselves to a belief that they 'feel' white. This tendency for black people to slip into negative appraisals of blackness is discussed in detail elsewhere (Nayak, 1993, 1997). For Fanon, the psychic 'splitting' endured by black subjects in a racist society is an intensely traumatic process of dislocation: 'What else could it be for me but an amputation, an excizion, a haemorrhage that spattered my whole body with black blood?' (1993:222). As Fanon evocatively explains, 'splitting' becomes a corporeal act of self-mutilation. Moreover, the process of fragmentation can involve a disturbing sense of 'loss', as seen when students continued their discussion of Balbir Singh.

> Jolene: He lost something. You can't really pretend you're something else just cos you're hanging 'round with friends. You gotta be your own person and they gotta like you for who you are.
>
> Chris: Then again, your person isn't your colour.
>
> Jolene: I know. But that's not the way he was. He came out with it cos he was hanging 'round with people.
>
> Chris: His mind might have been thinking that, cos he'd been in such a white community all his life.

The portraits of young people's cultural identities drawn up here and in the previous chapter suggest complex identifications that may transcend colour. In particular the responses suggest geographies of racial identification, in which place and locality are significant factors shaping young people's cultural attachments.

Pedagogy, Place and Practice

In order to make the question of race and ethnicity meaningful in predominantly white preserves it was necessary to engage with white-Anglo ethnicities. One way in which this could be done was by developing a detailed 'pedagogy of place'.

Exposing the diverse geographies and histories of white students upon Tyneside could be a productive exchange where the immediate heritage of respondents was discussed. The recognition that 'English' identities had changed over time allowed these students to feel less threatened by the prospect of black British settlement. Projects directed by young people that drew on familial life-history accounts were particularly interesting and may be of use to anti-racist practitioners, who can also share their personal biographies. Encouraging students in mainly white areas to sensitively trace their ethnic and social-class lineage was found to be a fruitful way of deconstructing whiteness.[44] Even so, I remain in agreement with Gillborn that, firstly, 'no strategy is likely to be completely successful, and second, that an effective strategy in one context, may fail in another context or at another time' (1995:89). With these provisos in place, the approach deployed was sensitive to the local culture of the community and subject to my particular relationship with students. I found that imploding white ethnicities offered a way of contextualizing anti-racism, and helped to develop an interest amongst students in race relations they felt they could have a personal stake in. In changing times a place-specific pedagogy is imperative, for, as Hall has noted, 'We are all, in that sense, *ethnically* located and our ethnic identities are crucial to our subjective sense of who we are' (1993:258).

The value of historical geographies was made known to me when new inflections upon an assumed, coherent English ethnicity began to unfold. Although a number of students identified as white-English[45] in general parlance, their subjective deconstructions acted as fertile ground upon which to yield syncretic youth identities.

[12 years]

Danielle: Mine parents were born in Germany, cos me nanna used to travel o'er abroad.

Brett: I used to have an Italian granddad.

Alan: Me next name's O'Maley an' that isn't English.

[...]

Nicola: I tell yer I'm English, but I'm part German. My granddad came over as a prisoner of war, he was working over at Belsey Park and my grandma was teaching.

[...]

James: Some white people have got black people in their family. Like, say, my aunty married a black person and had babies.

---

44. In US higher educational establishments, Kristin Crosland Nebeker found that such 'counter-stories' can 'question the role of whites in the dialogical process'. For further examples of biographical and story-telling critiques of whiteness, see also (hooks, 1993 [1992]), Ware (1993), Nayak (1997).

45. This would support the abandonment of 'cold' interviewing methods in favour of the use of long-term ethnographic research where the researcher can gradually get to know respondents. It may also be of use to speak to young people both in groups and individually to grasp the various situations in which multiple ethnic identifications can arise.

Michelle: I've got one in my family.
[. . .]
Sam: I'm a quarter Irish, a quarter Scottish, a quarter English and a quarter Italian.

Through utilizing a 'pedagogy of place' that focused on migration, hybridity and difference, it was found that the implosion of white ethnicities could offer alternative historical trajectories that many students had a self-fascination with. Tracing their familial past was a means of personalizing history, making it relevant to their life experiences to date. In the course of this process it was not unusual for students to refer to generational elements of racism within their family lineage. Many students mentioned parents or grandparents with pronounced racist opinions, allowing for further points of critique and discussion between young people. Although many whites may lay claim to the identity of white-Englishness, the narratives illustrated how these ethnicities were discursively constituted in the present situation. According to Hickman and Walter (1995), it is this failure to deconstruct whiteness that has led to the invisibility of Irish ethnicities in contemporary Britain. The deconstruction of white identity became, then, a means of splicing Englishness, whiteness and ethnicity.

Although the fragmented, 'hyphenated' identities of white youth (Anglo-Irish, Scotch-Irish, Anglo-Italian) has particular resonance to the local culture of the North East, this did not mean that Englishness itself was left untouched. Alan (10 years) pointed to the hybrid history of English identity and its absence from contemporary debate when he remarked, 'It's all a mixed breed in England cos we've had the Vikings and the Saxons come across . . . France, Denmark, them places'. In turn I could further share knowledge of the locality by discussing the longstanding migrant settlement in the region and the resistance to Fascism during the interim war period and beyond (see Chapter 3). Conversations concerning the locality and the labouring heritage of the area were particularly productive. This would support Burgess's claim that 'historical sources can provide the field researcher with a rich vein of material to complement the ethnographic present and provide deeper sociological insights into the way in which people lived their lives' (1982:134).

With older students it was possible to engage in a critical dialogue with whiteness itself. Ema and Jolene each identified as working-class young women. Ema's father was in the army and during the fieldwork period she too decided to sign up in preference to completing her Sixth Form education. Jolene's father, meanwhile, had a masculine occupation that reflected the depleting infrastructure of the region, working as a bailiff. Both Ema and Jolene engaged in an appraisal of their own racial identities, which at times disrupted the association of Britishness/Englishness with whiteness.

|16 years|

Jolene: There's different colours of white.

Anoop: What d'you mean?

Jolene: Like Chinese. Do you know what I mean, what colour are they? There isn't a colour – we're not proper white.

Ema: Different shades really.

Jolene: There's Chinese; there's other people; there's us; naturally dark skins who are white.

Ema: People say like, 'I'd hate to be black' and everything but when they go on the sun-bed and get tanned, they love to be tanned.

Jolene: Yeah! People go on the sun-bed just to get browned.

The critical deconstruction of whiteness undertaken by Ema and Jolene fractures monolithic notions of white identity through a recognition that so-called 'whites' are comprised of 'different shades really'. Instead of seeing white as colourless, as it is all too frequently regarded (Dyer, 1993, 1997), the young women introduced a wide spectrum of colour symbols which at its most extreme included bronzed, sun-tanned figures who still manage to 'claim' the elusive emblem of whiteness. The question of what colour Chinese people are further disrupts the fixed polarization of race as a discourse shared solely between black and white citizens.[46] Moreover, whiteness is seen as a term socially ascribed to certain groups rather than an accurate mode of racial classification. The social construction of whiteness is also apparent here, where students recognize that, strictly speaking, they are not 'proper white' (whatever that might be).

Engaging with the materiality of place was also a means to challenge the pervasive belief that blacks embodied distinct biological qualities (see Chapter 6). In view of widespread youth assumptions that blacks were superior athletes on the basis of racial 'essences', I consciously brought to light the interstices of race, place and social class by asking:

[16–17 years]

Anoop: Why might there be a lot of good black baskteball players but not say tennis players or swimmers?

Chris: Class. It's about class.

Anoop: What d'you mean?

---

46. Frank Dikotter (1992) has provided detailed historical evidence of ancient landed-gentry Chinese people who frequently deployed the symbol of whiteness as a signifier of bodily beauty. Thus, skin, teeth and other anotomical parts were compared to 'white jade', 'tree grubs', 'melon seeds', 'congealed ointment', 'silkworm moths' or 'young white grass' (p. 10). However, the author also makes clear that the notion of a 'yellow race' came via missionaries but was taken up willingly by sections of the Chinese who equated the colour with the positive signification of gold.

Chris: Having money. Tennis seems to be for a higher class.[47]

Suzanne: Swimming, you'd need a pool in your own house to train everyday, don't you? Something that's yours that you can use.

Anoop: So, something like basketball you could just play anywhere?

Chris: Just in the streets. There's lots of them [basketball courts] in America, that's why America's got the best team.

The reflexive, theory-led discussions encouraged students to move beyond myths of black sexual or physical prowess by focusing instead upon the lived geographies of place and daily habitation. Overall, nesting anti-racism within the localized cultures of young people in the North East permitted a discussion of 'Geordie' identity, whiteness and Englishness to come about, and as such offered a broader strategy of participation. Experimental artists such as the Multiple Occupancies Collective (1998) have used song, poetry and the medium of painting to recount the multiple configurations which come to make up their new ethnicities in Britain. The notion of white youth as also inhabiting 'multiple occupancies' may enable them to feel included in the term 'ethnicity', without having to resort to an unflinching nationalist rhetoric. Jane Ifekwunigwe, a co-member of the Collective, claims to 'encourage others with multiple identifications to acknowledge rather than to deny these affiliations' (p. 95). This call is taken up in Lorraine Ayensu's poems, where autobiographies of the local are a central part of the work. She explains:

> I was conceived as a result of my White English birth-mother's extramarital relationship with my Black Ghanaian father. She was married to a White English man. . . . My ethnic and cultural identities are strongly rooted in White Geordie (native Tyneside) culture. Embracing my Geordie experiences involves both a racialized critique of my ironic circumstances and an affirmation of my origins and my complex realities. (pp. 96–7)

Ayensu's knowing attempt to embrace a Tyneside identity acts at once as a 'racialized critique' of the whiteness of 'Geordie'. At the same time it points to the multiple heritages that may be concealed in seemingly monolithic terms such as 'Geordie', 'whiteness' or 'Englishness'. I would suggest that making slippery the frozen status of white-Anglo ethnicity may allow for new points of connection to emerge for white youth. Moreover, if these emergent ethnicities can be encouraged to flourish outside the ideological nexus that merges whiteness, racism and nationhood, there remains cause for hope.

47. Black American tennis stars such as Arthur Ashe, and, most recently, Serena and Venus Williams are rare exceptions who challenge these stereotypes. A similar comparison can be made in golf with Tiger Woods.

Concluding Remarks

The ethnographic data suggest that young people are responding differently to global change and economic restructuring and that these responses are in turn shaped by race, place, gender and generation. Referring to Paul Gilroy's (1995 [1987]) book *There Ain't No Black in the Union Jack* (a title derived from a National Front slogan), Stuart Hall closes his essay on 'new ethnicities' with the claim that until relatively recently he 'didn't care, whether there was any black in the Union Jack. Now not only do we care, we must' (1993:258). By the same token, if white students are to feel able to contribute to anti-racism whatever their nationality may be, they must have subjective investments in a politics that, at times, has passed them by. Deconstructing the identities of ethnic majorities with as much purpose and vigour as that of minority groups should be a vital component of anti-racist practice. A stumbling block that needs to be removed is the perception that many white students (and parents) have of anti-racism as a bourgeois, *anti-white* practice. Here, suppressed white grievances could give way to an under-standing that while racism 'works both ways', anti-racism does not. A more fruitful route to pursue in mainly white preserves may be to connect anti-oppressive policies with local histories and the 'lived' culture of the community. As Raphael Samuel has noted, 'Local history also has the strength of being popular. . . . People are continually asking themselves questions about where they live, and how their elders fared' (1982:136–7). Embracing the popular in this way may entail a clearer understanding of the specificities of white, British Northern ethnicities, and engender a perspective which is hopefully more sensitive to marginal working-class experiences. Despite its reputation for racist violence, Tyneside also boasts a legacy of anti-Fascist resistance, a history of organized marches against national-ist extremists such as Enoch Powell and Oswald Mosley, and a rarely acknowl-edged past of black settlement and habitation. Moreover, the multiple styles of whiteness evoked by young people even in largely white enclaves implies that a more sophisticated treatment of racism and anti-racism is required. Exposing the multiplicity and mutability of white experience remains imperative where the only recognizable forms of white, English identity for young men and women appear to be the 'Nazi Skinhead' or the 'blonde bimbo'.

–8–

Youth Cultures Reconsidered

Introduction

This book has explored how young people are negotiating change in uncertain times. It has shown how labour market restructuring, migration and the cultures of globalization have impacted upon contemporary youth formations. In this respect, the landscape of youth has been radically reshaped in a post-industrial era characterized by 'risk', uncertainty and insecurity. Nevertheless, the study has also demonstrated that young people are not the passive recipients of social transformations, as may have been assumed, but are responding to change in a variety of ways that draw upon the signs, symbols and motifs made available at local, national and international scales.

Race, Place and Globalization also attempts to further debates in race and ethnic studies. Where a number of subcultural studies have focused upon gender, class and generation as formative processes influencing young people's relationships (Chapter 2), ethnicity was also found to play a salient role in youth cultures. This was evident where musical dispositions, sporting affiliations or fashion preferences could become racially encrypted scripts for the performance and interpretation of a particular youth identity. Moreover, the grammar of race could also translate into spatial practices used to demarcate 'territory', neighbourhoods and urban areas. In many ways, the process of *racialization* was a means through which young people 'made sense of' themselves, one another and their changing habitations. The intricate patterning of gender, class, sexuality and ethnicity variegated the practice of racialization. As such, racialization was an *organizing principle* in youth relations regulating who was 'respectable' and who was not, who behaved appropriately and who was a *Wigger*, which places were 'safe' and which were 'risky', who went out with whom and what the moral costs of these associations were. Underpinning these daily relations was an implicit understanding that racialization could position young people within differing dominant or subordinate locations, positions that were themselves contingent upon time, place and circumstance. Thus, the valorized white appropriation of 'black cool' in one context may be undermined by its enactment in other racially marked spaces.

This book has sketched out three 'moments' of social, economic, political and cultural change in young lives. It began by considering 'passing times' and the theoretical debates surrounding materialist and postmodernist accounts of youth identities. This involved documenting the old and new landscapes of the North East of England and their relationship to globalization, economy and culture. The process of transition was signalled in 'changing times' by reflecting on young people's resistance, survival and adaptation to transformation. Finally, attention has turned to 'coming times' and the new ways of thinking about youth cultural identities beyond colour-based binaries. To pursue some of these debates a little further, I would like to conclude this section by elaborating upon three thematic areas that emerged from the research. These include: the issue of *change and continuity*, the question of *white ethnicities*, and the subject of *place and identity*. Disentangling these strands may enable a more detailed understanding of race and youth cultural identity to emerge in the late-modern era.

Change and Continuity

> Embodied aspects of restructuring may prompt individuals into action . . . .
> Equally, individuals may resist the new culture, promote alternative versions of
> change or construct their own individualized escape attempts which do not
> involve direct challenge or confrontation but, none the less, constitute a rejection
> of the new identities . . . .
>
> Susan Halford and Mike Savage 'Rethinking Restructuring' (1997)

Recent theories on social change have pointed to the dismantling of traditional industries, the increased dispersal and fragmentation of modern societies and developing transformations in the domestic sphere as evidence that we are living in 'new times'. There is little dispute that these changes are both widespread and of major consequence to Western late-modernity. However, the extent of these changes should not occlude us from observing everyday, taken-for-granted patterns of continuity. Thus, the perseverance of an older, established 'way of life' has led Sara Delamont to conclude that we still live in an age when most people 'marry, most are close to their families, most work for most of their lives, and so on' (2001:111). Moreover, 'class does not disappear just because traditional ways of life fade away' (Beck, 1998 [1992]: 99). To entice a flavour of change and continuity, the present volume has concentrated on enduring processes of transition referred to as passing, changing and coming times. Traces with the past were exemplified in the subcultural case studies when older attachments to place, locality and an imaginary working-class community prevailed. Felt investments in the familiar, the local and the 'traditional' were now 'spoken' through the discursive matrices and embodied practices of whiteness, masculinity and the culture of labour. These insights should act as a timely brake that curbs the rush to theorize 'new times' and cultural transformations as if some major cleavage has recently occurred, or, more beguilingly, is 'just around the corner'. At the same time theories of change need to address the spatial unevenness described and the significance of regional cultures, local histories and dissonant identities.

The ethnographic portraits of modern young people presented here provide a more contingent though less clear-cut image of social change than is evident in current theories of transformation. Their lives offer a patchy, rugged profile that speaks of change and continuity, trust and insecurity, place and 'placelessness'. So what, if anything, has changed for young men and women? Over twenty-five years ago, in his classic study of white working-class males, Paul Willis (1977) disclosed the functional relationship that existed between young men, schools and the labour market. For a counter-culture of 'lads', trickery, subversion and having a 'laff' at school were the tools of the trade through which young men 'learned to labour' and so reproduce their social class subordination (see Chapter 2). Angela McRobbie's early study of white working-class girls suggested it was by 'elevating and living out their definition of "femininity"'(1991 [1977]:51) in romance, pop music and fashion that girls and young women became drawn towards a culture of domesticity based on marriage and motherhood. In the de-industrial moment, the book suggests that new patterns youth subjectivity are now coming to the fore.

Race, Place and Globalization has found that young people are no longer 'learning to labour' or embarking upon a secure 'career' of marriage in ways that they once might have done. In a post-Fordist world the expectations surrounding work and home-life are now increasingly uncertain. If manual labour and early marriage were once characterized by Marxist and feminist scholars as arenas in which blocked opportunities, 'drudge' and a life-long service to either the factory or family prevailed, this emphasis is now increasingly redundant. Rather than providing an increased freedom of opportunity, at present the break-up of these state institutions is leading to greater insecurity and uncertainty in young lives. For many young people, inhabiting the de-industrial landscapes where my research was undertaken, life-long labour and community ties to the mill or colliery would now appear to offer welcome respite against unemployment, insecurity and a sense of dislocation. This is not to romanticize the masculine industrialized past, but to draw attention to the growing disparity of wealth, income and opportunity.

Changes in the domestic sphere also mean that the traditional nuclear family based on a male breadwinner and supportive housewife has now become the subject of an older heterosexual 'romance'. The increasing popularity of sit-coms and soap operas focusing upon thirty-something singles and families with multiple ties and step-relationships gives some flavour of these changing perceptions. Indeed, a number of my respondents had experienced divorce and family break-up and were either living with single parents or negotiating new relationships with step-parents, partners and siblings (see Frosh *et al.*, 2002). Prison sentences also impinged upon family life when a head of household was intermittently present. Teenage pregnancy and the numbers of children born out of wedlock were recognizably high in the deprived areas in which the research had been undertaken. However, the limited availability of well-paid unskilled work meant that few young mothers could afford to work or expect to rely upon their young male partners for financial support. In the estate in which I lived a number of young women had managed to get council housing for themselves, partner and child. However, the independence ascribed to 'setting up home' was tightly restricted by the necessity of state benefits and a lack of social mobility underscored by an extended reliance upon the older parental family. Thus, many young mothers continued to live in the parental home or had chose to live a few doors away. In the absence of work for either themselves or their partners, crime and 'scams' were often the uneasy resolution to these dynamics (Chapter 5).

Despite popular representations that domestic and workplace transformations are combining with contemporary media images to create new possibilities for a new gender order to prevail, my findings remain more prosaic. Discussions revealed that many young people were sceptical of change and sought, in time, to instil the values of their parental generation upon their future offspring. Though a number were adamant about the need to be economically independent, the modernist, traditional family was still regarded as the desirable, culminating point of stability. The commitment to 'domestic respectability' (McDowell, 2002b: 115) meant that possibilities for new masculinities, new femininities and new ethnicities were still highly contingent upon class, locality and culture. If security, routine and regulation were detested in the schooling system, they appeared much more desirable attributes to be had elsewhere, under the pressures of increased flexibility and greater adaptability. This was evident in the existing leisure patterns and future life-course aspirations of respondents. In many places global change and economic restructuring have exacerbated rather than eradicated socio-economic polarization. The ethnographic evidence seems to suggest that while post-industrial cities may feature developing urban quarters where loft-living, high-speed banking and multinational trade occur, they invariably contain economically deprived areas and highly localized communities where crime, unemployment and social exclusion proliferate. To this extent, the degree of contemporary youth insecurity is temporally and spatially variable.

While many of the aspects of globalization are in themselves not entirely new – international migration, the spread of cultures, technological advancements, and so forth – there has been an acceleration and intensification in these processes to the extent that most lifestyles are now intricately tied to a web of global relations. Thus, despite the seemingly white parochialism of their lives, few youth could escape the shadow of multiculturalism and its influence upon their language, dress and musical affiliations. As the *Real Geordies* were discovering, the traditional regional industries their forefathers had worked in could no longer function as a stalwart for local and national pride in the post-industrial epoch. The new micro-electronic industries were not embedded in the community as of old but were 'footloose' and keen to develop their own unique brand of business cultures. Though it would be premature to write off working-class youth as 'schooling for the dole' (Bates, 1984), as had once seemed the case in a New Right era when unemployment was interpreted as an 'economic necessity', genuine jobs were not easy to come by. In the eyes of certain employees there remained a critical gap between skills, training and knowledge, and the broader aspirations of young people.

As we saw in Chapter 5, the representations and activities of *Charver Kids* could also only be understood through a local–global nexus which had seen Nailton succumb to a diverse array of diasporic movement and settlement, including the influx of asylum seekers, and a longstanding process of de-industrialization. The racialization of *Charvers* as a 'white trash' underclass was filtered through these relations and the new cultural geographies of urban living in the post-colonial city. The influence of a global youth culture was most openly manifest in the subcultural styles and practices of the *White Wannabes*. The cultural 'flows' of global change had become the new rhythms through which these young people increasingly came to understand their lives. For these outwardly looking youth, globalization was producing imaginative spaces in which the intermingling of new identities, ethnicities and multicultural alliances could occur. In this respect, the degree and quality of change was contingent upon subcultural affiliation as well as the role of race, place, class and gender in young lives.

Whiteness

> They used to rule the world. Now they don't know who they are.
>
> Darcus Howe, *White Tribe*, Channel 4, 13 January 2000

When I was growing up in Thatcherite Britain during the eighties, so-called 'race riots' were by no means unusual. The Toxteth district in my hometown of Liverpool, St Paul's in Bristol, Aston Leazels in Birmingham and Brixton in London represent just some of the urban zones in which major uprisings occurred. Indeed, if the title of Cashmore and Troyna's (1982) early edited collection is to be believed, the perception amongst the political Right and Left was united at this point around the construction of *Black Youth in Crisis*.

But perhaps the 'crisis', if indeed there is one, has less to do with black youth and more to do with the social, political and economic challenges facing white youth in the English state. Confronted with the end of empire, the challenge of integration, mass unemployment and the enduring problem of 'those inner cities', it could be argued that it is whiteness and Englishness that is being called into question. For as Mercer has famously declared, 'identity only becomes an issue when it is in crisis, when something assumed to be fixed, coherent and stable is replaced by the experience of doubt and uncertainty' (1994:259). Globalization, devolution, the 'hollowing out' of the nation state and post-colonial resettlement represent just some of the fault lines fragmenting the imagined coherence of white English identities. If it was once black youth who were in crisis, this condemnation has radically shifted to encompass their white counterparts. Yet the idea of 'white crisis' is surely as limited a catch-all when applied to the lives of the ethnic majority as it was when it first congealed in a distinctive configuration to racialize the behaviour of 'crisis-ridden' black youth, 'caught between two cultures'. In attempting to move beyond the dramatic discourse of 'crisis' (a word that has been applied to such far-ranging topics as the nation state and masculinities), it may be worth pausing while reflecting upon the longstanding history of youth 'moral panics' (Chapter 2). Here, it would appear from academic studies of 'deviance', newspaper reports and cultural representations that youth are perpetually 'in crisis' when more intelligent criticism is required.

In recent years ethnic minorities, and particularly those groups identified as 'black', have tended to be over-represented in studies of race and ethnicity. Indeed, it is a feature of those groups who carry the embodied ascription of privilege – masculinity, heterosexuality or whiteness, say – that the ascendant aspects of their identities are rendered normal or 'invisible', so allowing them to inhabit seemingly de-gendered, de-sexualized or de-racialized discursive positions (Bonnett, 1996; Richardson, 1996; Dyer, 1997). For example, Stuart Hall has noted how 'the embattled, hegemonic conception of "Englishness" . . . because it is hegemonic, does not represent itself as an ethnicity at all' (1993:257). Perhaps of all of these ascendant categories the assertion that white people live racially structured lives, precariously positioned in multiple, mobile structures of privilege, remains particularly difficult for many white-skinned people to fully comprehend (Morrison, 1992; hooks, 1993 [1992]; McIntosh, 1997). In my own experience white folk are more likely to position themselves as 'women', 'Irish', 'lesbian' or 'working-class' first, in a racial disavowal of whiteness that is as silent as it is powerful. Curiously enough, perhaps because of this racial displacement, visible minorities have a sharper appreciation of what constitutes whiteness and a more intimate understanding of the multi-layered range of privileges it affords (hooks, 1993 [1992]; Nayak, 1997; Nebeker, 1998).

Though retaining a central focus upon race, place and socio-economic transformations, this book has also illustrated the 'doing' of whiteness. In particular it has shown how whiteness is produced, consumed, regulated, adapted and transgressed in the lives of contemporary generations. This led me to consider the new subject positions available to white youth in the present post-imperial moment. For it seems to me that many white-Anglo youth have uncertainties and experience difficulties when articulating a positive ethnicity in a manner that does not reinscribe 'white pride' by pulling upon the ideologies of racism, nationalism and white exclusivity. Making whiteness visible can unhinge it from its location as transparent, dominant and ordinary, by placing a renewed emphasis upon it as an activity or practice. In this respect whiteness and Englishness have come to represent *the ethnicity that is not one*. 'Seeing' whiteness, then, may offer a positive challenge to 'doing' whiteness. But beyond this, the ethnography has revealed how whiteness can be questioned, done differently, not done at all or, on occasion, 'undone'.

The 'doing' of identity is developed in Queer Theory and philosophical work undertaken by Judith Butler discussing 'the performativity of gender' (1990: 139). For Butler, 'There is no gender identity behind the expressions of gender; that identity is performatively constituted by the very "expressions" that are said to be its results' (p. 25). In other words, there is no pre-given subject, no 'man' or 'woman' who pre-figures action, no 'doer behind the deed' (p. 142). In Butler's reading, masculinities and femininities are corporeal activities that are enacted on the surface of bodies through multiple 'styles of the flesh' (p. 139) and congeal over time to provide the illusion of a substantive gender identity. Here, 'gender is an "act", as it were, that is open to splittings, self-parody, self-criticism, and those hyperbolic exhibitions of the "natural" that in their very exaggeration, reveal its fundamentally phantasmatic status' (pp. 146–7). Similarly, the actions of the *Real Geordies*, *Charvers* and *Wannabes* suggest that the category of race, and in this case whiteness, is performatively conveyed through repetition, stylized gestures, parodic reiterations and corporeal enactments that purport that these racial inscriptions are somehow 'real'. However, if Butler's work has focused on gender and sexuality at the expense of race and class, the ethnography indicates that performativity may also need to be understood as geographically bounded and materially situated.

In view of the difficulties (theoretical, political and pedagogical) of engaging with white-Anglo identity, the question is how can we delicately capture the varied experience of white ethnicity without alienating white youth or evoking a relativist racial equivalence? The strategies discussed in the previous chapter used deconstructionist and materialist insights to elicit an historically embedded and place-specific approach to youth cultural identity. In arguing for a critical engagement with white identity, the study seeks to remove whiteness from its privileged place as normal, transparent and invisible. 'Seeing' white power and privilege offers a starting point for challenging such racially inscribed inequalities. Clearly, such a project must avoid indulging in a navel-gazing fetish that reifies the category of whiteness. In arguing against the recuperation of whiteness as a distinct cultural identity, my aim is not to resurrect the phantom of whiteness but to exorcize it. For as long as colour-based racisms continue to preside, whiteness cannot hold equal status within the multicultural corridors of youth culture.

As we saw in the previous chapter, many white working-class youth are unable to reconcile themselves as the 'privileged' subjects designated by traditional anti-racist models. The assumption that 'being white' equates with 'being racist' and having power is increasingly unsustainable in 'new times' where 'a more sensitive and sophisticated approach to questions of *white* ethnicity' (Gillborn, 1995:11) is patently required. For as the Burnage Report illustrates, 'heavy-handed' forms of anti-racism have tended to treat white students as implicitly racist on the basis of their whiteness, 'whether they are ferret-eyed fascists or committed anti-racists' (MacDonald *et al.*, 1989:402). Indeed, the subcultural case studies undertaken already contradict simplistic notions of 'white privilege' and disclose the cultural contingency of white identities structured not only in relation to blackness, but also in relation to other forms of white subjectivity.

In the quest for social justice in 'new times' I have provided pedagogical pointers for future policy and practice in the field of whiteness, race and ethnicity. These are drawn from the research, existing literature and discussions with youth workers, teachers and other practitioners. It is hoped that this will create a starting point from which a new multiculturalism can emerge that is more in touch with contemporary youth cultures in a changing world. To become more inclusive such practices must:

- engage with the identities and everyday local cultures of young people;
- draw upon existing networks and be sensitive to the organic, 'felt' needs of students, teachers, parents and the wider community;
- move beyond the black–white colour paradigm, to appreciate new ethnic and religious differences;
- recognize that all students have an ethnicity and live racially structured lives;
- appreciate that young ethnicities are multiply positioned in changing relationships of dominance and subordination, marked across lines of gender, class, sexuality and dis/ability;
- illustrate the historical relations of power underpinning contemporary racisms;
- distinguish between 'being white' and 'acting white';
- avoid 'moral policing' and instead be seen to liberate and promote equality for all;
- recognize that contemporary racisms and ethnicities are shot through with ambivalence and contradiction;

- be geographically attentive to the particularity of place and differences at the local, national and international scale;
- continue to adapt and develop through a reflexive engagement with theory and practice.

Place and Identity

The empirical research conducted in Northeast England observed that there is a highly meaningful relationship between place and identity. This contrasts some-what with postmodernist theories suggesting we are living in 'placeless' times, characterized by simulation, artifice and hyper-realities. Here, contemporary society is no longer bound to the rigidities of an industrial community designed around the pit, shipyard or factory but comprises 'virtual communities', more mobile populations and increasingly remote relationships between kith and kin. The complexity of 'living the global city' (Eade, 1997) seems to have now given way to 'new ethnicities', changing morphologies and new cultural attachments. However, although young people's sense of place may be mediated through the information superhighway and new cultural circuits of global display – including advertising, film, fashion and music – there are strong indications that place and locality are of significant importance in young lives. In a period where the barriers of time and space are disintegrating and the 'flows' of people, capital and goods grow ever more intensified, the ethnography indicates that place retains a material and symbolic prominence in young lives.

The significance of place relations is evident in the subcultural histories. For the *Real Geordies*, local cultures are an integral part of their individual and collective identities. Support of NUFC and the adaptation of older, industrial drinking practices are a vital means of resuscitating local pride and breathing new life into the meaning of white 'Geordie' masculinity in seemingly uncertain times. More-over, these locally specific practices have resulted in the reinvention of the region from a place associated with coal, cloth-caps and pigeon-racing to a region renowned for drinking, partying and celebration. Crucially, participation in this transformation is possible as it does not obliterate class cultural codes but imagina-tively draws upon, and then elaborates, these signs, in the arena of leisure and consumption. Shared family histories and intersecting labour biographies then enrich the social 'stickiness' of place. Despite processes of de-industrialization and the new employment emphasis being assigned to mobility, opportunism and individualism, the 'pride in place' instilled in being a *Real Geordie* is as meaning-ful now as it has ever been.

Intra-regional differences in youth cultures are evident in the distinctions drawn between *Real Geordies* and *Charver Kids*. The place-specific qualities of the

Charver subculture may be extending, but the associations with inner-city crime and the lower-class culture of the Nailton district remains. For some of these youth, their reliance upon the immediate locality is such that a number do not venture outside their estate and have little sense of events outside their neighbourhood boundaries. Moreover, in the de-industrialized landscapes of Nailton, *Charver Kids* are seen to *rework* the habitations in which they reside by developing an informal economy designed around the 'culture of the street'. This alternative economy has undoubtedly divided local communities, but it is also a knife-like response to global change and labour market restructuring. In many ways this is de-industrialization in its rawest, most naked form with transformations undressing unashamedly before the looking glass of the local community.

In contrast, for those youth developing emerging ethnicities in Chapter 6, the new spaces of consumption available in the global economy, including music, fashion and sport, are especially influential. Satellite communication, MTV and the screening of basketball games, skateboarding competitions, Hip-Hop music and other global youth activities have certainly hastened cross-cultural identification in the region. But although these youth may have looked to Africa, Asia and America for inspiration, it is in 'local' spaces – the basketball court, the Hip-Hop venue, playground and local music scenes – that these identities are 'tried out' and made to cohere in embodied form specifically adapted to the immediate vicinity. The research indicates that whilst youth cultures may draw inspiration from the global marketplace when it comes to dress, music, hairstyles and fashion, these values are invariably appraised at the prosaic level of the 'local', where the inflections of race, class, gender, and so forth, remain evident. These different youthscapes reveal how young lives are fashioned by way of a 'power geometry' (Massey, 1996 [1991]), in which groups and individuals are placed in distinct and unequal relations to the flows and interconnections that cohere around their social worlds.

Despite the homogenizing aspects of globalization and the perceived 'Mc-Donaldization' of society, there remains compelling evidence to suggest that youth cultures continue to be complex, place-related phenomena. Recent work has suggested that we can no longer think of place, locality or communities as securely 'bounded'. Instead, locales are porous and open-ended 'meeting places' within which a whole host of social interactions cross-cut and reconfigure our 'sense of place' (Massey, 1996 [1991]). Rather than being fixed or stable points, they comprise a series of interchanging discourses. Indeed, the geographical boundaries drawn around places, regions, nations and communities are, at best, 'imaginary'. Local places are not, then, tightly 'bounded' hermetic zones that can be neatly demarcated from national, international and even global processes in occurrence. Instead, a central feature of globalization is the manner in which social relations become 'disembedded' from their local constituents. Nevertheless, the ethnography is indicative of the intense 'structures of feeling' young people maintain with their environments and the simultaneous practices of *re-localization* that occur in the local–global nexus. This is illustrated in the strident localism of the *Real Geordies* and the enduring ability of *Charver Kids* to resurrect an inner-city working-class community reliant upon older family and kinship networks, 'scams' and door-to-door 'trading'.

This study has shown that in a changing world, young people's identities continue to be defined through the material cultures of daily life. Neighbourhood networks, the institution of schooling, familial relations, local labour markets and place and locality continue to shape and fashion young people's ethnicities. These identities can acquire richer meaning in the enactment and take-up of a recogniz-able subcultural style. In these cases, youth cultures become particularly significant as young people define themselves through and against one another in the immed-iate and intense space of the 'local'. Postmodern interpretations of youth styles as designed in a chaotic bazaar where eclecticism, multiculture, *bricolage* and pastiche predominate only go some way to describing the evident material patterning of youth relations. These 'felt' understandings of difference are embodied in the 'oblique' postures of subculture, an encoded practice that relies upon mutual forms of youth recognition. In global times the enactment of a subcultural persona seems then, a thoroughly *modernist* way of imposing a rationale sense of order and stability in a changing world.

By drawing upon historical, structural and cultural perspectives, *Race, Place and Globalization* has sought to open up a space for a 'transdisciplinary' debate on youth. It has sought to map a new type of *spatial cultural studies*. In doing so it has developed insights from human geography concerning space, place and global change and allied these to youth cultural studies and the wider sociology of race and ethnic relations. The work has argued that the current cultural studies fascina-tion with dance, music and consumption could yet benefit from being more securely anchored to the multi-dimensional and changing material cultures of young lives. Research on young people and the labour market, the family, schooling or neighbourhood offer complementary zones in which we can map out more extensive portraits of youth cultures beyond the dancehall or shopping mall. The analysis of local political economy cautions against a belief that young people's lifestyles are fluid to the point where place, institutions and material cultures are no longer of consequence. These insights, achieved at a local scale, can add important detail to open-ended depictions of 'youth lifestyles' as endlessly produced, performed and repackaged through world-wide commodity chains and global consumer cultures.

Nevertheless, structural approaches to youth cannot rely solely on statistics and the place-specific qualities of particular institutions within the labour market. These reports need to be placed more firmly within the immediate context of everyday youthscapes where the fluidity, complexity and ambiguities of individual and collective biographies are brightly illuminated. Here, the 'centrality of identity and the subtle interplay of individual agency, circumstance and social structure' (Thompson *et al.*, 2002:336) should be of primary significance to transitional accounts. In global times, where young people may take inspiration from products, events or happenings that occur outside their immediate spatial vicinity, cultural studies is key to understanding these interlocking local–global complexities. Recent research in post-colonial theory, feminism, post-structuralism and psycho-analysis provides fresh and exciting ways for 'rethinking the youth question' (Cohen, 1997). If the findings in my own research are anything to go by, these discussions need to engage more closely with lived experience and the changing cultural and material geographies of young lives. Grasping this challenge in-evitably involves blending 'good theory' with an impassioned and committed approach to young people. For if future debates on race, place and global change are to ripen, such passion will be indispensable.

Appendices

Appendix 1: The Ethnography

Methods

The ethnography incorporates observation, interviews and 'thick' description of people and place.

1. *Participant observation* was undertaken as part of a multi-site analysis in schools, city-centre and neighbourhood spaces. These techniques were enriched through my time spent living on the Nailton estate and the day-to-day activities of moving between spaces and interacting with the landscape, services and people.
2. *Semi-structured interviews* were conducted by way of a series of individual and focus group interviews. There was a longitudinal dimension to the study familiar to ethnography. All respondents were interviewed two to four times according to the willingness of the participant, the researcher rapport and the quality of information provided. Interviews were organized around set themes (e.g. education, family, locality, employment) but were consistently revised and reflexively refined according to the material generated. This enabled invaluable discussions on topics such as football, local music scenes and *Charver* sub-cultures to develop that could otherwise have been omitted.
3. *'Thick' description* was deployed to enable a more embodied account of young lives to emerge. There were two key advantages to this. Firstly, 'thick' description of people and place provided a contextual location from which to explore youth subjectivities. Secondly, the move away from standard interviewing meant action as well as speech could be recorded, normally through the use of fieldwork journals and on rare occasions through memory work. In particular, secondary sources such as local histories, press reportage, census data and other studies in the field was used to cross-reference information but also as a technique for the emplacement and layering of accounts.

Appendix 2: The Institutional Interviews

School-Based Data: Emblevale School

Emblevale is a multi-ethnic middle school that draws upon children from leafy residential suburbs and impoverished inner-city districts. It has a large number of 'special needs' students, many of whom have visual impairments. Approximately three-quarters of the students are white, though, in addition to English students this includes a number from Irish, Welsh and Scottish backgrounds as well as a smaller number who had Scandinavian, Polish, German and Italian ancestry. The remainder are South Asian (including those of Indian, Pakistani and Bangladeshi descent), with a fraction of African-Caribbean and East Asian students.

Intake range: 9–12 years.

Total number of students: 405 equally split by gender.

Ethnicity, social class and dis/ability characteristics may be cautiously derived from the following broad indicators:

- Number of students requiring special educational needs (SEN): 118.
- Percentage of students for whom English is an additional language: 11.
- Percentage of students receiving free school meals: 24.

Emblevale School (9–10 years)

Aisha
Alan
Alistair
Andrew
Brett
Danielle
Fern
Jane
Kirsty

Emblevale School (11–12 years)

James
Lucy
Michelle
Nicola/Nicky
Sam
Sara

Appendices

School-Based Data: Snowhill Comprehensive

Snowhill Comprehensive is a large, ostensibly white state school. At the time of research it had 1,936 pupils of whom 1,869 were white, UK citizens. The school contained an equal number of boys and girls, the majority of whom were from working-class backgrounds.

Intake range: 11–18 years (mixed gender).
Total number of students: 1,936.
White ethnic majority: 1,869.

Snowhill Comprehensive Sixth Form
Total number of students: 270 of whom 15 were identified as ethnic minority.
255 classified as white, UK citizens.
6 classified as Indian.
5 classified as Chinese.
2 classified as Pakistani.
2 classified as 'Other minority'.

Snowhill Comprehensive, masculine familial labouring background in brackets (16–17 years)
Bill (sheet-metal worker)
Cambo (skilled construction)
Carl (skilled construction)
Chris (unemployed)
Dave (skilled construction)
Duane (car mechanic)
Ema (armed forces)
Fat Mal (factory foreman)
Filo (central-heating fitter)
Helena (care-taker)
Jason (small business)
John (site manager)
Jolene (bailiff)
Jono (cab driver)
Lucy (small business)
Paul (public sector)
Shaun (publican)
Spencer (skilled construction)
Steve (electrician)
Suzanne (skilled labour)

Appendix 3: Data Analysis

Transcription code
edited break in text
... participant pause in text
[*italics*] description of on-going action

All institutional interviews were tape-recorded, transcribed and analysed by the author. The data were biographically indexed and then thematically arranged to sharpen the interpretative focus. However, as many themes cross-cut, it was important not to bind these strands too rigidly.

The ethnographic interviews were interpreted in four main ways: firstly, at a *structural* level to undergird the relationship between an individual, specific institutional structures and the wider social world; secondly, at an *historical* level to enable connections between the past and present to be identified, thus allowing hitherto unmarked patterns to come to light; thirdly, at a *cultural* level to trace the dynamic and multiple refashioning of young identities; and finally, at a *theoretical* level bringing together insights from cultural studies, geography and sociology. As new themes and perspectives emerged, it was necessary to rethink and at times reposition this interpretative place-matrix. This occurred more frequently as themes were revisited through further group and individual interviews. Even so, the place-matrix acted as a useful grid through which to underpin the more descriptive elements of ethnography.

Bibliography

Alexander, C. (1996) *The Art of Being Black: The creation of black British youth identities* (Oxford, Clarendon Press).

Alexander, C. (2000) *The Asian Gang: Ethnicity, identity, masculinity* (Oxford, Berg).

Allen, R. (1992) *The Complete Richard Allen Volume One* (Dunoon, Skinhead Times Publishing).

Allen, T. (1994) *The Invention of the White Race* (London, Verso).

Amos, V. and Parmar, P. (1984) Challenging imperial feminism, *Feminist Review*, 17, pp. 3–19.

Anderson, B. (1984 [1983]) *Imagined Communities: Reflections on the origin and spread of nationalism* (London, Verso).

Appadurai, A. (1990) Disjuncture and difference in the global economy, *Theory, Culture and Society*, 7, pp. 295–310.

Atkinson, P. (1990) *The Ethnographic Imagination: Textual constructions of reality* (London, Routledge).

Atkinson, P. (1992) *Understanding Ethnographic Texts* (London, Sage).

Back, L. (1990) Racist name-calling and developing anti-racist initiatives in youth work, *Centre for Racial and Ethnic Relations* 14 (Coventry, University of Warwick).

Back, L. (1996) *New Ethnicities and Urban Culture: Racism and multiculture in young people's lives* (London, UCL Press).

Back, L. and Nayak, A. (1999) Signs of the Times? Violence, graffiti and racism in the English suburbs, in T. Allen and J. Eade (eds) *Divided Europeans: Understanding ethnicities in conflict* (The Hague, Kluwer Law International).

Ball, S. (1990) *Politics and Policy Making in Education: Explorations in political sociology* (London, Routledge).

Barker, M. (1981) *The New Racism* (London, Junction Books).

Bates, I. (1984) *Schooling for the Dole? The new vocationalism* (London, Macmillan)

Bath, L. and Farrell, P. (1996) The attitudes of white secondary school students towards ethnic minorities, *Educational and Child Psychology*, 13(3), pp. 5–13.

Bauder, H. (2001) Culture in the labour market: Segmentation theory and perspectives of place, *Progress in Human Geography*, 25 (1), pp. 37–52.

Bean, D. (1971) *Tyneside: A biography* (London, Macmillan).

Bean, D. (1980) *Newcastle 900: A portrait of Newcastle upon Tyne* (Newcastle, Newcastle upon Tyne City Council).

Beck, U. (1998 [1992]) *Risk Society: Towards a new modernity* (London, Sage).

Becker, H.S. (1973 [1963]) *Outsiders: Studies in the sociology of deviance* (New York, Free Press).

Bell, D. (1990) *Acts of Union: Youth culture and sectarianism in Northern Ireland* (Basingstoke, Macmillan).

Bennett, A. (1999a) Subcultures or neo-tribes? Rethinking the relationship between youth, style and musical taste, *Sociology*, 33(3), pp. 599–617.

Bennett, A. (1999b) Rappin' on the Tyne: White hip hop culture in northeast England: an ethnographic study, *Sociological Review*, 47, pp. 1–24.

Bennett, A. (2000) *Popular Music and Youth Culture: Music, identity and place* (Baskingstoke, Macmillan).

Bhabha, H.K. (1984) Signs taken for wonders: Questions of ambivalence and authority under a tree outside Delhi, May 1817, in F. Baker *et al., Europe and Its Others*, Vol. 1 (Essex, Essex Sociology of Literature).

Bhabha, H.K. (1990) The third space – Interview with Homi Bhabha, in J. Rutherford (ed.) *Identity: Community, culture, difference* (London, Lawrence & Wishart).

Bhabha, H.K. (1994) *The Location of Culture* (London, Routledge).

Blackman, S. (1997) 'Poxy Cupid!' An ethnographic and feminist account of a resistant female youth culture: The New Wave Girls, in T. Skelton and G. Valentine (eds) *Cool Places: Geographies of youth* (London, Routledge).

Bonnett, A. (1993a) *Radicalism, Anti-Racism and Representation* (London, Routledge).

Bonnett, A. (1993b) 'Forever "white"?' Challenges and alternatives to a 'racial' monolith, *New Community*, 20(1), pp. 173–80.

Bonnett, A. (1993c) The formation of public professional radical consciousness: The example of anti-racism, *Sociology*, 27(2), pp. 281–97.

Bonnett, A. (1996) 'White studies': The problems and projects of a new research agenda, *Theory, Culture and Society*, 13(2), pp. 145–55.

Bonnett, A. and Nayak, A. (2003) Cultural geographies of racialization: The territory of race, in K. Anderson, M. Domosh, S. Pile and N. Thrift (eds) *Handbook of Cultural Geography* (London, Sage).

Booth, C. (1976 [1890]) In Darkest England and the Way Out, in P. Keating (ed.) *Into Unknown England 1866–1913* (Manchester, Manchester University Press).

Bourke, J. (1994) *Working-Class Cultures in Britain 1890–1960: Gender, class and ethnicity* (New York, Routledge).

Bradford, M. and Burdett, F. (1989) Privatization, education and the north–south divide, in J. Lewis and A. Townsend (eds) *The north–south Divide: Regional change in Britain in the 1980s* (London, Paul Chapman).

Bradley, H., Erickson, M., Stephenson, C. and Williams, S. (2000) *The Myth of Globalization* (Cambridge, Polity Press).

Brah, A. (1996) *Cartographies of Diaspora: Contesting identities* (London, Routledge).

Brake, M. (1993 [1985]) *Comparative Youth Culture: The sociology of youth subcultures in Britain and Canada* (London, Routledge).

Bromley, R. (1988) *Lost Narratives: Popular fictions, politics and recent history* (London, Routledge).

Brown, M. (1997) Basketball, Rodney King, Simi Valley, in M. Hill (ed.) *Whiteness: A critical reader* (New York, New York University Press).

Bryson, J., Henry, N., Keeble, D. and Martin, R. (eds) (1999) *The Economic Geography Reader* (Chichester, Wiley).

Burgess, R.G. (1982) Personal documents, oral sources and field research, in R.G. Burgess *Field Research: A sourcebook and field manual* (London, George Allen & Unwin).

Butler, J. (1990) *Gender Trouble: Feminism and the subversion of identity* (New York, Routledge).

Campbell, A. (1991 [1984]) *The Girls in the Gang* (Oxford, Blackwell).

Campbell, B. (1993) *Goliath: Britain's dangerous places* (London, Methuen).

Campbell, B. (1995) Old fogeys and angry young men: A critique of communitarianism, *Soundings* 1, pp. 47–64.

Canaan, J.E. (1986) Why a 'slut' is a 'slut': Cautionary tales of middle-class girls' morality, in H. Varenne (ed.) *Symbolizing America* (Nebraska: Indiana University Press).

Canaan, J.E. (1996) 'One thing leads to another': Drinking, fighting and working-class masculinities, in M. Mac an Ghaill (ed.) *Understanding Masculinities* (Buckingham, Open University Press).

Carby, H. (1982) White woman listen! Black feminism and the boundaries of sisterhood, in Centre for Contemporary Cultural Studies, *The Empire Strikes Back: Race and racism in 70s Britain* (London, Hutchinson).

Carr, B. (1992) Black Geordies, in R. Colls and B. Lancaster (eds) *Geordies: Roots of regionalism* (Edinburgh, University of Edinburgh Press).

Cashmore, E. and Troyna, B (eds) (1982) *Black Youth in Crisis* (London, Allen & Unwin).

Castells, M. (1997) *The Power of Identity* (Oxford, Blackwell)

Centre for Contemporary Cultural Studies (1982) *The Empire Strikes Back: Race and racism in 70s Britain* (London, Hutchinson).

Chambers, I. (1988 [1986]) *Popular Culture: The metropolitan experience* (London, Routledge).

Chang, T.C. (1999) Local uniqueness in the global village: Heritage tourism in Singapore, *Professional Geographer*, 51(1), pp. 91–103.

Chatterton, P. and Hollands, R. (2001) *Changing Our 'Toon': Youth, nightlife and urban change in Newcastle* (Newcastle, University of Newcastle upon Tyne)

Chatterton, P. and Hollands, R. (2002) Theorizing urban playscapes: Producing, regulating and consuming youthful nightlife city spaces, *Urban Studies*, 39(1), pp. 95–116.

Clarke, G. (1981) Defending of ski-jumpers: A critique of theories of youth subcultures, Stencilled Paper 72, Centre for Contemporary Cultural Studies, University of Birmingham.

Clarke, J. (1974) Subcultural symbolism: Reconceptualizing 'youth culture', unpublished MA thesis, Centre for Contemporary Cultural Studies (Birmingham, University of Birmingham).

Clarke, J. (1977 [1975]) The skinheads and the magical recovery of community, in *Resistance through Rituals* S. Hall and T. Jefferson (eds) (London, Hutchinson/ University of Birmingham, Centre for Contemporary Cultural Studies).

Clarke, J., Hall, S., Jefferson, T. and Roberts, B. (1977 [1975]) Subcultures, cultures and Class: A theoretical overview, in S. Hall and T. Jefferson (eds) *Resistance Through Rituals: Youth subcultures in post-war Britain* (London, Hutchinson/University of Birmingham, Centre for Contemporary Cultural Studies).

Clarke, K.B. and Clarke, M.K. (1939) The development of consciousness of self and the emergence of racial identification in Negro preschool children, *Journal of Social Psychology*, SPSSI Bulletin 10, pp. 591–9.

Clarke, K.B. and Clarke, M.K. (1947) Racial identification and preference in Negro children, in T. Newcomb and E. Hartley (eds), *Readings in Social Psychology* (New York: Holt, Rinehart and Winston.

Coard, B. (1982) What the British school system does to the black child, in A. James and R. Jeffcoate (eds) *The School in the Multicultural Society* (London, Harper & Row/Open University Press).

Coffield, R., Borrill, C. and Marshall, S. (1986 [1985]) *Growing Up at the Margins: Young adults in the North East* (Milton Keynes, Open University Press).

Cohen, A. (1997 [1955]) A general theory of subcultures, in K. Gelder and S. Thornton (eds) *The Subcultures Reader* (London, Routledge).

Cohen, P. (1972) Subcultural conflict and the working-class community, *Working Papers in Cultural Studies*, 2 (Centre for Contemporary Cultural Studies, University of Birmingham).

Cohen, P. (1993 [1988]) The perversions of inheritance: Studies in the making of multi-racist Britain, in P. Cohen and H. Bains (eds) *Multi-racist Britain* (Basingstoke, Macmillan).

Cohen, P. (1993) 'It's racism what dunnit': Hidden narratives in theories of racism, in J. Donald and A. Rattansi (eds) *'Race', Culture and Difference* (London, Open University Press).

Bibliography

Cohen, P. (1997) *Rethinking the Youth Question: Education, labour and cultural studies* (Basingstoke/London, Macmillan).

Cohen, P. (ed.) (1999) *New Ethnicities, Old Racisms* (London, Zed Books).

Cohen, S. (ed.) (1971) *Images of Deviance* (Harmondsworth, Penguin).

Cohen, S. (1973 [1972]) *Folk Devils and Moral Panics* (St Albans, Paladin).

Collier, R. (1998) *Masculinities, Crime and Criminology* (London/Thousand Oaks/New Delhi, Sage).

Colls, R. (1992) Born again Geordies, in R. Colls and B. Lancaster (eds) *Geordies: Roots of regionalism* (Edinburgh, University of Edinburgh Press).

Colls, R. and Lancaster, B. (eds) (1992) *Geordies: Roots of regionalism* (Edinburgh, University of Edinburgh Press).

Connell, R.W. (1989) Cool guys, swots and wimps: The interplay of masculinity and education, *Oxford Review of Education*, 5 (3), pp. 291–303.

Connell, R.W. (1995) *Masculinities* (Cambridge, Polity Press).

Connolly, P. (1998) *Racism, Gender Identities and Young Children: Social relations in a multi-ethnic inner-city primary school* (London, Routledge).

Conrad, J. (1994 [1902]) *Heart of Darkness* (London, Penguin).

Corrigan, P. (1981 [1979]) *Schooling the Smash Street Kids* (Basingstoke, Macmillan).

Daniel, S. and McGuire, P. (eds) (1972) *The Paint House: Words from an East End gang* (Harmondsworth, Penguin).

Davis, M. (1991) *City of Quartz* (London, Verso).

Dawley, S. (2000) Labour market responses to foreign direct investment, (dis)-investment and re-investment: The case of the semiconductor industry in the North East region 1989–2000, unpublished paper presented at the Global Conference on Economic Geography, Singapore, 5–8 December.

Delamont, S. (2001) Changing Women, Unchanged Men?: Sociological Perspectives on Gender in a Post-industrial Society (Buckingham, Open University Press)

Department of Education and Science (1985) *Education for All: The Swann Report* (London, HMSO).

Dikotter, F. (1992) *The Discourse of Racism in Modern China* (London, Hurst)

Donbrow, M. (1988 [1972]) *They Docked at Newcastle and Wound Up in Gateshead* (Gateshead, Portcullis Press).

Douglas, M. (1992 [1966]) *Purity and Danger: An analysis of the concepts of purity and taboo* (London, Routledge).

Driver, G. (1982) Classroom stress and school achievement: West Indian adolescents and their teachers, in A. James and R. Jeffcoate (eds) *The School in the Multicultural Society* (London, Harper & Row/Open University Press).

Dyer, R. (1993) White, in *The Matter of Images: Essays on representations* (London, Routledge).

Dyer, R. (1997) *White* (London, Routledge).

Eade, J. (ed.) (1997) *Living the Global City: Globalization as a local process* (London, Routledge).

Ely, P. (1997) Food for Thought: Identity and the cultural politics of Chinese cuisine in Newcastle's Chinatown, unpublished undergraduate dissertation (Newcastle, Department of Geography at the University of Newcastle upon Tyne).

Epstein, D. (1993) *Changing Classroom Cultures: Anti-racism, politics and schools* (Stoke on Trent, Trentham Books).

Fanon, F. (1967 [1952]) *Black Skin, White Masks* (New York, Grove).

Fanon, F. (1993) The fact of blackness, in J. Donald and A. Rattansi (eds) *'Race', Culture and Difference* (London, Open University Press).

Featherstone, M. (1998 [1991]) *Consumer Culture and Postmodernism* (London, Sage)

Foucault, M. (1980) Truth and power, in C. Gordon (ed.) *Power/Knowledge: Selected interviews and other writings 1972–77* (Brighton, Harvester Press).

Foucault, M. (1988) Technologies of the self, in L. Martin, H. Gutman and P. Hutton (eds) *Technologies of the Self: A seminar with Michel Foucault* (London, Tavistock).

Frankenberg, R. (1994) *White Women, Race Matters: The social construction of whiteness* (Minneapolis, University of Minnesota Press).

Frosh, S., Phoenix, A. and Pattman, R. (2002) *Young Masculinities: Understanding boys in contemporary society*, (Basingstoke, Palgrave).

Fryer, P. (1984) *Staying Power: The history of black people in Britain* (London/ New Leichardt, Pluto Press).

Fuller, M. (1982) Black girls in a London comprehensive, in A. James and R. Jeffcoate (eds) *The School in the Multicultural Society* (London, Harper & Row/Open University Press).

Fyvel, T.R. (1963 [1961]) *The Insecure Offenders: Rebellious youth in the welfare state* (Harmondsworth, Penguin).

Gaine, C. (1987) *No Problem Here: A practical approach to education and 'race' in white schools* (London, Hutchinson Education).

Gaine, C. (1995) *Still No Problem Here* (Stoke on Trent, Trentham Books).

Garrahan, P. and Stewart, P. (1994) *Urban Change and Renewal: The paradox of place* (Avebury, Aldershot).

Gelder, K. (1997) Introduction to part three, in K. Gelder and S. Thornton (eds) *The Subcultures Reader* (London/New York, Routledge).

Gelder, K and Thornton, S. (eds) (1997) *The Subcultures Reader* (London/New York, Routledge).

Giddens, A. (1991) *Modernity and Self-identity in the Late Modern Age* (Cambridge, Polity).

Gillborn, D. (1990) *'Race', Ethnicity and Education: Teaching and learning in multi-ethnic schools* (London, Unwin-Hyman/Routledge).

Gillborn, D. (1995) *Racism and Antiracism in Real Schools* (Buckingham, Open University Press).

Gillborn, D. (1996) Student roles and perspectives in antiracist education: A crisis of white ethnicity, *British Educational Research Journal*, 22(2), pp. 165–79.

Gilroy, P. (1994 [1992]) The end of antiracism, in J. Donald and A. Rattansi (eds) *'Race', Culture and Difference* (London, Sage/Open University Press)

Gilroy, P. (1995 [1987]) *There Ain't no Black in the Union Jack* (London, Hutchinson).

Giroux, H. (1997a) Rewriting the discourse of racial identity: Towards a pedagogy and politics of whiteness, *Harward Educational Review*, 67(2), pp. 285–319.

Giroux, H. (1997b) Racial politics and the pedagogy of whiteness, in M. Hill (ed.) *Whiteness: A critical reader* (New York, New York University Press).

Gissing, G. (1889) *The Nether World: A novel* (London, Smith, Elder and Co.).

Gissing, G. (1992 [1891]) New Grub Street, in J. Halperin (ed.) *New Grub Street/ George Gissing* (Halifax, Ryburn).

Gordon, P. and Klug, F. (1986) *New Right New Racism* (Nottingham, Searchlight Publications).

Gordon, T., Holland, J. and Lahelma, E. (2000) *Making Spaces: Citizenship and difference in schools* (Basingstoke, Macmillan).

Gough, B. and Edwards, G. (1998) The beer talking: Four lads, a carry-out and the reproduction of masculinities, *The Sociological Review*, 46(3), pp. 409–35.

Gray, R. (1981) *The Aristocracy of Labour in Nineteenth-Century Britain 1850– 1914* (London/Basingstoke, Macmillan).

Greenwood, J. (1976 [1874]) The Wilds of London, in P. Keating (ed.) *Into Unknown England 1886–1913* (Manchester, Manchester University Press).

Griffin, C. (1985) *Typical Girls? Young women from school to the job market* (London, Routledge & Kegan Paul).

Griffin, C. (1993) *Representations of Youth: The study of youth and adolescence in Britain and America* (Cambridge, Polity Press).

Halford, S. and Savage, M. (1997) Rethinking restructuring: Embodiment, agency and identity in organizational change, in R. Lee and J. Wills (eds) *Geographies of Economies* (London, Arnold).

Hall, S. (1993) New ethnicities, in J. Donald and A. Rattansi (eds), *'Race', Culture and Difference* (London, Sage/Open University Press).

Hall, S. and Jefferson, T. (1977 [1975]) *Resistance through Rituals* (London, Hutchinson/Centre for Contemporary Cultural Studies, University of Birmingham)

Hall, S., Critcher, C., Jefferson, T., Clarke, J. and Roberts, B. (1979 [1978]) *Policing the Crisis: Mugging, the state, and law and order* (London, Macmillan).

Hammersley, M. and Atkinson, A. (1989 [1983]) *Ethnography: Principles in practice* (London, Routledge).

Hargreaves, D.H., Hester, S. and Mellor, F. (1975) *Deviance in Classrooms* (London, Routledge & Kegan Paul).

Harris, J. (1994 [1993]) *Private Lives, Public Spirit: Britain 1870–1914* (Harmondsworth, Penguin).

Harvey, D. (1990 [1989]) *The Condition of Postmodernity: An enquiry in the origins of cultural change* (Cambridge, MA: Blackwell).

Healy, M. (1996) *Gay Skins: Class, masculinity and queer appropriation* (London/ New York, Cassell).

Hebdige, D. (1977) Reggae, Rastas and Rudies, in S. Hall and T. Jefferson (eds) *Resistance through Rituals* (London, Hutchinson/ University of Birmingham Centre for Contemporary Cultural Studies).

Hebdige, D. (1987 [1979]) *Subculture: The meaning of style* (London, Methuen).

Henriques, J., Hollway, W., Urwin C., Venn, C. and Walkerdine, V. (1998 [1984]) *Changing the Subject: Psychology, social regulation and subjectivity* (London, Routledge).

Herbert, S. (2000) For ethnography, *Progress in Human Geography*, 24(4), pp. 550–68.

Hewitt, R. (1986) *White Talk Black Talk* (Cambridge, Cambridge University Press).

Hewitt, R. (1996) *Routes of Racism: The social basis of racist action* (Stoke on Trent, Trentham Books).

Hey, V. (1997) *The Company She Keeps: An ethnography of girls' friendships* (Buckingham, Open University Press).

Hickman, M.J. and Walter, B. (1995) Decconstructing whiteness: Irish women in Britain, *Feminist Review*, 50, pp. 5–19.

Hirst, P. and Thompson, G. (1999 [1996]) Globalization – A necessary myth?, in J. Bryson, N. Henry, D. Keeble and R. Martin (eds) *The Economic Geography Reader* (Chichester, Wiley)

Hobsbawm, E.J. (1982 [1968]) *Industry and Empire* (Hardmondsworth, Penguin).

Hoggart, R. (1966 [1957]) *The Uses of Literacy* (Harmondsworth, Penguin).

Hollands, R. (1990) *The Long Transition* (Basingstoke, Macmillan).

Hollands, R. (1995) *Friday Night, Saturday Night: Youth cultural identification in the post-industrial city* (Newcastle, Department of Social Policy at the University of Newcastle upon Tyne).

Hollands, R. (1997) From shipyards to nightclubs: Restructuring young adults' employment, household and consumption identities in the North-East of England, *Berkeley Journal of Sociology*, 41, pp. 41–66.

Hollingshead, J. (1986) *Ragged London in 1861* (London, Everyman History).

Holohan, A., Pledger, G. and Watson, D. (1988) Health and health provision, in F. Robinson (ed.) *Post-Industrial Tyneside: An economic and social survey of*

Tyneside in the 1980s (Newcastle, Newcastle upon Tyne City Libraries and Arts).

hooks, b. (1993 [1992]) *Black Looks* (New York, Routledge).

Hudson, R. (2000) *Production, Places and Environment: Changing perspectives in economic geography* (Harlow, Longman).

Humphries, S. (1981*) Hooligans or Rebels? An oral history of working-class history and youth 1889–1939* (Oxford, Blackwell).

Ignatiev, N. (1995) *How the Irish became White* (New York, Routledge).

Ingham, J., Purvis, M. and Clarke, D.B. (1999) Hearing places, making spaces: Sonorous geographies, ephemeral rhythms, and the Blackburn warehouse parties, *Environment and Planning D: Society and Space*, 17, pp. 283–305.

International Searchlight (2002) North East round up April, no. 322, p. 17

Jackson, P. (1993) The concept of 'race', in P. Jackson and P. Penrose (eds) *Constructions of Race, Place and Nation* (London, UCL Press).

Jackson, P. (1995 [1989]) *Maps of Meaning: An introduction to cultural geography* (London, Unwin Hyman).

Jameson, F. (1991) Postmodernism, or, The Cultural Logic of Late Capitalism (London, Verso).

Jarvis, H., Pratt, A.C. and Chen-Chong Wu, P. (2001) *The Secret Life of Cities: The social reproduction of everyday life* (Harlow, Prentice Hall).

Jay, A.O.M. (1891) *Life in Darkest London* (London, Webster and Cable).

Jeater, D. (1992) Roast beef and reggae music: The passing of whitness, *New Formations*, 18, pp. 107–21)

Jeffcoate, R. (1982) Evaluating the multicultural curriculum: Pupils' perspectives, in A. James and R. Jeffcoate (eds) *The School in the Multicultural Society* (London, Harper & Row/Open University Press).

Johnson, R., McLennan, G., Schwarz, W. and Sutton, D. (eds) (1982), *Making Histories: Studies in history-writing and politics* (London, Hutchinson).

Jones, S. (1988) *Black Culture, White Youth: The reggae tradition from JA to UK*, (Basingstoke, Macmillan).

Katz, C. (1994) Playing the field: Questions of fieldwork in geography, *Professional Geographer*, 46(1), pp. 67–72.

Keating, P. (ed.) (1976) *Into Unknown England 1866–1913* (Manchester, Manchester University Press).

Kehily, M.J. (2002) *Sexuality, Gender and Schooling: Shifting agendas in social learning* (London, Routledge).

Kehily, M.J. and Nayak, A. (1997) 'Lads and laughter': Humour and the production of heterosexual hierarchies, *Gender and Education*, 9(1), pp. 69–87.

Kerouac, J. (2003 [1958]) *On the Road* (Harmondsworth, Penguin).

King, A.D. (1997 [1991]) Introduction: Spaces of culture, spaces of knowledge, in A.D. King (ed.) *Culture, Globalization and the World System: Contemporary conditions for the representation of identity* (Minneapolis, University of Minnesota Press).

Klein, N. (2000) *No Logo* (London, Flamingo)

Kobayashi, A. (1994) Colouring the field: Gender, 'race' and the politics of fieldwork, *Professional Geographer*, 46(1), pp. 73–80.

Labour Party (1992) .

Lacey, C. (1970) *Hightown Grammar: The school as a social system* (Manchester, Manchester University Press).

Lancaster, B. (1992) Newcastle – Capital of what? in R. Colls and B. Lancaster (eds) *Geordies: Roots of regionalism* (Edinburgh, Edinburgh Press).

Lanigan, C. (1996) Placing identity in North East regionalism, *Northern Economic Review*, 25, pp. 3–24.

Lawless, R.I. (1995) *From Ta'izz to Tyneside: An Arab community in the North-East of England during the early twentieth century* (Exeter, University of Exeter Press).

Lees, S. (1986) *Losing Out: Sexuality and adolescent girls* (London, Hutchinson).

Lefebvre, H. (2001 [1974]) *The Production of Space* (Oxford, Blackwell).

Lewis, J.L. and Townsend, A. (eds) (1989) *The North–South Divide: Regional change in Britain in the 1980s* (London, Paul Chapman).

Leyshon, A. (1995) Annihilating space? The speed-up of communications, in J. Allen and C. Hamnet (eds) *A Shrinking World? Global unevenness and inequality* (Milton Keynes, Open University Press).

Lydon, J. (1994) *Rotten: No Irish – No Blacks – No Dogs* (New York, St Martin's Press).

Lyotard, J.F. (1991 [1984]) *The Postmodern Condition: A report on knowledge* (Manchester, Manchester University Press)

Mac An Ghaill, M. (1988) *Young, Gifted and Black* (Milton Keynes, Open University Press).

Mac An Ghaill, M. (1991) Schooling, sexuality and male power: Towards an emancipatory curriculum, *Gender and Education*, 3, pp. 291–309.

Mac An Ghaill, M (1997 [1994]) *The Making of Men: Masculinities, sexualities and schooling* (Milton Keynes, Open University Press).

Mac An Ghaill, M. (1999) *Contemporary Racisms and Ethnicities: Social and cultural transformations*, (Buckingham, Open University Press).

Mac an Ghaill, M. and Haywood, C. (1997) The end of anti-oppressive education? A differentialist critique, *International Studies in Sociology of Education*, 7(1), pp. 21–34.

MacDonald, I., Bhavani, R., Khan, L. and John, G. (1989) *Murder in the Playground: The Burnage Report* (London, Longsight).

MacDonald, R. (1999) The road to nowhere: Youth, insecurity and marginal transitions, in J. Vail, J. Wheelock and M. Hill (eds) *Insecure Times: Living with insecurity in contemporary society* (Routledge, London).

MacDonald, R., Mason, P., Shildrick, T., Webster C., Johnstone, L. and Ridley, L. (2000) Snakes & Ladders: In defence of studies of youth transition, http://www.socresonline.org.uk/5/4/macdonald.html

McDowell, L. (2000) Learning to serve? Employment aspirations and attitudes of young working-class men in an era of labour market restructuring, *Gender, Place and Culture*, 7(4), pp. 389–416

McDowell, L. (2002a) Transitions to work: Masculine identities, youth inequality and labour market change, *Gender, Place and Culture*, 9(1), pp. 39–59.

McDowell, L. (2002b) Masculine discourses and dissonances: Strutting 'lads', protest masculinity, and domestic respectability, *Environment and Planning D: Society and Space*, 20, pp. 97–119.

McEwan, C. (2001) Geography, culture and global change, in P. Daniels, M. Bradshaw, D. Shaw and J. Sidaway (eds) *Human Geography: Issues for the 21st Century* (Harlow, Prentice Hall).

McGuinness, M. (2000) Geography Matters? Whiteness and contemporary geography, *Area*, 32(2), pp. 225–30.

McHugh, K.E. (2000) Inside, outside, upside down, backward, forward, round and round: A case for ethnographic studies in migration, *Progress in Human Geography,* 24(1), pp. 71–89.

McIntosh, P. (1997) White privilege and male privilege: A personal account of coming to see correspondences through work in women's studies, in R. Delgado and J. Stefancic (eds) *Critical White Studies: Looking behind the mirror* (Philadelphia, Temple University Press).

MacPherson, W. (1999) *The Stephen Lawrence Inquiry*, Cm. 42621 (London, HMSO).

McRobbie, A. (1991 [1977]) The culture of working-class girls, in *Feminism and Youth Culture: From 'Jackie' to 'Just Seventeen'* (Basingstoke, Macmillan).

McRobbie, A. (1991) *Feminism and Youth Culture: From 'Jackie' to 'Just Seventeen'* (Basingstoke, Macmillan).

McRobbie, A. (1996 [1994]) *Post-modernism and Popular Culture* (London, Routledge).

McRobbie, A. (1997) Different, youthful subjectivities, in H.S. Mirza (eds.) *Black British Feminism: A reader* (London, Routledge).

McRobbie, A. and Garber, J. (1977 [1975]) Girls and subcultures: An exploration, in S. Hall and T. Jefferson (eds) *Resistance through Rituals* (London, Hutchinson Centre for Contemporary Cultural Studies, University of Birmingham).

Maher, F.A. and Tetreault, M.K. (1997) Learning in the dark: How assumptions of whiteness shape classroom knowledge, *Harvard Educational Review*, 62(2), pp. 321–49.

Mailer, N. (1970 [1957]) The White Negro, in *Advertisements for Myself* (London, Panther Books).

Malbon, B. (1999) *Clubbing: Dancing, ecstasy and vitality* (London, Routledge).

Martino, W. and Meyenn, B. (2001) *What About the Boys? Issues of masculinities in schools* (Buckingham, Open University Press).

Massey, D. (1995 [1984]) *Spatial Divisions of Labour: Social structure and the geography of production* (Basingstoke, Macmillan).

Massey, D. (1995) The conceptualization of place, in D. Massey and P. Jess (eds) *A Place in the World?* (Milton Keynes, Open University Press).

Massey, D. (1996 [1991]) A global sense of place, in S. Daniels and R. Lee (eds) *Exploring Human Geography* (London, Arnold).

Massey, D. (1998) The spatial construction of youth culture, in T. Skelton and G. Valentine (eds) *Cool Places: Geographies of youth cultures* (London, Routledge).

Massey, D. and Allen, J. (1994 [1984]) *Geography Matters!* (Cambridge, Cambridge University Press/Open University Press).

Massey, D. and Meegan, R. (1984) *The Anatomy of Job Loss* (London, Methuen).

Mayhew, H. (1950) *London's Underworld: Being selections from 'Those that will not work'. The fourth volume of London labour and the London poor* (London, Spring Books).

Media Research Group (1987) *Media coverage of London councils* (London, Goldsmiths College, University of London).

Mercer, K. (1994) *Welcome to the Jungle: New positions in black cultural studies* (London, Routledge).

Miles, R. (1995) *Racism* (London, Routledge).

Miles, S. (2000) *Youth Lifestyles in a Changing World* (Buckingham, Open University Press).

Mirza, H. (1992) *Young, Female and Black* (London, Routledge).

Modood, T. (1988) 'Black', racial equality and Asian identity, *New Community*, 14(3), pp. 397–404.

Moore, D. (1994) *The Lads in Action: Social processes in an urban youth subculture* (Aldershot, Arena).

Morgan, D. (1981) Men, masculinity and the process of sociological enquiry, in H. Roberts (ed.) *Doing Feminist Research* (London, Routledge & Kegan Paul).

Morrison, B. (1997) *As If* (London, Granta Books).

Morrison, T. (1992) *Playing in the Dark: Whiteness in the literary imagination* (London, Harvard University Press).

Mould, W. (1987) The Swann Report: An LEA response, in T. Chivers (ed.) *Race and Culture in Education* (Windsor, NFER).

Muggleton, D. and Weinzierl, R. (in press) *The Post-Subcultures Reader* (Oxford, Berg).

Multiple Occupancies Collective (1998) Multiple occupancies: Locating home base, *New Formations*, 33, pp. 90–108.

Nast, H. J. (1994) Women in the field: Critical feminist methodologies and theoretical perspectives, *Professional Geographer*, 46(1) pp. 54–66.

Nayak, A. (1993) Narratives of Racism, Cultural Studies from Birmingham, 2, pp. 124–54.

Nayak, A. (1997) Tales from the darkside: Negotiating whiteness in school arenas, *International Studies in Sociology of Education*, 7(1), pp. 57–80.

Nayak, A. (1999a) White English ethnicities: Racism, anti-racism and student perspectives, *Race Ethnicity and Education*, 2(2), pp. 177–202.

Nayak, A. (1999b) 'Pale warriors': Skinhead culture and the embodiment of white masculinities, in A. Brah, M.J. Hickman and M. Mac an Ghaill (eds) *Thinking Identities: Ethnicity, racism and culture* (Basingstoke, Macmillan).

Nayak, A. and Kehily, M.J. (1996) Playing it straight: Masculinities, homophobias and schooling, *Journal of Gender Studies*, 5(2), pp. 211–30.

Nayak, A. and Kehily, M.J. (2001) 'Learning to laugh': A study of schoolboy humour in the English secondary school, in W. Martino and B. Meyenn (eds) *What About the Boys? Issues of masculinity in schools* (Buckingham, Open University Press).

Nebeker, K.C. (1998) Critical race theory: A white graduate student's struggle with this growing area of scholarship, *Qualitative Studies in Education*, 11(1), pp. 25–41.

Nederveen Pieterse, J. (1995) Globalization as hybridization, in M. Featherstone, S. Lash and R. Robertson (eds) *Global Modernities* (London, Sage).

Osgerby, B. (1998) *Youth in Britain since 1945* (Oxford, Blackwell).

Panayi, P. (1991) Middlesborough 1961: A British riot of the 1960s?, *Social History*, 16(2), pp. 139–53.

Parker, D. (1995) *Through Different Eyes: The cultural identities of young Chinese in Britain* (Aldershot, Avebury).

Parker, H.J. (1974) *View from the Boys* (London/Vancouver, David & Charles).

Patterson, S. (1965 [1963]) *Dark Strangers: A study of West Indians in London* (Harmondsworth, Penguin).

Pearson, G. (1976) 'Paki-bashing' in a North East Lancashire cotton town: A case study and its history, in G. Mungham and G. Pearson (eds) *Working Class Youth Culture* (London, Routledge).

Phoenix, A. (1997) 'I'm white! So what?' The construction of whiteness for young Londoners, in M. Fine, L. Weis, L. Powell and L. Mun Wong (eds) *Off White* (New York, Routledge).

Pickard, T. (1982) *Jarrow March* (London/New York, Allison & Busby).

Pollert, A. (1981) *Girls, Wives, Factory Lives* (Basingstoke, Macmillan).

Powell, E. (1972) *Still to Decide*, ed. J. Wood (London, Batsford).

Pratt, M. L. (1992) *Imperial Eyes: Travel writing and transculturation* (London, Routledge).

Raban, J. (1975 [1974]) *Soft City* (Glasgow, Fontana/Collins).

Rattansi, A. (1993) Changing the subject? Racism, culture and education, in J. Donald and A. Rattansi (eds) *'Race', Culture and Difference* (London, Sage/ Open University Press).

Redhead, S. (1990) *The End-of-the-Century Party: Youth and pop towards 2000* (Manchester, Manchester University Press)

Redhead, S. (ed.) (1993) *Rave Off: Politics and deviance in contemporary youth culture* (Aldershot, Ashgate).

Redhead, S. (1995) *Unpopular Cultures: The birth of law and popular culture* (Manchester, Manchester University Press).

Redhead, S. (1997) *Subculture to Clubcultures* (Oxford, Blackwell).

Rex, J. and Tomlinson, S. (1979) *Colonial Immigrants in a British City* (London, Routlege & Kegan Paul).

Richardson, D. (1996) *Theorizing Heterosexuality*, (Buckingham, Open University Press).

Robertson, R. (1997 [1995]) Glocalization: Time–space and homogeneity– heterogeneity, in M. Featherstone, S. Lash and R. Robertson (eds) *Global Modernities* (London, Sage).

Robins, D. and Cohen, P. (1978) *Knuckle Sandwich: Growing up in the working-class community* (Harmondsworth, Pelican Books).

Robins, K. (1991) Tradition and translation: National culture in its global context, in J. Corner and S. Harvey (eds) *Enterprise and Heritage: Crosscurrents of national culture* (London, Routledge).

Robinson, F. (1988) *Post-industrial Tyneside: An economic and social survey of Tyneside in the 1980s* (City of Newcastle upon Tyne, Newcastle).

Robinson, V. (1987) Race, space and place (the geographical study of UK ethnic relations 1957–1987), *New Community*, XIV(1/2), pp. 186–97.

Roediger, D. (1992) *The Wages of Whiteness: Race and the making of the American working class* (London, Verso).

Roediger, D. (1994) *Towards the Abolition of Whiteness* (London, Verso).

Roman, L.G. (1993) White is not a colour! White defensiveness, postmodernism and anti-racist pedagogy, in C. McCarthy and W. Critch low (eds) *Race, Identity and Representation in Education* (London, Routledge).

Rutherford, J. (1997) *Forever England: Reflections on masculinity and empire* (London, Lawrence & Wishart).

Said, E.W. (1993) *Culture and Imperialism* (London, Vintage).

Said, E.W. (1995 [1978]) *Orientalism: Western conceptions of the Orient* (Harmondsworth, Penguin).

Samson, B. (1994 [1993]) Foreword in D. Moore, *The Lads in Action: Social processes in an urban youth subculture* (Aldershot, Arena).

Samuel, R. (1982) Local history and oral history, in R.G. Burgess (ed.) *Field Research: A sourcebook and field manual* (London, George Allen & Unwin).

Sewell, T. (1997) *Black Masculinities and Schooling: How black boys survive modern schooling* (Stoke on Trent, Trentham Books).

Short, G. and Carrington, B. (1992) Towards an antiracist initiative in the all-white primary school: A case study, in D. Gill, B. Mayor and M. Blair (eds) *Racism and Education: Structures and strategies* (London, Sage/Open University Press).

Sibley, D. (1995) *Geographies of Exclusion: Society and difference in the West* (London, Routledge).

Silverman, D. (1994 [1993]) *Interpreting Qualitative Data: Methods for analysing talk, text and interaction* (London, Sage).

Skeggs, B. (1997) *Formations of Class and Gender: Becoming respectable* (London, Sage).

Skelton, C. (2000) 'A passion for football': Dominant masculinities and primary schooling, *Sport, Education and Society*, 5(1), pp. 5–18.

Skelton, C. (2001) *Schooling the Boys: Masculinities and primary education* (Buckingham, Open University Press).

Skelton, T. (2000) 'Nothing to do, nowhere to go?' Teenage girls and 'public' space in the Rhondda Valleys, South Wales, in S.L. Holloway and G. Valentine (eds) *Children's Geographies: Playing, living, learning* (London, Routledge).

Skelton, T. and Valentine, G. (eds) (1998) *Cool Places: Geographies of youth cultures* (London, Routledge).

Sleeter, C.E. (1993) How white teachers construct race, in C. McCarthy and W. Critchlow (eds) *Race, Identity and Representation in Education* (London, Routledge).

Solomos, J. and Back, L. (1995) *Racism and Society* (Basingstoke/London, Macmillan).

Spivak, G.C. (1990) Can the subaltern speak? In P. Williams and L. Chrisman (eds) *Colonial Discourse and Post-Colonial Theory* (London, Prentice Hall).

Stanley, L. and Wise, S. (1983) *Breaking Out: Feminist consciousness and feminist research* (London, Routledge & Kegan Paul).

Stedman Jones G. (1984 [1971]) *Outcast London: A study of the relationship between classes in Victorian society* (Oxford, Clarendon Press).

Sunderland, P.L. (1997) 'You may not know it but I'm black': White women's self-identification as black, *Ethnos*, 62(1/2), pp. 32–58.

Tailor, H. (1992) Sporting heroes, in R. Colls and B. Lancaster (eds) *Geordies: Roots of Regionalism* (Edinburgh, Edinburgh University Press).

Taylor, I. and Jamieson, R. (1997) 'Proper Little Mesters': Nostalgia and protest masculinity in de-industrialized Sheffield, in S. Westwood and S. Williams (eds) *Imagining Cities: Scripts, signs, memory* (London, Routledge).

Taylor, I., Evans, K. and Fraser, P. (1996) *A Tale of Two Cities: Global change, local feeling and everyday life in the north of England. A study of Manchester and Sheffield* (London, Routledge).

Taylor, J.H. (1976) *The Half-Way Generation: A study of Asian youths in New-castle upon Tyne* (Windsor, NFER).

Taylor, P.J. (1993) The meaning of the North: England's 'foreign country' within, *Political Geography*, 12(2), pp. 136–55.

Thompson, E.P. (1982 [1968]) *The Making of the English Working Class* (Ayles-bury, Pelican Books).

Thompson, R., Bell, R., Holland, J., Henderson, S., McGrellis, S. and Sharpe, S. (2002) Critical moments: Choice, chance and opportunity in young people's narratives of transition, *Sociology*, 36(2), pp. 335–54.

Thornton, S. (1995) *Club Cultures: Music, media and subcultural capital* (Cam-bridge, Polity Press).

Thornton, S. (1997) General introduction, in K. Gelder and S. Thornton (eds) *The Subcultures Reader* (London, Routledge).

Thrift, N. (1989) The geography of international economic disorder, in R. Johnston and P. Taylor (eds) *A World in Crisis: Geographical Perspectives* (Oxford, Blackwell).

Todd, N. (1995) *In Excited Times: The people against the Blackshirts* (Tyne and Wear, Bewick Press/TWAFA).

Tolson, A. (1990) Social surveillance and subjectification: The emergence of 'subculture' in the work of Henry Mayhew, *Cultural Studies*, 4(2), pp. 113–27.

Tomaney, J. and Ward, N. (2001) *A Region in Transition: North East England at the millennium* (Aldershot, Ashgate).

Tomaney, J., Pike, A. and Cornford J. (1998) Plant closure and the local economy: the case of Swan Hunter on Tyneside, *Regional Studies*, 33(5), pp. 401–11.

Tomlinson, S. (1990) *Multicultural Education in All-white Areas* (Aldershot, Avebury).

Trenchard, L. and Warren, T. (1984) *Something to Tell You* (London, Gay Teenag-ers Group).

Troyna, B. and Hatcher, R. (1992a) *Racism in Children's Lives: A study of mainly white primary schools* (London, Routledge/National Children's Bureau).

Troyna, B. and Hatcher, R. (1992b) It's only words: Understanding 'racial' and racist incidents, *New Community*, 18(3), pp. 493–6.

Twine, F.W. (1996) Brown skinned white girls: Class, culture and the construction of white identity in suburban communities, *Gender, Place and Culture*, 3(2), pp. 205–44.

Unks, G. (1995) *The Gay Teen: Educational practice and theory for lesbian, gay and bisexual adolescents* (London, Routledge).

Urry, J. (2000) Mobile sociology, *British Journal of Sociology*, 51(1), pp. 185–203.

Vail, J., Wheelock, J. and Hill, M. (eds) (1999) *Insecure Times: Living with insecurity in contemporary society* (London, Routledge).

Valentine, G., Skelton, T. and Chambers, D. (1998) Cool places: An introduction to youth and youth cultures, in T. Skelton and G. Valentine (eds) *Cool Places: Geographies of youth cultures* (London, Routledge).

Walkerdine, V. (1990) *Schoolgirl Fictions* (London, Verso).

Walter, I. (1998) Resisting disicipline? The use of the body in gang girls' self-presentations, paper presented at the British Sociological Association Annual Conference 6–9 April, University of Edinburgh.

Ware, V. (1993) *Beyond the Pale: White women, racism and history* (London, Verso).

Waters, M. (1995) *Globalization* (London, Routledge)

Watson, D. and Corcoran, J. (1996) *An Inspiring Example: The North East of England and the Spanish Civil War 1936–1939* (unspecified, The McGuffin Press).

Watt, P. (1998) Going out of town: Youth, 'race', and place in the South East of England, *Environment and Planning D: Society and Space*, 16, pp. 687–703.

Werbner, P. (1997) Introduction: The dialectics of cultural hybridity, in P. Werbner and T. Modood (eds) *Debating Cultural Hybridity: Multicultural identities and the politics of anti-racism* (London, Zed Books).

Westwood, S. (1990) Racism, black masculinity and the politics of space, in J. Hearn and D. Morgan (eds) *Men, Masculinities and Social Theory* (London, Unwin Hyman).

Wheelock, J. (1994) Is Andy Capp dead? The enterprise culture and household responses to economic change, in P. Garrahan and P. Stewart (eds) *Urban Change and Renewal: The paradox of place* (Avebury, Aldershot).

Whyte, W.F. (1981 [1943]) *Street Corner Society: The social structure of an Italian slum*, (Chicago, University of Chicago Press).

Widdicombe, S. and Wooffitt, R. (1995) *The Language of Youth Subcultures* (Hemel Hempstead, Harvester Wheatsheaf).

Wilkinson, E.C. (1939) *The Town that was Murdered: The life-story of Jarrow* (London, Victor Gollancz).

Williams, R. (1973 [1961]) *The Long Revolution* (Harmondsworth, Penguin/ Chatto & Windus).

Williams, R. (1985 [1973]) *The Country and the City* (London, The Hogarth Press).

Willis, P. (1977) *Learning to Labour: How working class kids get working class jobs* (London, Saxon House).

Willis, P. (1978) *Profane Culture* (London/Boston, Routledge & Kegan Paul).

Willis, P. with Jones, S., Canaan, J. and Hurd G. (1990) *Common Culture: Symbolic work at play in the everyday cultures of the young* (Milton Keynes, Open University Press).

Bibliography

Willott, S and Griffin, C. (1996) Men, masculinity and the challenge of long-term unemployment, in M. Mac an Ghaill (ed.) *Understanding Masculinities* (London, Open University Press).

Wills, J. (1999) Political economy I: Global crisis, learning and labour, *Progress in Human Geography*, 23(3), pp. 443–51.

Winlow, S. (2001) *Badfellas: Crime, tradition and new masculinities* (Oxford, Berg).

Wohl, A.S. (1986) [1861] Introduction to J. Hollingshead, *Ragged London in 1861* (London, Everyman History).

Wulff, H. (1995) Inter-racial friendship: Community youth styles, ethnicity and teenage femininity in South London, in V. Amit-Talai and H. Wulff (eds) *Youth Cultures: A cross-cultural perspective* (London, Routledge).

Young, C.M. (1977) Rock is sick and living in London, *Rolling Stone*, 20 October.

Young, J. (1972 [1971]) *The Drugtakers* (London, Paladin).

Young, L. (1995) Environmental images and imaginary landscapes, *Soundings*, 1, pp. 99–110.

Young, R. (1995) *Colonial Desire: Hybridity in theory culture and race* (London, Routledge).

Author Index

Adorno, T. 16
Alexander, C. 25
Allen, R. 22–3
Allen, T. 62
Althusser, L. 15
Amos, V. and Parmar, P. 24, 118
Anderson, B. 72, 81
Appadurai, A. 35
Atkinson, P. 29–30
    see also Hammersley, M. and Atkinson, P.
Ayensu, L. 165

Ball, S. 7
Back, L. 7, 26, 54, 61, 75, 105, 139, 145, 149,
    152, 153n42, 158
    see also Solomos, J. and Back, L.
Barker, M. 153, 156, 159
Bates, I. 171
Bath, L. and Farrel, P. 42
Bauder, H. 58
Bean, D. 36, 37, 47, 54, 66–7
Beck, U. 4, 33, 59, 168
Becker, H. 14
Bell, D. 139
Benjamin, W. 16
Bennett, A. 19, 28, 33, 44, 75, 105
Blackman, S. 24
Bhabha, H. 121, 132
Bonnett, A. 38, 43, 146–7, 150, 152, 154n43,
    172
Bonnett, A. and Nayak, A. 32, 105, 121
Booth, W. 76, 102
Bourke, J. 41
Bradford, M. and Burdett, F., 53
Bradley, H., Erickson, M., Stephenson, C. and
    Williams, S. 5
Brah, A. 35, 105
Brake, M.19, 24
Bromley, R. 70
Brown, M. 108

Bryson, J., Henry, N., Keeble, D. and
    Martin, R. 105
Burgess, R. 163
Butler, J. 173

Campbell, A. 23
Campbell, B. 38, 41, 43–4, 47, 62, 79–81, 83,
    88, 90, 96, 158
Canaan, J.E. 24, 71
Carby, H. 118
Carr, B. 36, 41, 46–7
Cashmore, E. E. and Troyna, B. 171
Castells, M 36
Centre for Contemporary Cultural Studies,
    15–17, 20–1, 159
Chambers, I. 77, 84
Chang, T. C., 35
Chatterton, P. and Hollands, R. 28, 33, 56, 66
Clarke, J. 16–17, 32
    Clarke, J., Hall, S. Jefferson, T. and
        Roberts, B. 16
Clarke, K. B. and Clarke, M. K. 186
Coard, B. 146, 160
Coffield, R., Borrill, C. and Marshall, S. 44, 62,
    66, 71n20
Cohen, A. 14
Cohen, P. 16, 22, 25, 54, 61, 69, 71–2, 77, 95,
    139, 152
    see also Robins, D. and Cohen, P.
Cohen, S. 14–15, 78, 145, 178
Collier, R. 47, 79, 83–5
Colls, R. 37
    Colls, R. and Lancaster, B. 60, 157
Connell, R., 7, 64n16, 70, 90
Connolly, P. 139, 152
Corrigan, P. 33, 37, 81

Daniel, S. and McGuire, P.22
Davis, M. 87
Dawley, S. 58

Author Index

Mac an Ghaill, 18, 24, 25, 75, 139, 144, 146, 156
Mac an Ghaill and Haywood, 149
MacDonald, R. 4, 33, 65, 71n20, 86
    MacDonald, R., Mason, P., Shildrick, T., Webster, C., Johnstone, L. and Ridley, L. 61, 71n20
MacDonald, I., Bhavani, R., Khan, L. and John, G. 141, 144, 147, 153, 174
    see also Burnage Report
McDowell, L. 4, 53–4, 97, 170
McEwan, C. 5, 35
McGuinness, 105
McHugh, 29
McIntosh, P. 172
McRobbie, A. 17, 18, 19, 23–4, 30, 32–3, 113, 169
    see also McRobbie, A. and Garber, J. 22–4, 64n16, 117
Maher, F. A. and Tetreault, M. K. 144
Malbon, B. 28, 33
Martino, W. and Mayenn, B. 53n10
Masterman, C. F. G. 84
Mayhew, H. 18, 89
Marcuse, H. 16
Marx, K. 15
    see also Marxism
Massey, D. 7, 27, 35, 55, 69, 108, 111, 176
Massey, D. and Allen, J. 5
Massey, D. and Meegan, R. 56
Mercer, K. 116, 172
Miles, R. 152
Miles, S. 28, 32–3
Mirza, H., 18
Modood, T. 144–5
Moore, D. 26–7, 94
Morgan, D. 23
Morrison, B. 83n24
Morrison, T. 172
Mould, W. 42
Muggleton, D. and Weinzierl, R., 20
Multiple Occupancies Collective 165

Nast, H. 30, 121
Nayak, A. 7, 22, 54, 105, 122, 142n41, 161, 162n44, 172
Nayak, A. and Kehily, M. J. 25, 64n16, 68, 71

see also Bonnett, A. and Nayak, A.
see also Kehily, M. J. and Nayak, A.
Nebecker, K. C. 162n44, 172

Osgerby, B. 14

Panayi, P. 42
Parker, D. 39
Parker, H. J. 23
Patterson, S. 159
Pearson, G. 21–2
Phoenix, A. 140n39
Pickard, T. 46
Pieterse, J. N. 122
Pollert, A. 23
Pratt, M. L. 121–2

Raban, J. 76
Rattansi, A. 141n40, 142, 145, 153–4
Redhead, S. 19, 20–1, 33
Rex, J. and Tomlinson, S. 160
Richardson, D. 172
Robertson, R. 5
Robins, D. and Cohen, P. 16, 22
Robins, K. 35, 105
Robinson, F. 55, 58, 88
Robinson, V. 7–8
Roediger, D. 62
Roman, L. 152
Rutherford, J. 141, 145, 159

Said, E. 80–1, 121
Samuel, R. 166
Sewell, T. 25, 95, 139, 144, 146
Sibley, D. 43, 84
Silverman, D. 29
Simms, G. R. 77
Short, G. and Carrington, B. 146
Skeggs, B. 58, 61, 89, 91
Skelton, C. 65
Skelton, T. 56
    Skelton, T. and Valentine, G. 33, 54
Sleeter, C. 146
Solomos, J. and Back, L. 160
Spivak, 121
Stanley, L. and Wise, S. 23
Stedman Jones, G. 77
Sunderland, P. 133

Author Index

Tailor, H. 63–4
Taylor, J. H. 38, 42
Taylor, P. J. 36
Taylor, I. and Jamieson, R. 59, 70
  Taylor, I., Evans, K. and Fraser, P. 36, 37n7, 71, 100
Thompson, E. P. 60–1, 91–2
Thompson, R., Bell, R., Holland, J., Henderson, S., McGrellis, S. and Sharpe, S. 178
Thornton, S. 19, 33, 94
  see also Gelder, K. and Thornton, S.
Thrift, N. 57
Todd, N. 45
Tolson, A. 18
Tomaney, J, and Ward, N. 58
  Tomaney, J. Pike, A. and Cornford, J. 55
Tomlinson, S. 146
Trenchard, L. and Warren, T. 24
Troyna, B. and Hatcher, R. 146, 148–9, 151, 158
Twine, F. W. 161

Uncks, 24
Urry, J. 27–8

Vail, J. Wheelock, J. and Hill, M. 4

Valentine, G., Skelton, T. and Chambers, D. 28
  see also Valentine, G. and Skelton, T. 33

Wade, M. 41
Walkerdine, V. 143
Walter, I. 23
Ware, V. 162
Waters, M. 4, 35
Watson, D. and Corcoran, J. 47
Watt, P. 28, 54, 105
Werbner, P. 132
Westwood, S. 89–90
Wheelock, J. 56
Whyte, W.F. 14
Widdicombe and Woofitt, 19, 26
Wilkinson, E. 46
Williams, R. 15, 70–1, 76, 108
Willis, P. 7, 17, 33, 53–4, 65, 111, 169
  Willis, P, with Jones, S., Canaan, J. and Hurd, G., 90
Willott, S. and Griffin, C. 61, 95
Wills, J. 33n6
Winlow, S. 87, 98
Wulff, H. 105, 113, 115n34

Young, J. 15
Young, R. 19n2, 121

General Index

General Index

ethnography, 6, 17, 27–30, 58, 60, 105, 139, 162n45, 163, 166, 170, 173, 175, 176, 179, 182
see also method
ethnoscape, 35

factories/manufacturing, *see* industry and labour markets
family/kinship, 33, 36, 42, 58–63, 65, 71, 73, 86–8, 96, 103, 110, 129, 163, 168, 169–70, 175, 177, 179, 181
Far–Right, 166
British National Party, 43–5
Fascism 42, 45, 46, 48, 163
National Front, 43–5, 139
Nazis, 140, 160, 166
Fascism, *see* Far–Right
feminism, 22–24, 31, 91, 144, 169
football, 8, 9, 18, 43, 43n9, 48–9, 54, 60, 63–6, 73, 78, 108, 112, 131
Frankfurt School, 13, 16

gay culture/identity, 24, 78, 107, 143, 170
see also Queer Theory
gender, 11, 22–25, 28, 59n12, 61, 64n16, 67n17, 88–9, 91, 93, 101, 112–14, 117, 121, 144, 147, 151, 166, 167, 169–71, 172, 173, 174, 176, 180–1
see also masculinities
Geordies, 9, 37, 43, 49–50, 53–73 passim, 122, 156, 157, 165
geography, 5, 7, 12, 26, 28–9, 33, 36, 43, 54, 72, 75, 81, 85, 103, 105, 121–2, 139, 150, 154, 161, 162–6, 171, 173, 175–8, 182
see also space
Gramsci, 15–16
Great Strike, 45, 48, 50

homology 110–12
Howe, Darcus 55, 171
humour, 68
hybridity, 105–35 passim
and globalization 39, 44, 75, 139, 145
and limitations of, 120–6
and possibilities, 126–35, 157, 163
and postmodernism 19, 19n2, 20, 31, 145
and music 93, 95

industry, 3, 17, 31, 53, 59, 79, 168, 171, 175
and ammunitions, 79
and coal mining, 38, 47, 55, 57, 59, 60, 64, 67, 69–70, 169, 175
see also Great Strike
and engineering, 57, 59, 67, 79
and micro–electronics, 57, 63, 71
and shipping, 39–41, 46–7, 55, 59, 61, 64, 70, 79, 175
and motorcars, 57, 57n11
and pubs, 59, 67
see also labour markets, apprenticeships
Irish, 35, 40, 40n8, 101, 150, 151, 163, 180

Jarrow March, 46, 50, 57
Jews, 39, 40, 45

Kerouac, Jack, 107

labour markets, 4, 7, 9–10, 21, 33, 53, 55–59, 135, 151, 163, 169, 175, 177, 181
see also industry
lesbians 24, 172
see also gay identity, sexuality

MacPherson Report, 140
manufacturing, *see* industry and labour markets
Mailer, Norman, 107
Marxism, 15, 17, 20–22, 21n3, 26, 31–2, 169
masculinism, 22–5, 68n18, 112
masculinities,
and 'crisis' 172
and family, 58–9, 62, 64, 163, 170
and fashion, 90, 100
and humour, 68–9, 71
and race, 89–90, 100–2, 107–8, 122–4, 144
see also whiteness
and sexuality, 24, 68, 71, 101
and sport, 64–6
and violence, 22, 25, 68, 71, 98, 100–1
see also crime
and work, 53–4, 56, 62–4, 69–72, 163, 169, 170
methods, 6–7, 23, 85, 140, 179–81
and cultural studies, 8
and ethnography, 27–30, 61n14, 162n45, 163, 179, 182
and subculture, 13

Anoop Nayak

RACE, PLACE AND GLOBALIZATION
YOUTH CULTURES IN A CHANGING WORLD

'Race, Place and Globalization is a critical ethnography of the construction of young white masculinities in North-East England. It provides a locally grounded understanding of the experience of globalization from the perspective of those at its cutting edge. The 'Real Geordies', 'Charver Kids', 'Wiggers' and 'Wannabees' who we encounter in the course of this most engaging book are no ciphers of some abstract social theory. In Anoop Nayak's skilful narrative, they emerge as real, live, embodied and contradictory identities. The author combines a geographical interest in the dynamics of place, space and location with a wider perspective on the cultural politics of race, class and gender. It makes compelling reading and deserves a wide audience.'
Peter Jackson, *University of Sheffield*

What does it mean to be young in a changing world? How are migration, settlement and new urban cultures shaping young lives? And in particular, are race, place and class still meaningful to contemporary youth cultures?

This path-breaking book shows how young people are responding differently to recent social, economic and cultural transformations. From the spirit of white localism deployed by de-industrialized football supporters, to the hybrid multicultural exchanges displayed by urban youth, young people are finding new ways of wrestling with questions of race and ethnicity. Through globalization is whiteness now being displaced by 'black' culture – in fashion, music and slang – and if so, what impact is this having on race politics? Moreover, what happens to those people and places that are left behind by changes in late modernity?

By developing a unique brand of spatial cultural studies, this book explores complex formations of race and class as they arise in the subtle textures of whiteness, respectability and youth subjectivity. This is the first book to look specifically at young ethnicities through the prism of local-global change. Eloquently written, its riveting ethnographic case studies and insider accounts will ensure that this book becomes a benchmark publication for writing on race in years to come.

Anoop Nayak, *University of Newcastle upon Tyne*

BERG

ISBN 1 85973 609 2
Cover Design: Raven Design

ISBN 1-85973-609-2

9 781859 736098 >

OXFORD NEW YORK